Whitchurch to Market Drayton

IN OLD PHOTOGRAPHS

Whitchurch to Market Drayton

IN OLD PHOTOGRAPHS

MARIANNE MORRIS

Alan Sutton Publishing Limited
Phoenix Mill · Far Thrupp · Stroud
Gloucestershire

First Published 1994

British Library Cataloguing in Publication Data.
A catalogue record for this book is available from the British Library.

ISBN 0 7509 0784 3

Typeset in 9/10 Sabon.
Typesetting and origination by
Alan Sutton Publishing Limited.
Printed in Great Britain by
The Guernsey Press Company Limited,
Guernsey, Channel Islands.

For the memory of Penny Dickerson and Mrs 'B' of Shawbury who opened my eyes to the reality of country life, the changing moods of the landscape, the physical region in which their minds and spirits were rooted.

There haunts within them secretly
One that lives while empires die,
A shrineless God whose song abides
Forever in the countryside.

Mary Webb

Contents

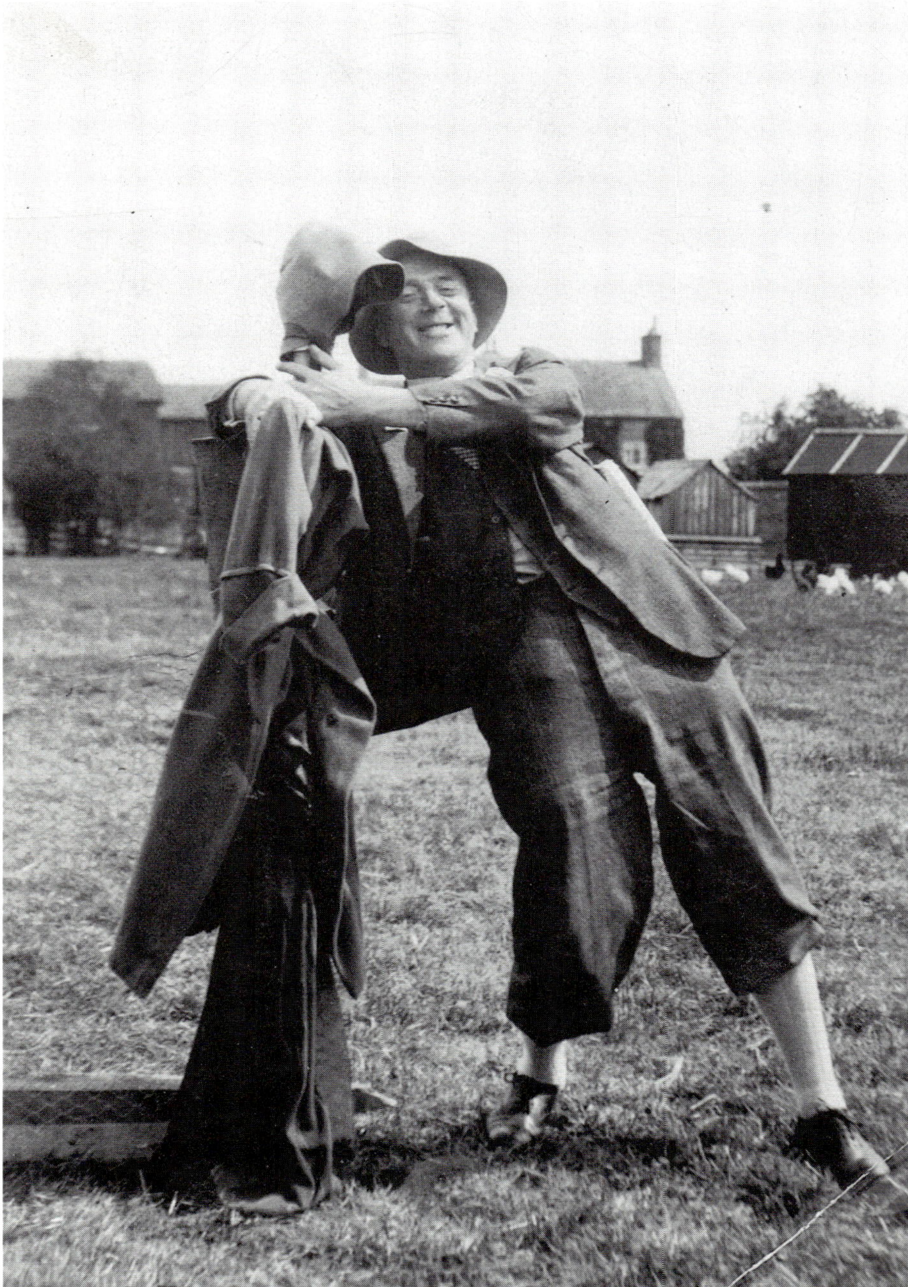

Jack Maddox, farmer of the Moss farm near Whitchurch, befriending a scarecrow in the 1930s.

Introduction

Looking at old photographs is like catching a glance of the corner of a room in the mirror – one sees fragments, familiar and yet remote. They can evoke a sentimental longing for the past, where time has softened reality, the knowledge of two wars, depression, social injustice and rigid Victorian moral values. Frozen, unsmiling faces come to life again; they speak to us. They speak to us of many things: the way they worked the land, the houses they lived in, the changing fashion and the transport they used before the arrival of the motor car. We recognize some of the schools, houses and churches still standing, and country lanes through which our forefathers walked.

A large section of the population remains, however, anonymous, not having been able to pay for the sitting in the photographer's studio. This subsequently changed with the innovation of the pocket camera; cheap, instant photography resulting in a larger variety of subject matter. The faster film speed made it possible to capture moving objects and natural smiling faces.

How wonderful it would be to see the interior of some of the more humble dwellings before the bulldozers reduced them to rubble, timber from ancient oak trees defying destruction. Pulled down in the name of progress they made way for supermarkets and car parks. Both in Whitchurch and Market Drayton and the villages around, you still find a large number of cottages that huddle together as if to protect each other. Not yet sanitized by the city commuter their many times painted walls talk of the bustle of everyday life. You can hear the cry of birth, the happiness of a Christmas celebration, and death repeated over and over again.

Shropshire, this beautiful county, is roughly divided into two parts by the River Severn: the hilly south and the plain with rich arable and pastureland to the north. They call Whitchurch and Market Drayton the 'forgotten towns' of Shropshire, not being connected to the motorway. Once, the Shropshire Union Canal, the markets and the railway played an important part in the development of that region. People came from miles around to sell their cattle, poultry, horses, pigs and farm produce. Clocks from Whitchurch and gingerbread from Market Drayton were exported to places all over the world. The many shops, inns and hotels of both towns prospered. The local gentry and the church both financed and promoted education. Famous visitors arrived to stay at the many fine houses, the preacher John Wesley built his first chapel in Whitchurch, and Thackeray stayed at the vicarage in Prees.

People here are proud of the place they live in, stoic in the face of hardship, independent and patriotic. They are proud of their famous and infamous sons.

John Talbot, 1st Earl of Shrewsbury, was born near Whitchurch in 1390 and lost his life in battle against Joan of Arc. His bodyguard, men from Whitchurch, returned with his body to the town where it remains today in a tomb in St Alkmund's Church. Randolph Caldecott, the illustrator and painter, and the composer of *Merrie England,* Sir Edward German, brought honour to the town of Whitchurch. Clive of India, born in 1725 at Styche near Market Drayton, is on the other hand affectionately called the first hooligan of Shropshire. His many youthful pranks included climbing the tower of St Mary's Church and holding local shopkeepers to ransom.

The great houses which succeeded the castles and abbeys were some of the finest in the country. Many, like Adderley Hall, home of the Corbet family after their arrival from France, have disappeared. For the communities the decline of the estates meant high unemployment. To go into service was one of the only options for young girls at the turn of the century. The demise of the railway and the canals, as well as the markets at a later stage, brought further economic hardship. Industry did not follow after the arrival of the motor car. The community spirit in that region has survived, however. Residents still know each other and give support when needed. Living close to the land, being close to nature, has formed the spirit of the people. They refuse stubbornly to let go of their heritage.

Here we have old photographs of 'ordinary' people with yet unique experiences. There are the two images of Evadna Etches, for example, as a young girl and later as a beautiful aspiring actress in London. She gave up her career to care for her ailing parents and never left Market Drayton again. More touching than any medieval relique is the black toy cat featured in one of the photographs and now in possession of the Civic Society. Harold Jones from Prees, proud in his new uniform at the age of 17, returned to his beloved Shropshire countryside from the Battle of the Somme, the only survivor from his village. For the rest of his long life he would never talk about the war.

We also celebrate with the images in this book all the women who, as teachers, suffragettes or just mothers, helped to pave the way for a better future for their daughters. Frances Shaw left behind material comfort and security to follow her heart and become the wife of a penniless canal boatman. With three young children to support, this courageous young woman tried to carry on the harsh business on her own after her husband's untimely death.

'Life is like that' people say in the area, waiting for spring to come, for the first green in the hedgerow and the return of the swallow: the rebirth of the countryside. Farming technology may have changed dramatically but it is still possible to walk through the quiet country lanes and imagine the binder pulled by horses, cutting the long sheaves of wheat, smell the stacks of hay instead of the instant plastic-covered bundles left behind by modern machinery. We look at the photographs in this book and remember, recognizing part of us – reality and fantasy side by side.

SECTION ONE

Whitchurch

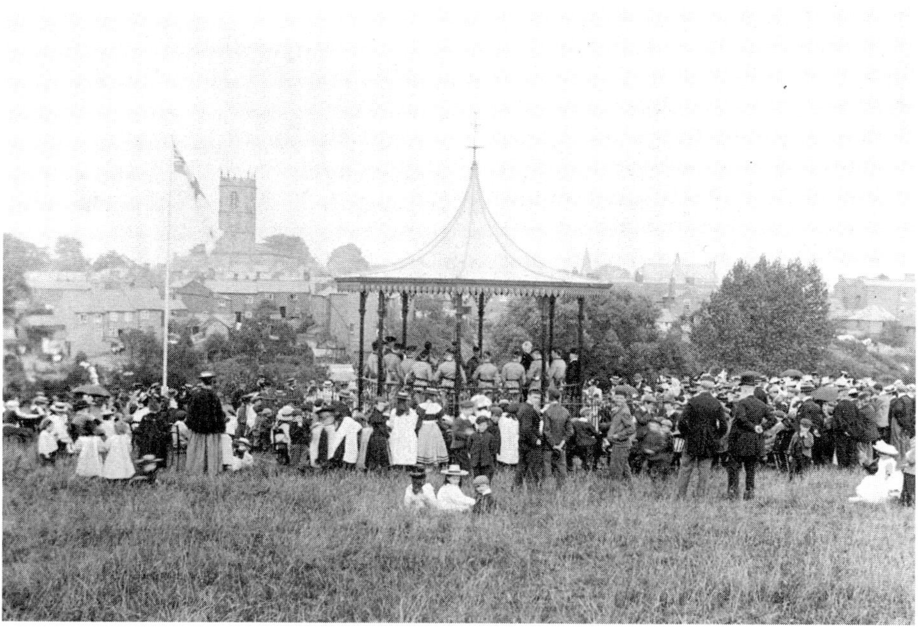

Jubilee Park in Whitchurch, *c.* 1900. The bandstand is still in the same position.

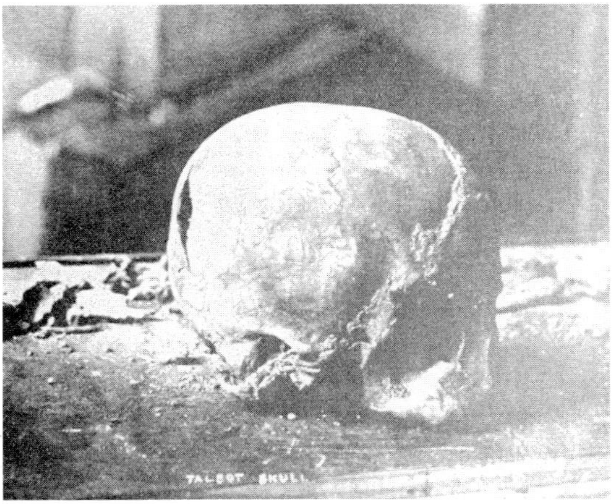

Sir John Talbot was born at Blakemere near Whitchurch in 1373, heir to John le Strange. He served under King Henry V and became Lord Lieutenant of Ireland. At the ripe old age of 80 he went to fight in France for the second time and in a heroic battle against Joan of Arc he and his son both lost their lives. His remains were brought back by his Whitchurch bodyguard and buried at St Alkmund's Church. The church collapsed in 1711 and after all the rubble had been cleared, a silver urn was found containing the embalmed heart of John Talbot. After restoration the heart was returned to his original resting place under a stone at the south porch. The tomb itself was only slightly damaged. The rector of the church for many years, Revd Edgerton, decided that on the occasion of the wedding in 1870 of Lady Adelaide, a descendant of John Talbot, the tomb should be repaired at their cost. The bones, including the skull, were neatly displayed in the vestibule. It was then discovered that the cause of death had been a blow from a battleaxe to the head. The remains were photographed (above) and returned to the now restored tomb.

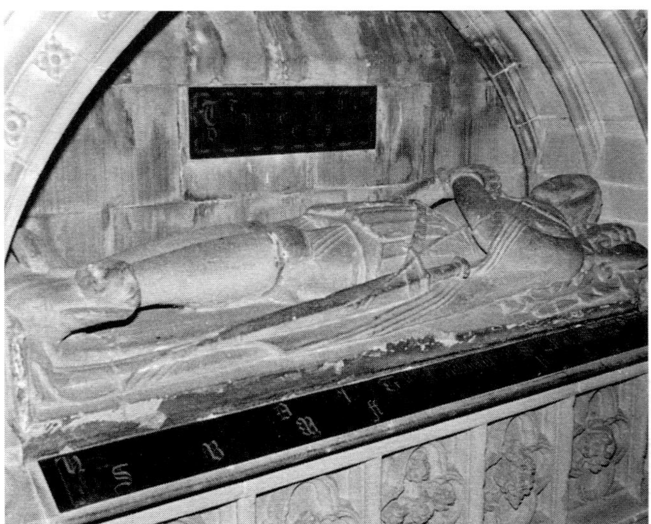

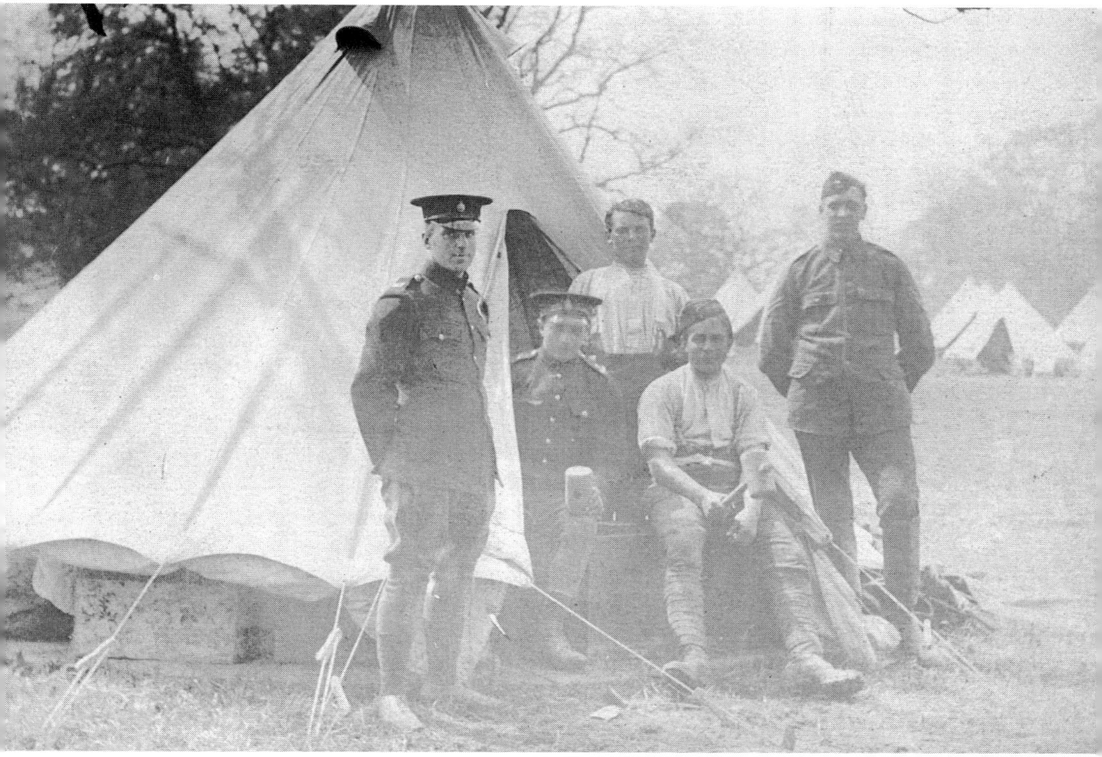

The Yeomanry Cavalry was raised in Shropshire at the time of Napoleon. In 1794 an act was passed through parliament that anybody who was assessed as the owner of ten horses, kept for the purpose of riding or driving, was obliged to supply one man and a horse for the Provisional Cavalry. It became an established custom to train for eight to ten days each year, either between spring seeding and hay harvest or after the corn harvest. In 1901 the Imperial Yeomanry changed from cavalry to mounted infantry; the sword was replaced by a short-end rifle. Annual training was increased from ten to eighteen days. At the opening of a riding school in Shrewsbury in 1913, Colonel Meyrick recited the following poem:

We have a ride together
We have ridden side by side
And it binds us all together
Like a lover to his bride.

Neither the precise date nor the training camp of this photograph are known but it features Jack Wynn with his fellow yeomen in 1914.

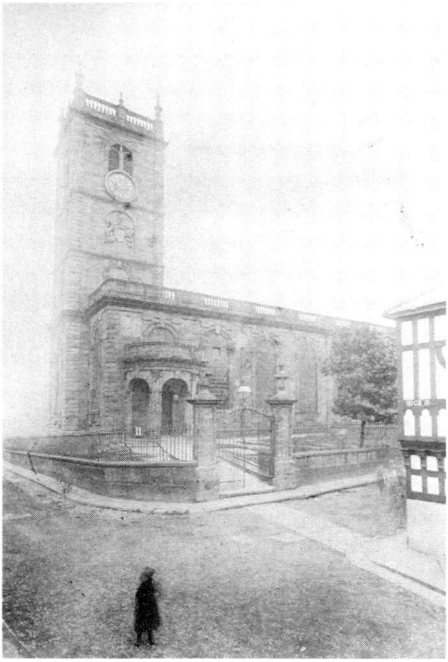

It is certain that a church was erected in 1088 on top of Weston Hill and that it was built of white stone, so giving the name to the town – Whitchurch. It was dedicated to Alkmund, the great-great grandfather of Ethelfleda, Queen of Mercia. He died a martyr. Nothing remains of the second church which collapsed in 1711, with the exception of the font, still used today for christenings, and the tomb of Sir John Talbot. The beautiful railings and the gate were removed during the Second World War as part of the war effort. It is said that wherever you are in Whitchurch you can always see the tower of St Alkmund's. On a plain wall we can read of one of the early Nonconformist ministers, Philip Henry, who began life in Whitehall and is buried here. As a boy he watched Charles I walk to his trial and then his last moments on the scaffold. There are letters by Philip Henry at Whitchurch Library. This photograph shows St Alkmund's Church, in around 1910.

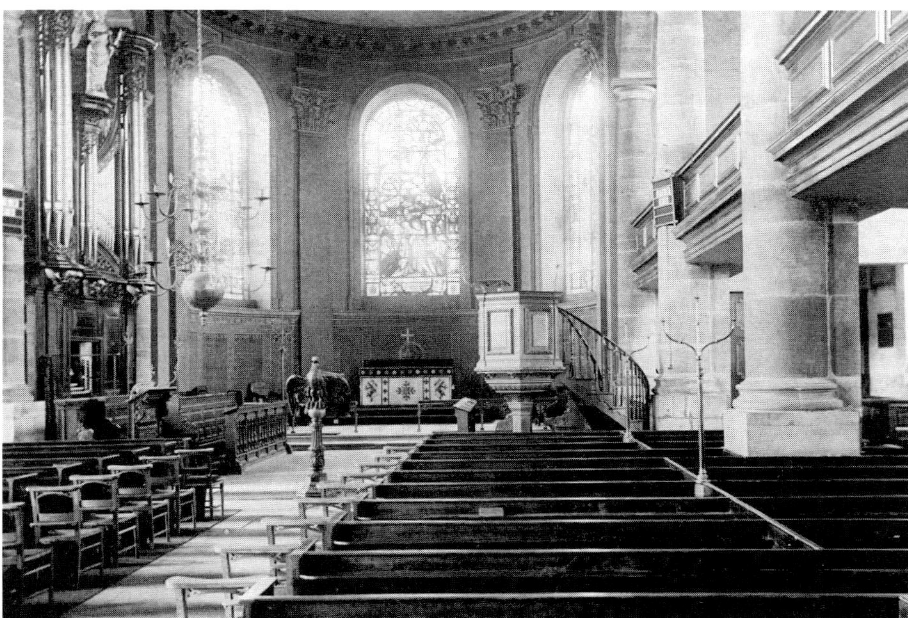

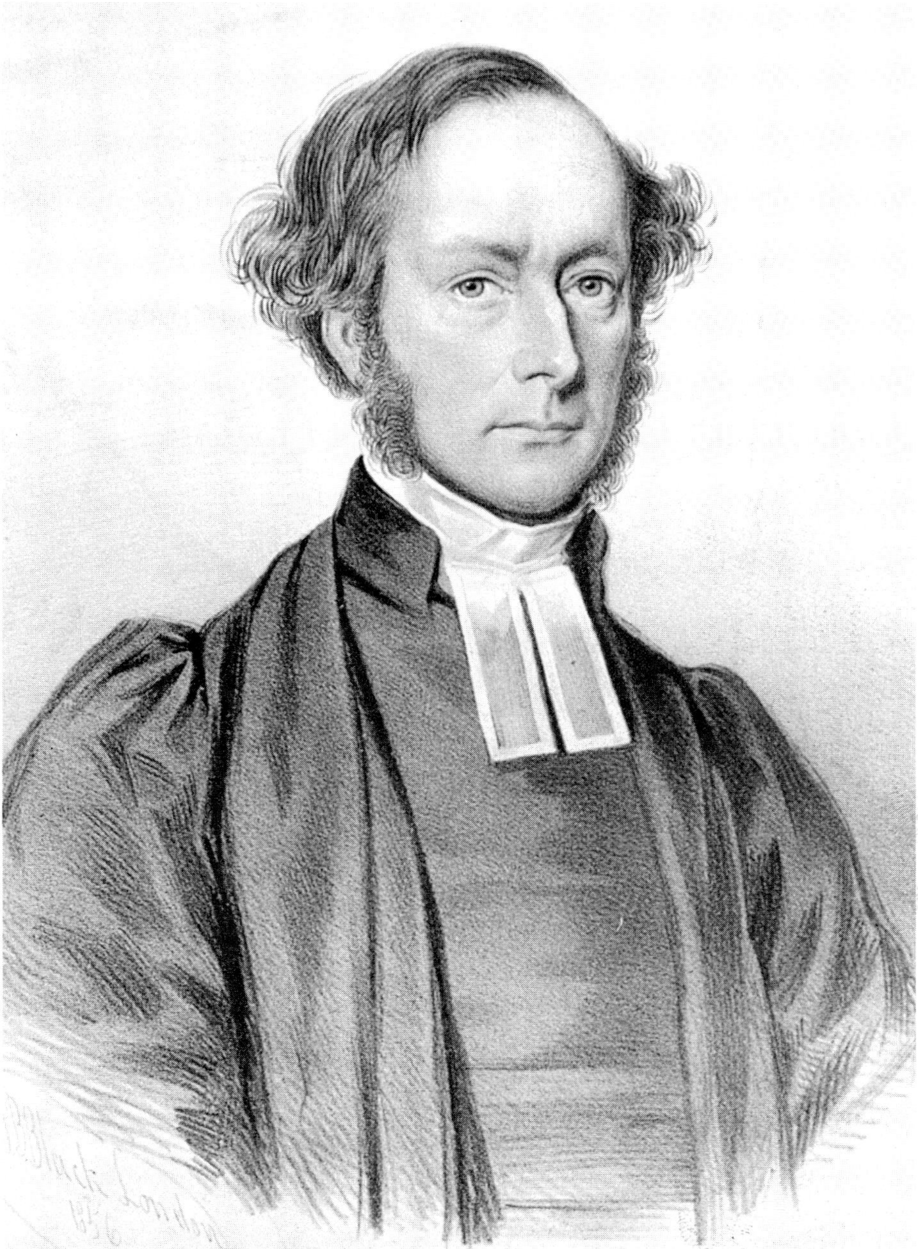

William Henry Edgerton was rector of St Alkmund's Church for sixty-two years and concerned himself with many of the affairs of the town, from education to architecture to everyday events. He lived to the ripe old age of 96. This portrait is from a drawing of 1870.

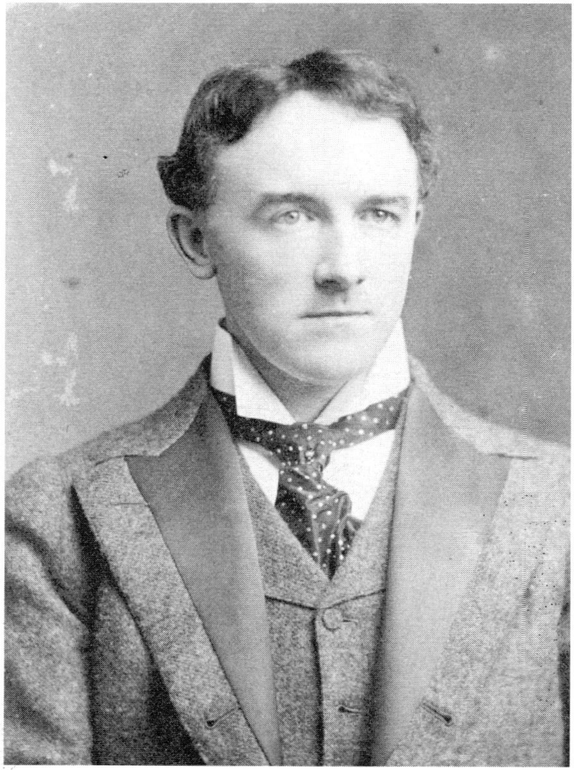

Sir Edward German was born in Whitchurch on 17 February 1862, the second of five children born to Mrs and Mr Jones. David Jones was at that time Honorary Organist and Choirmaster at the Congregational Church. Although baptized German Edward Jones he changed his name to Edward German while still living in Whitchurch. The beautiful organ in Shrewsbury Abbey was Edward German's first instrument; he also studied the violin and orchestration with Mr Hay. A talented young musician, he passed his entrance examination for the Royal Academy in London without any problem. As Musical Director for the Globe Theatre he wrote incidental music for Shakespeare's plays which made him famous. His greatest success was the patriotic operetta *Merrie England*. This he performed on the occasion of his fiftieth birthday with the Whitchurch Choral Society. In 1927 Edward German lost the sight in his right eye and took the baton as a conductor for the last time at a Bournemouth Symphony Concert. He received his knighthood in the New Year's Honours list in 1928. All through his life he stayed loyal to his home town that was so proud of his success as a composer. Edward German died in London in 1936 with his two sisters at his bedside and was laid to rest in the new cemetery in Whitchurch. He is commemorated by tablets in St Alkmund's Church and the Congregational Church.

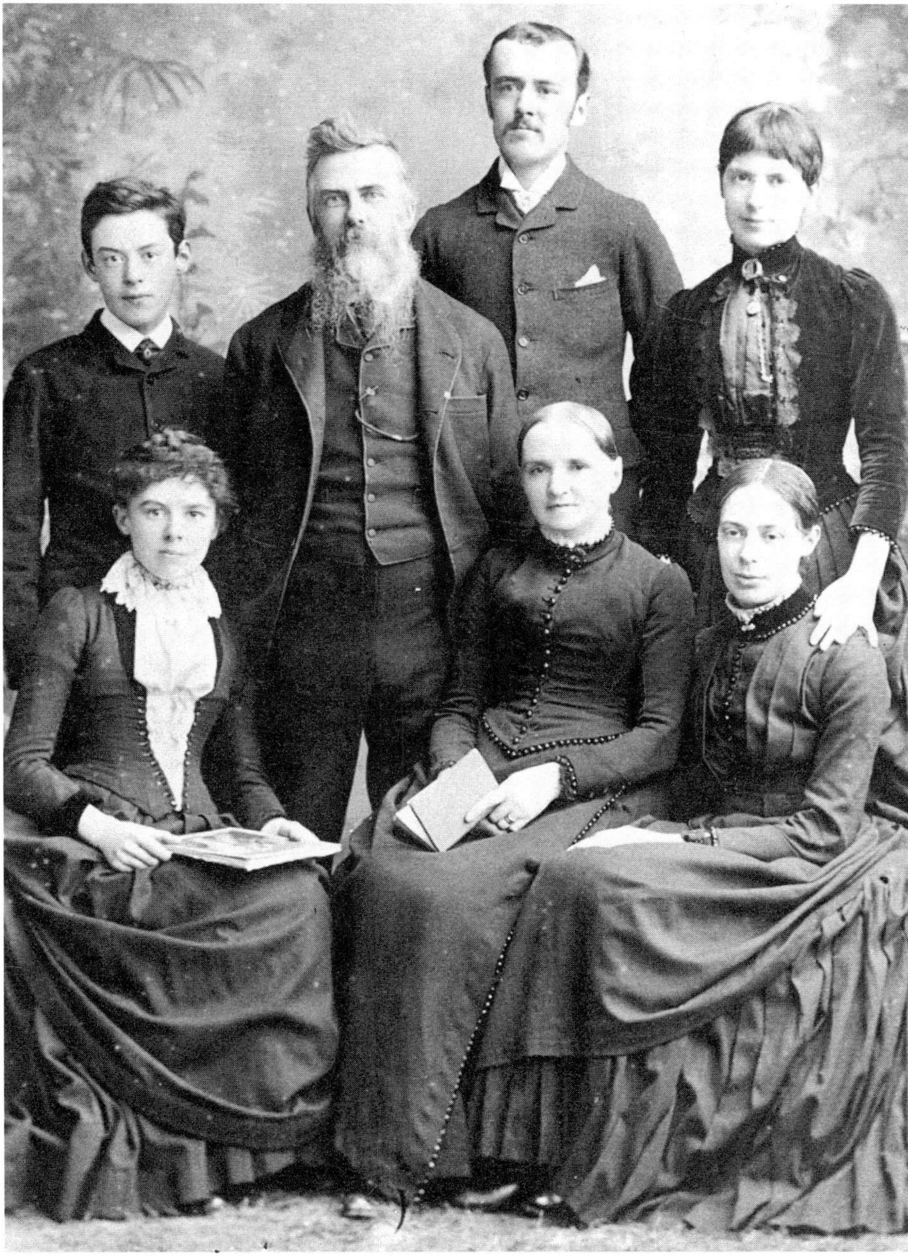

Edward German's uncle and his family. Standing, left to right: Ernest Jones, Edward Jones sen. (founder of the Bank Building Store), Edward jun., German's beloved cousin 'Ted'. Seated: daughter (name not known), Mrs Ernest Jones and a second daughter also remaining nameless. The exact date of the image is not known.

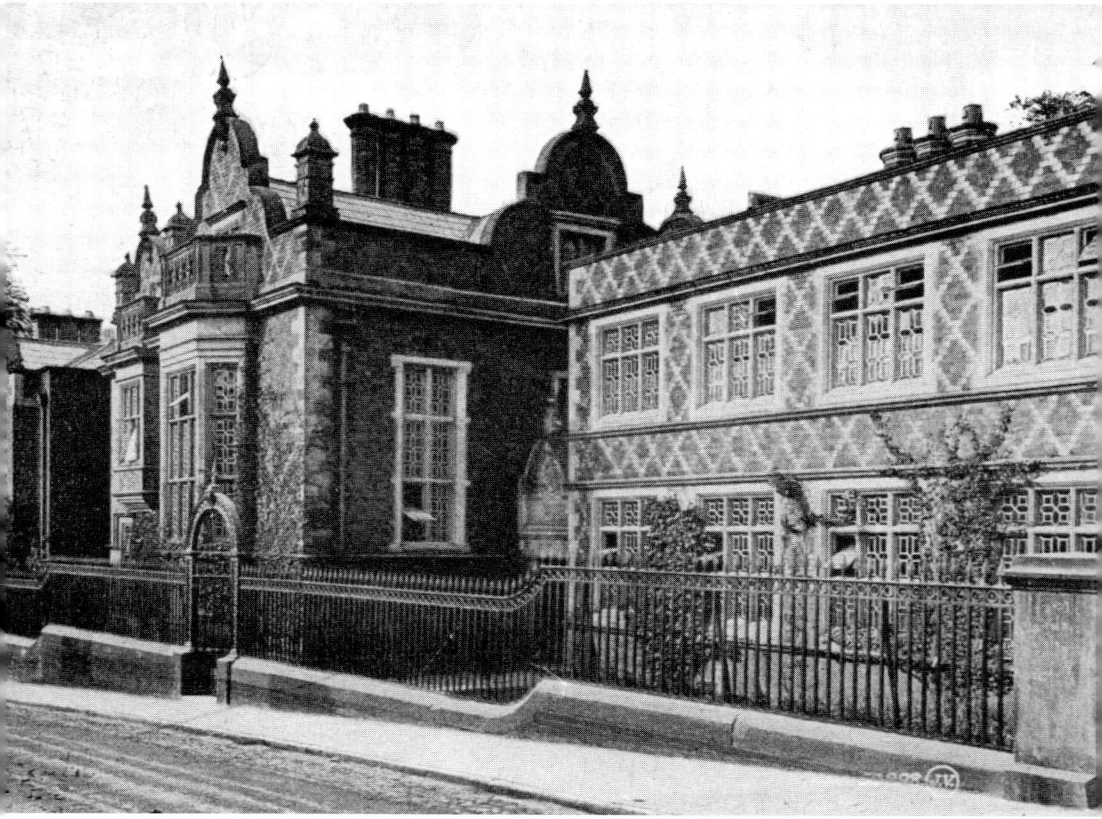

The Grammar School was founded in 1550 by Canon John Talbot. Research suggests that he was the illegitimate son of Sir Humphrey Talbot, the youngest son of John Talbot, 1st Earl of Shrewsbury. The school survived unchanged for three hundred years and was rebuilt in the same tudor style in 1848 at a cost of £1,595. One of its more illustrious 'old boys' was Robert Clive of Styche Hall near Market Drayton. The better-known Clive of India was his son. The school was brought under the secondary education system of the county in 1930. An inspector found the place crowded and unsanitary. It was decided in 1930 to build a new school at Mossfields, a house and grounds on the outskirts of the town. All the old oak pannelling and marble fireplaces were taken down and moved to the new building. This photograph was taken after the addition of a new science block in 1902.

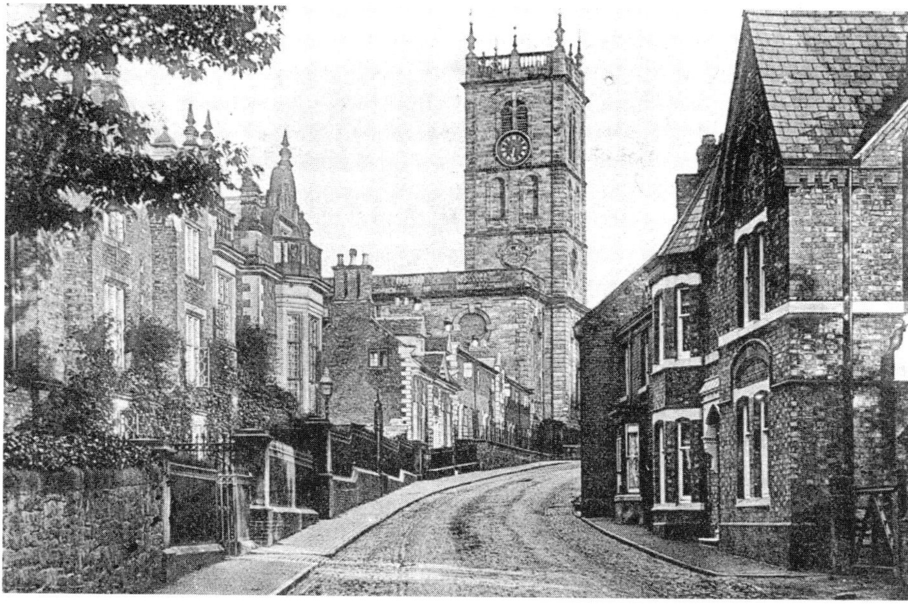

Bargates with the Grammar School and St Alkmund's Church in the background in 1901. The name of the road cannot be explained except that it is the road to 'Bar-mere'.

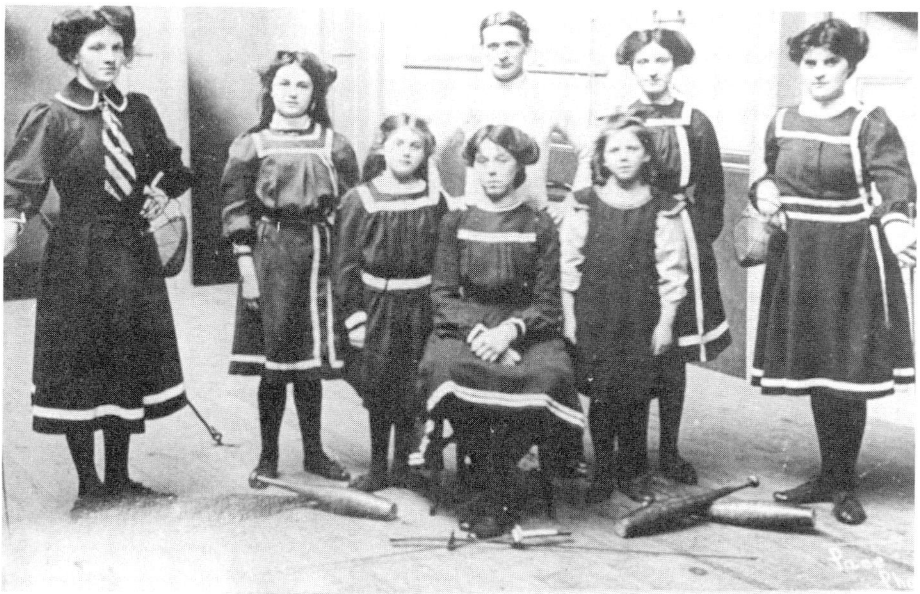

Gymnastic class in 1920 at the Drill Hall. The instructor was Mr W. Malam and the girls are wearing the uniform of the Girls High School. It appears that juggling and fencing were part of the exercises.

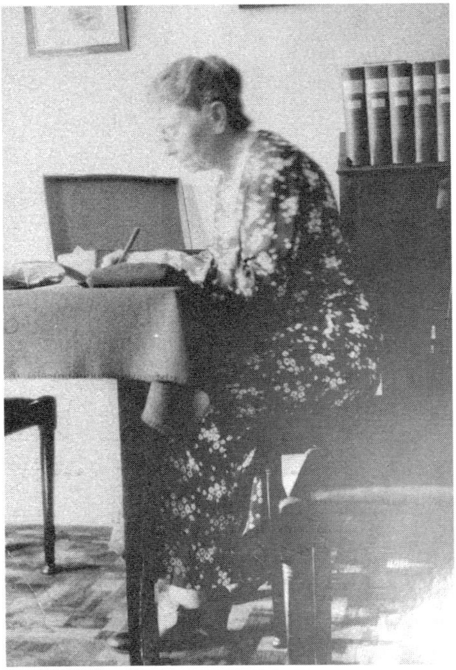

The Girls High School in Dodington's Mansion House was sold to Miss Keitley in 1894. Miss Keitley had been privately educated in Paris. Although the 1902 Education Act made it the responsibility of the County Council, it was still in essence a school for young ladies, with the emphasis on art, music and French. As a fee-paying school it was only accessible for girls from the wealthier families of the town and surrounding area. Moving to larger premises in St Mary's Street in Whitchurch, it was later incorporated into the new Council-run Girls Public High School, which opened in 1912. Bursaries were made available for those girls wanting to continue with their education as pupil-teachers or by joining a teacher training college. The photograph shows Miss Keitley at the new school around 1920.

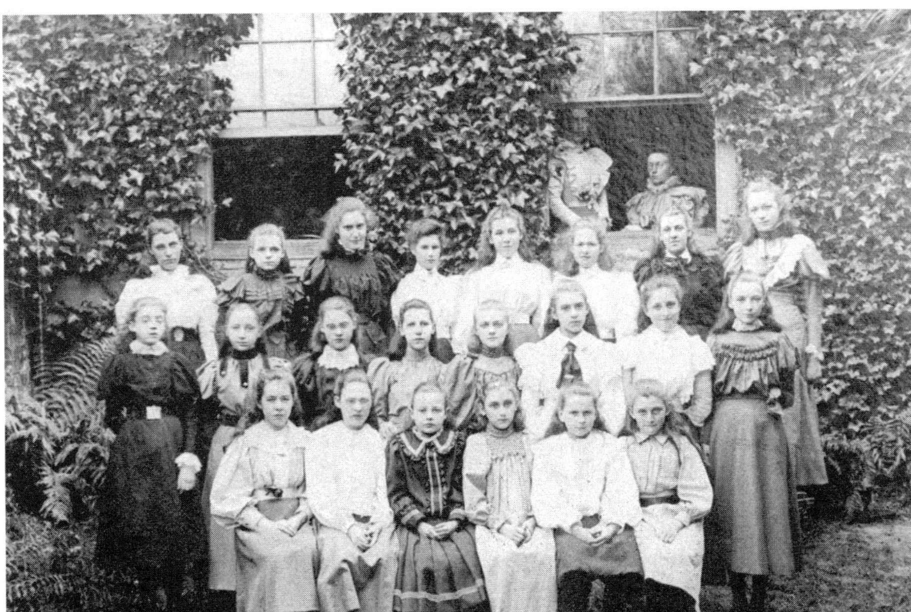

A class of around 1900 with Miss Keitley in the background.

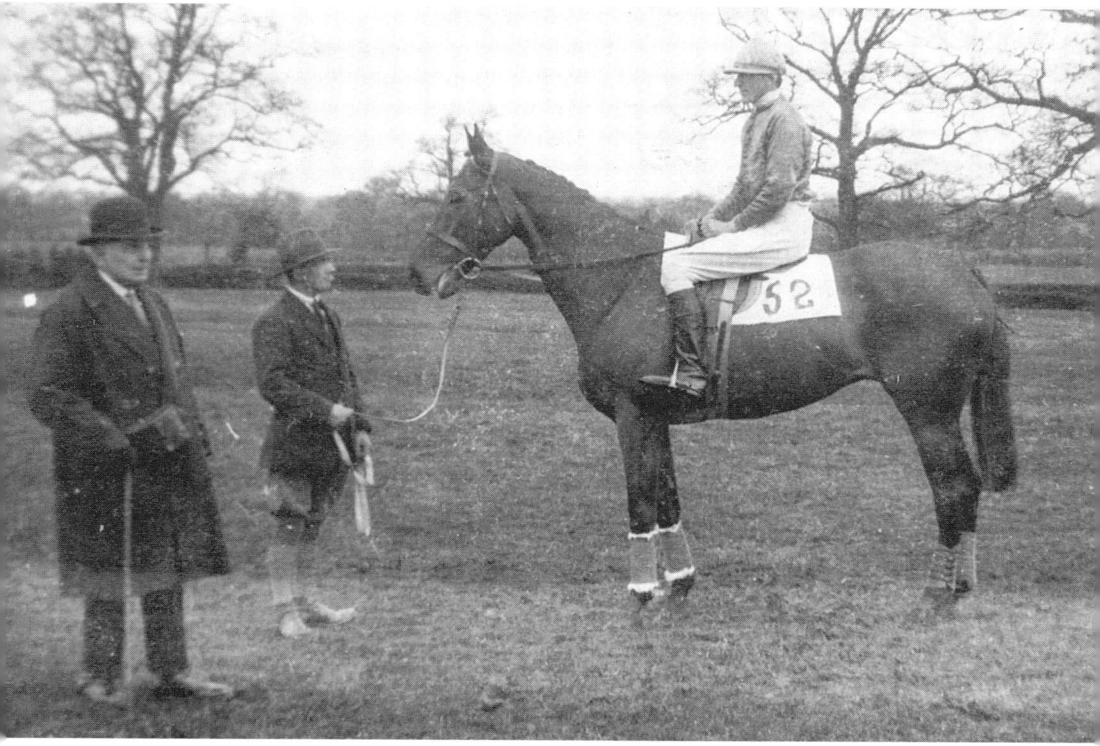

Tipperary Tim, bred in the county of Tipperary and owned by Harold Kenyon, was trained in Whitchurch by Joseph Dodd. In the 1928 Grand National the Americans were confident about winning the race with Billy Barton. The odds of 100/1 were a good reflection of what little chance Tipperary Tim had of winning the race for his jockey William Parker Dutton. It was one of the most disastrous races ever to be held; only a few horses were able to keep going and in the end only two made it to the finishing line, Tipperary Tim first and Billy Barton, a long distance behind. Mr Dutton, a solicitor from Chester, afterwards turned professional. Sadly no tribute was ever paid to Tipperary Tim, but the most searching questions were asked as to how such a mediocre horse could possibly succeed in racing's greatest event. The photograph, taken before the race in 1928, shows Mr Dodd, the trainer and Mr Dutton the jockey.

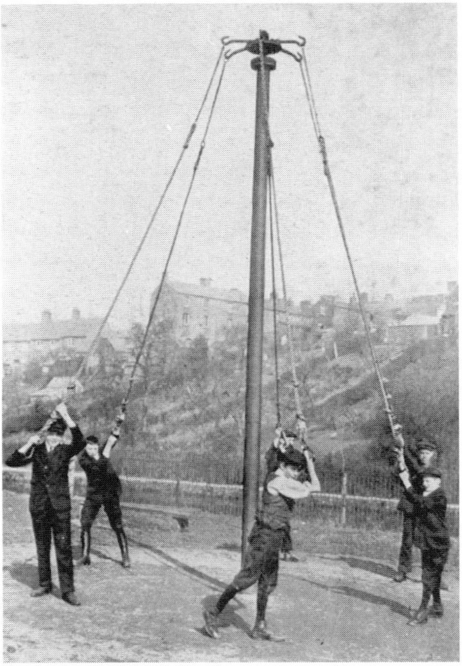

A boys' roundabout in the Jubilee Park, *c.* 1900. It would definitely not pass the health and safety regulations of today. The boys had to run fast around the pole until the heavy iron cables lifted them off the ground into the air.

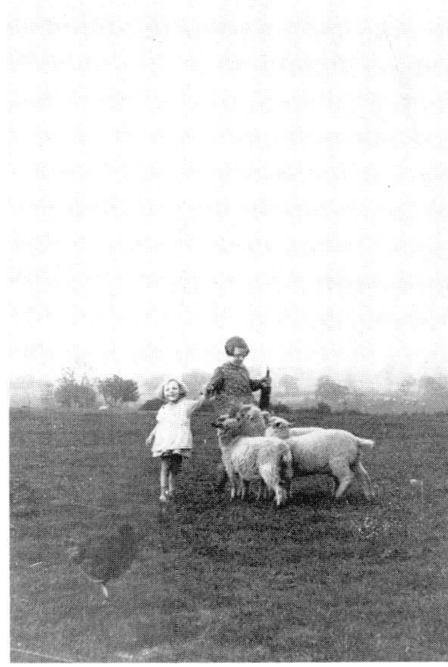

Diana and Biddy Wynn feeding the lambs in the 1930s. Children were involved in the work on the farm from a very early age; feeding the chickens, giving milk to the lambs and skinning rabbits for supper were just a few of their jobs. During harvest time most village schools would close, as the children's help was needed at home.

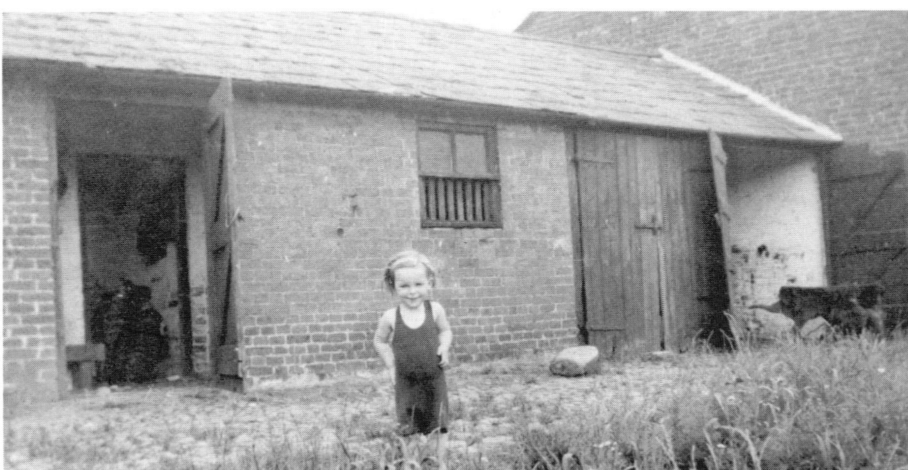

Diana in front of the barn at Hadley Farm.

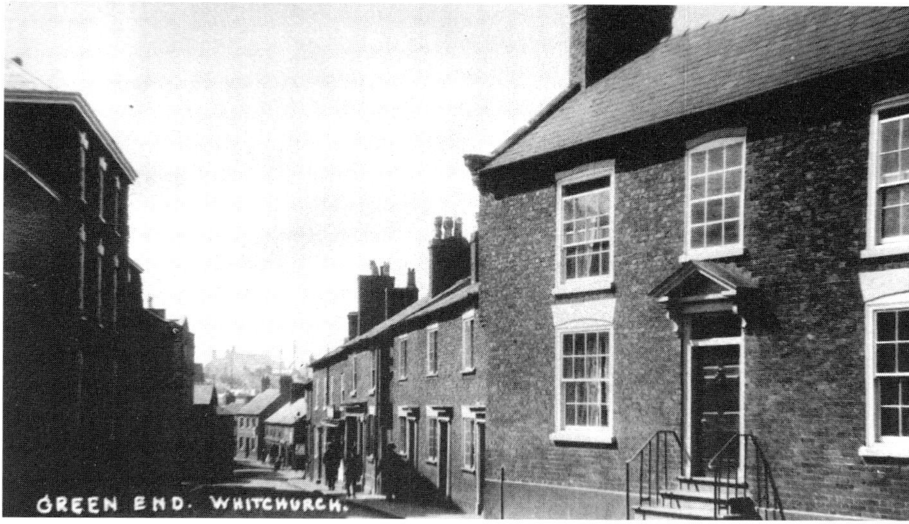

Green End at the turn of the century. Fountain House on the corner together with the adjoining cottages was demolished around 1930 to make way for a car park. Many residents still remember the 'Penny Bazaar' before the war, where everything was sold for a penny. It was in this shop that Hilda Cliff from Newtown started her working life.

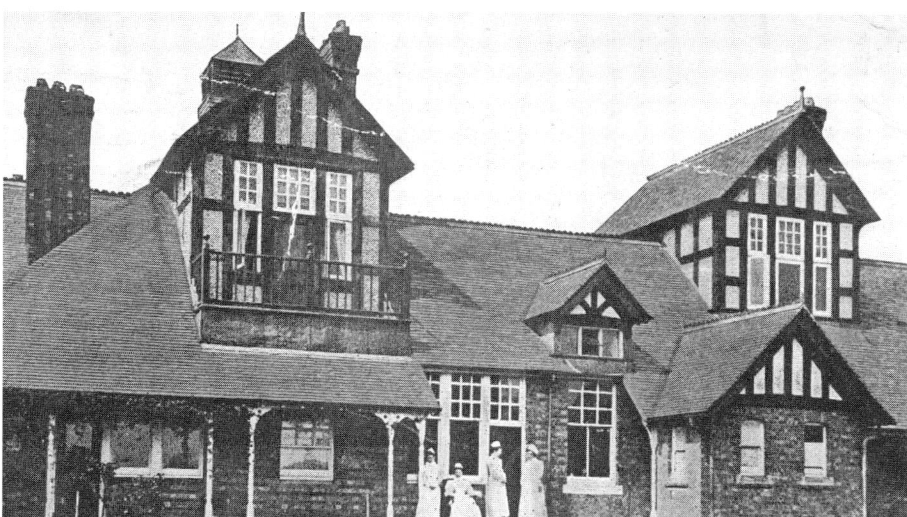

The Cottage Hospital in Brownlow Street was opened on 1 October 1886. The land was given by Lord Brownlow. The hospital was enlarged in 1897 in commemoration of the sixtieth year of the reign of Queen Victoria. In 1904 the accommodation included one private ward, six male beds, six female beds, one cot, rooms for matron, three nurses and two maids, and one X-ray machine. This photograph dates from around 1910. The hospital was closed two years ago and is now on the verge of being demolished.

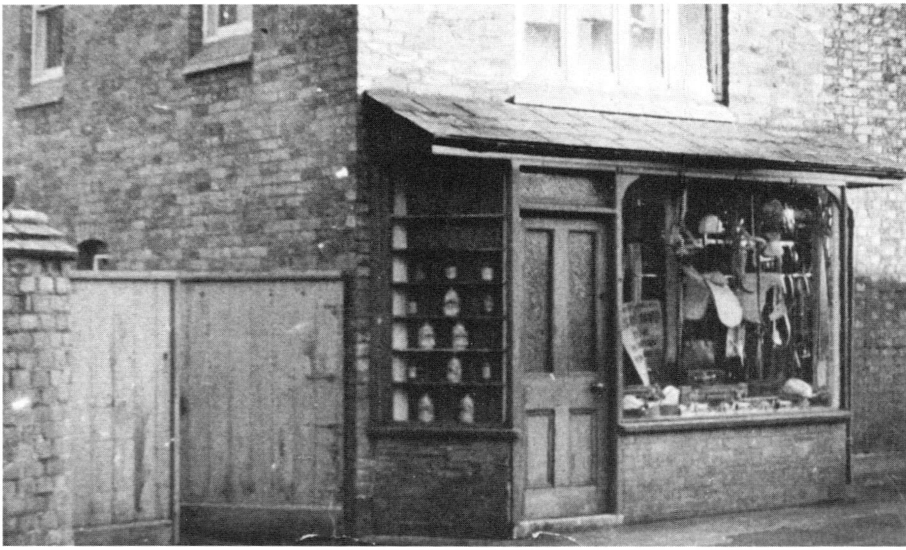

The tannery brought important trade to the town. Shoes were made for the Manchester market and saddles from Lewis's in St John's Street were popular in the whole county. The business was established around 1920 and the shop (seen here) was demolished in the 1960s. The flats built on the site are called Saddlers Court. This photograph was taken around 1938.

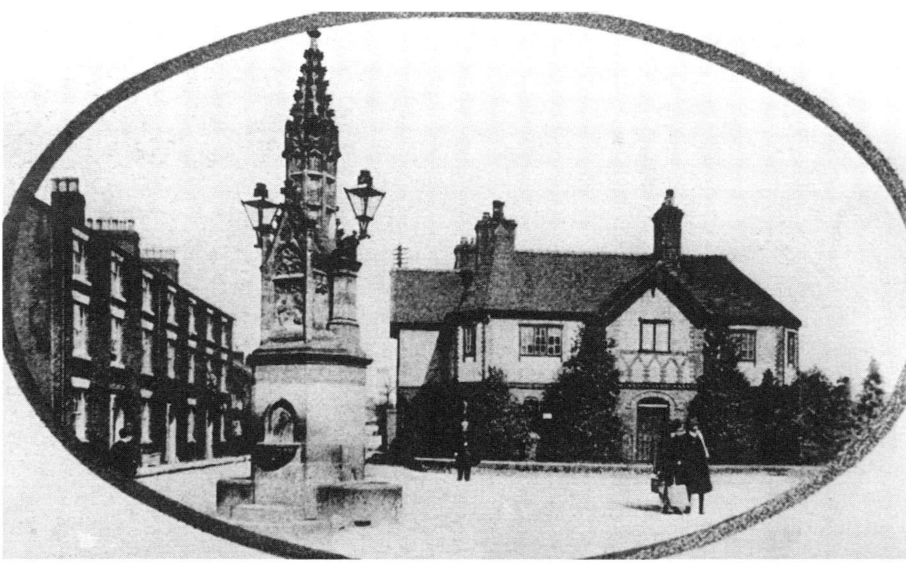

The fountain, originally at Green End, was erected as a memorial to the great cause of temperance. It was moved in 1928 to Brownlow Street, where it still is today. Before mains water was connected to Whitchurch, the fountain supplied the local residents. The photograph was taken around 1930.

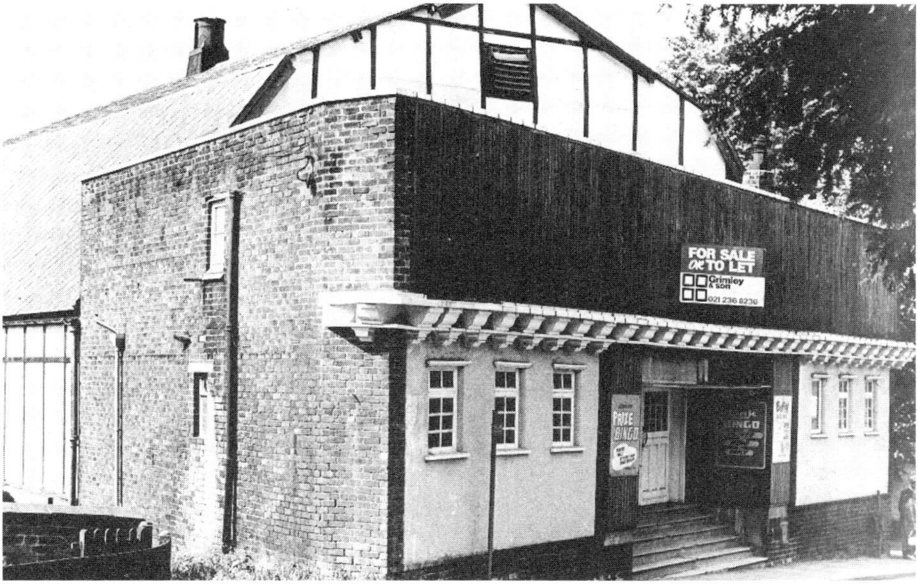

The cinema, or picture palace as it was known in Whitchurch, opened in 1918. Hilda Cliff, who worked there during the war, recalled that the biggest success was *Gone with the Wind*. The building, shown here in the 1960s, has been used since the closure of the cinema for many different enterprises, from bingo hall to furniture shop. It is surprising that nearly all the cinemas in the smaller country towns have now ceased to operate, particularly as there is very little other entertainment for young people.

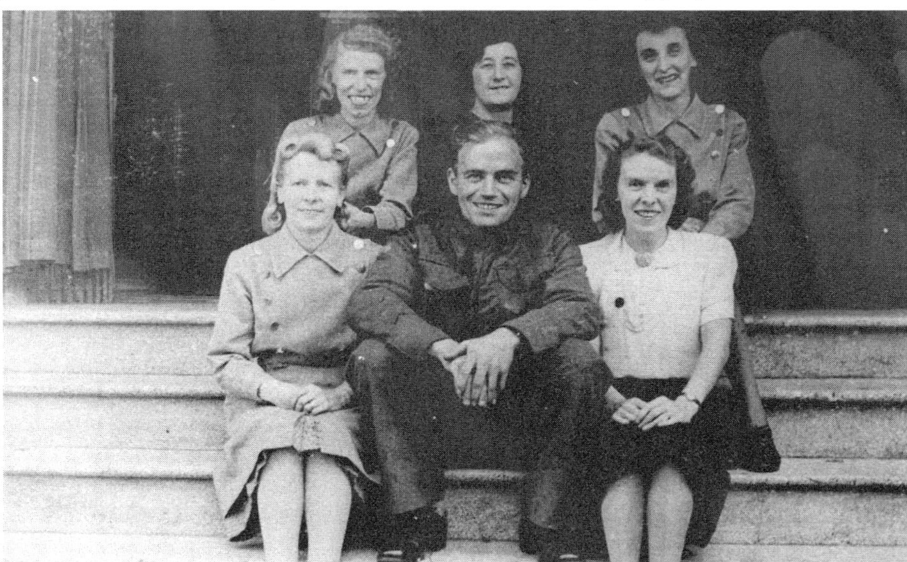

Hilda Cliff (bottom right) and friends sitting on the steps of the picture palace in 1942.

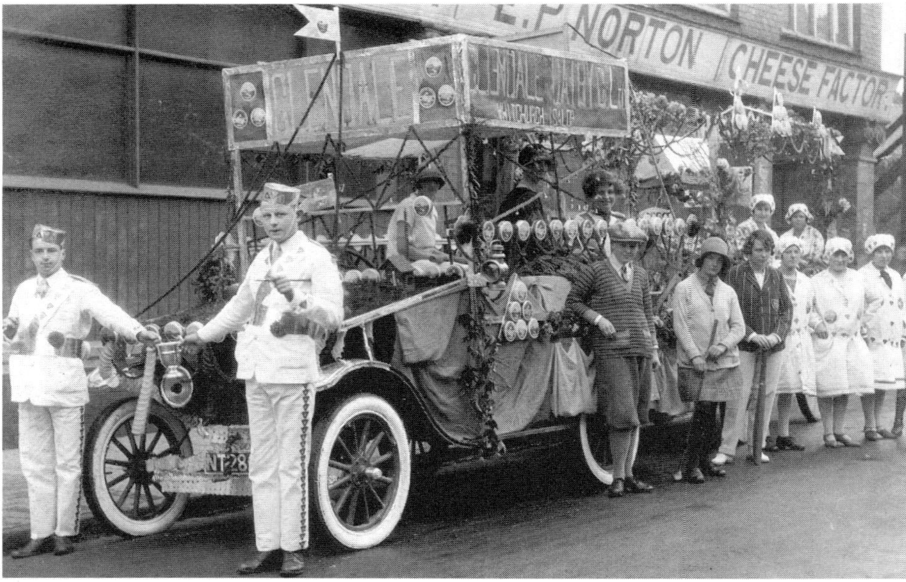

This 1930 carnival float belonged to Mr E.P. Norton, the well-known cheese manufacturer and entrepreneur, featured here in his plus-fours. This photograph was found among the papers of the late Miss Eileen Dyer, who worked for Mr Norton.

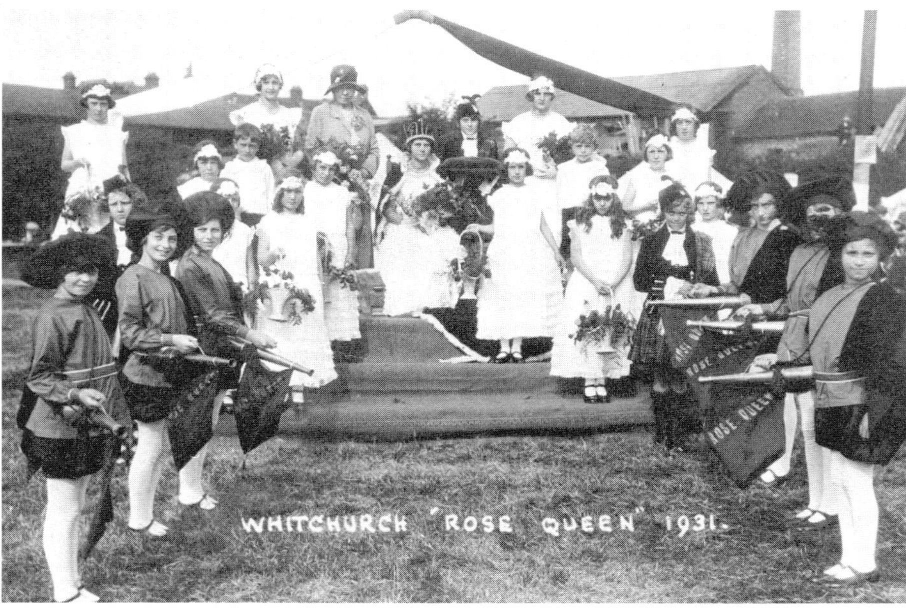

Crowning the 'Rose Queen' in 1931 in White Lion Meadow. Margaret Lewis was chosen that year and crowned by Mrs Dugdale of Terrick Hall (Chairwoman of the Governors of Whitchurch Girls High School).

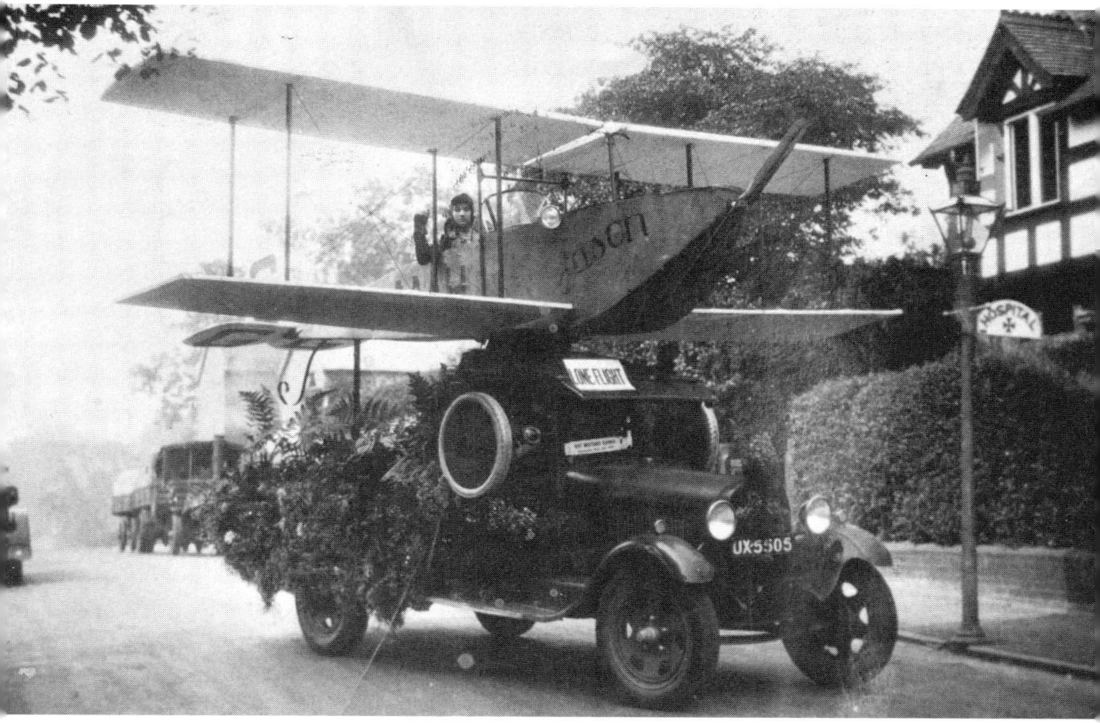

The carnival provided much-needed entertainment during the hard times of the 1930s. Photographed here outside the Cottage Hospital in 1930 is a float with a mock-up of Amy Johnson's aeroplane.

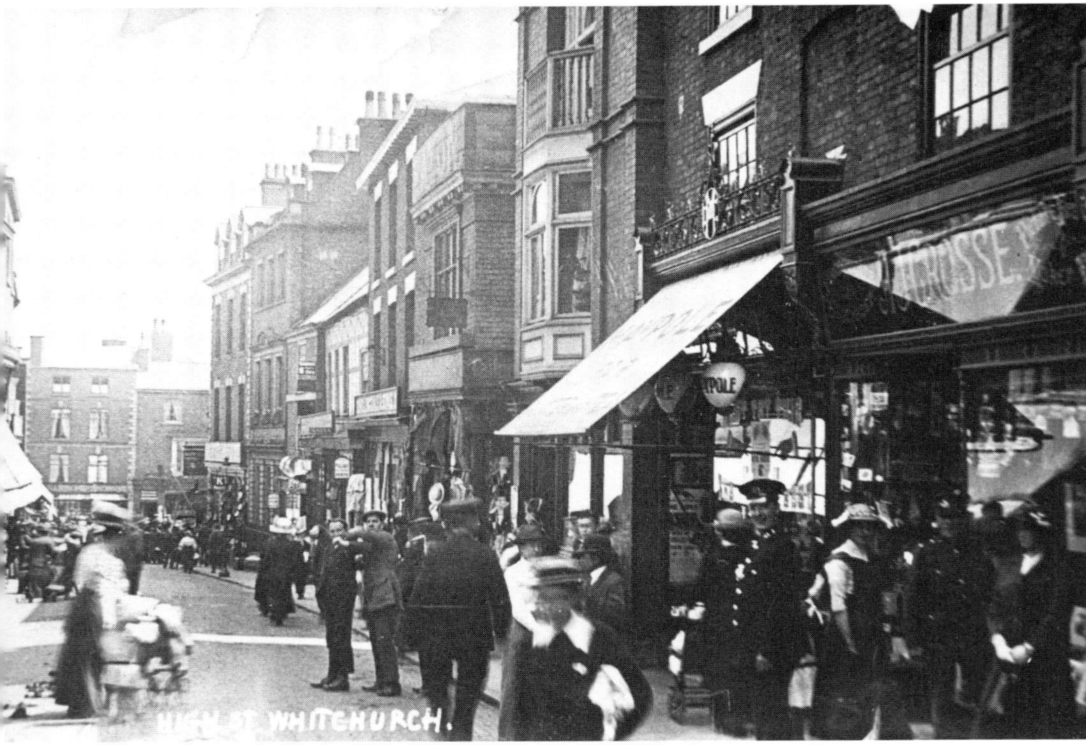

High Street, Whitchurch, *c.* 1920. An historic extract on Shropshire, dated 1837, describes the streets of Whitchurch as being 'far from great beauty or spaciousness but clean and respectable. The inns, tradesmen's shops and private dwellings show moderate wealth, good trade and friendly behaviour of the inhabitants'. The railway, the market and the canal all contributed to make Whitchurch a busy market town. The closure of the Cumbrian Railway line and the building of the bypass have resulted in reduced trade for many of the shops in town, and a large number have been empty for a long time. However, Whitchurch has just received a large grant that will help to promote it as a tourist attraction and bring new vitality to the place.

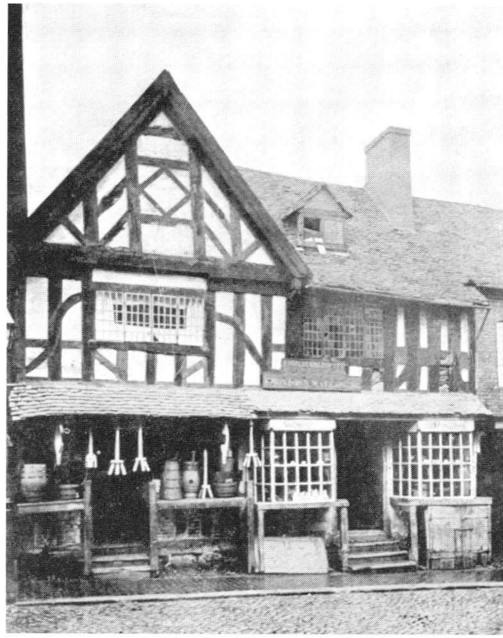

The Old Shop in the High Street, part of which was built in 1450 and the rest in 1650, when it was known as the Old Cooperage. This image was taken in 1911. Although the house is now much altered, it has not only avoided destruction but has also retained most of its character.

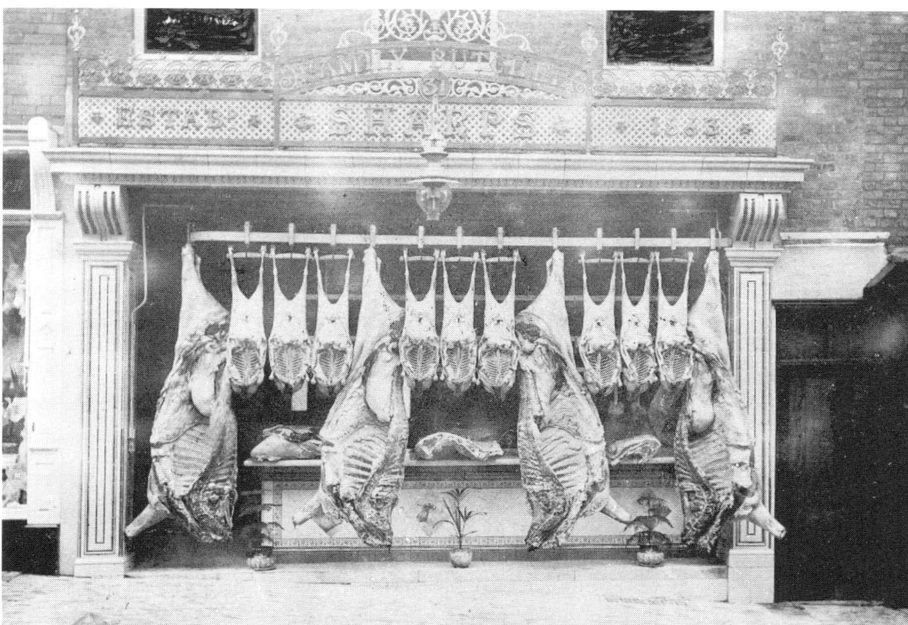

Sharps the butcher was established in 1863 and is still in existence in the High Street today. The display, luckily, has changed, however. This photograph was taken in 1930.

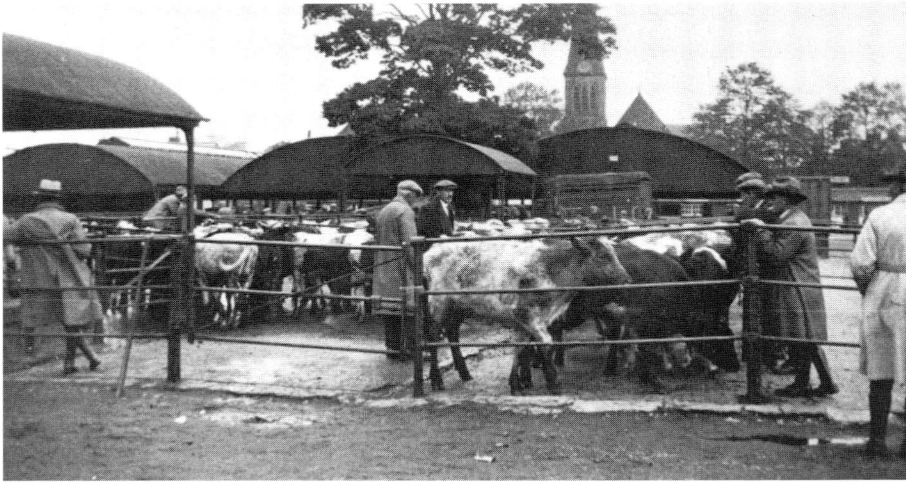

Smithfield Market in 1936. It was demolished in 1980 to make way for the Kwiksave supermarket and farmers now have to take their livestock to the cattle markets in Shrewsbury or Crewe. In 1761 we find an entry in the town map of a 'Swine Market' in Newtown. Geese were sold in Church Lane and horses and cattle in New Street and Bargates. To bring it all together, Smithfield Market was opened in 1877 with two entrances, at Brownlow Street and St John's Street.

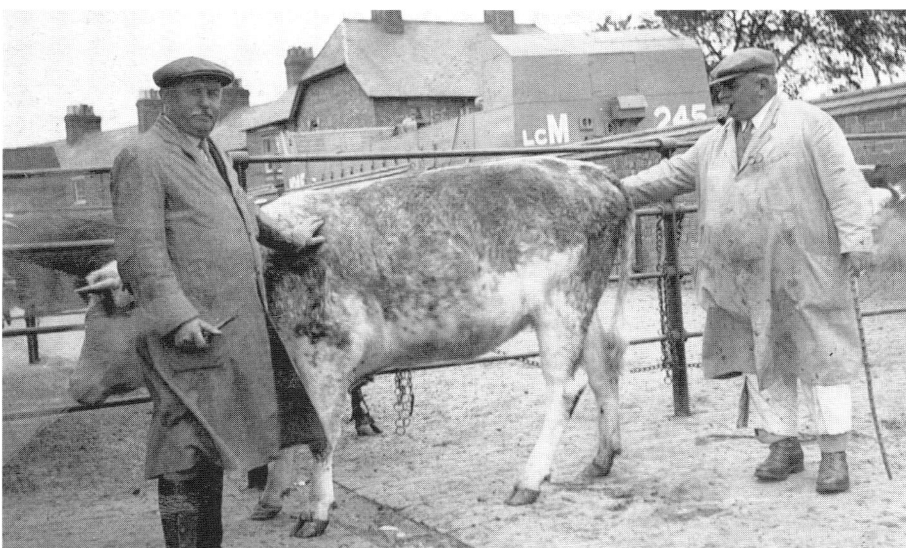

Two farmers at Smithfield Market in 1943 inspecting a bull. Herefords and Short-horns gave way to the Friesian cow, which provided a larger quantity of milk. The Friesian would be mated with a Hereford bull so that the calf would have more flesh on it. Now, of course, the bull comes in the shape of a sales representative with semen specimens from a large variety of breeds.

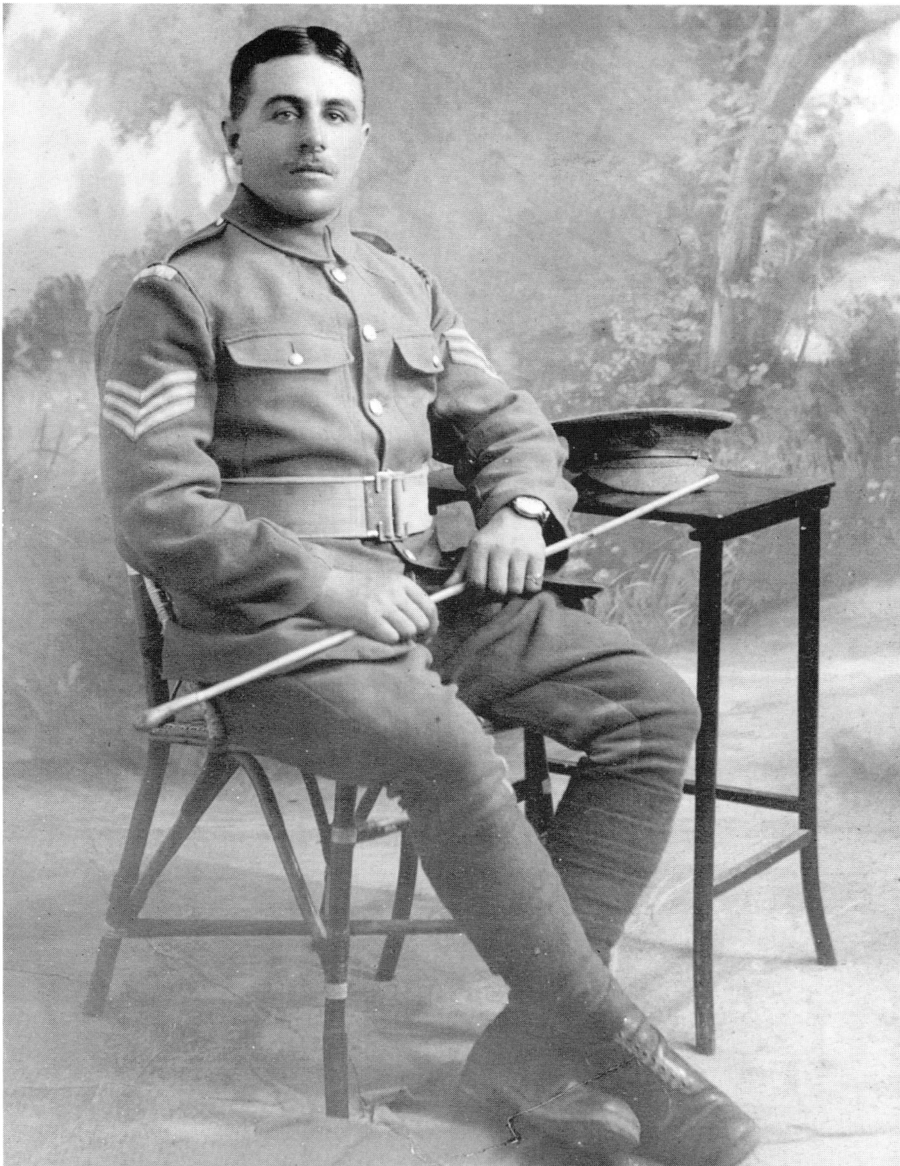

The following passage is taken from *The Shropshire Yeomanry 1795–1945* by E.W. Gladstone: 'During the First World War while stationed at Benacre the first confrontation with the war was a Zeppelin raid. There had been many before but not so close. Order was given in the camp to disperse. Sergeant Jack Wynn – who in those days weighed a mere 14 stone – was the first to get the section away. "Follow me, lads," he said, "I'll pull you through", and he did.' This photograph of Jack Wynn was taken in a studio in 1916.

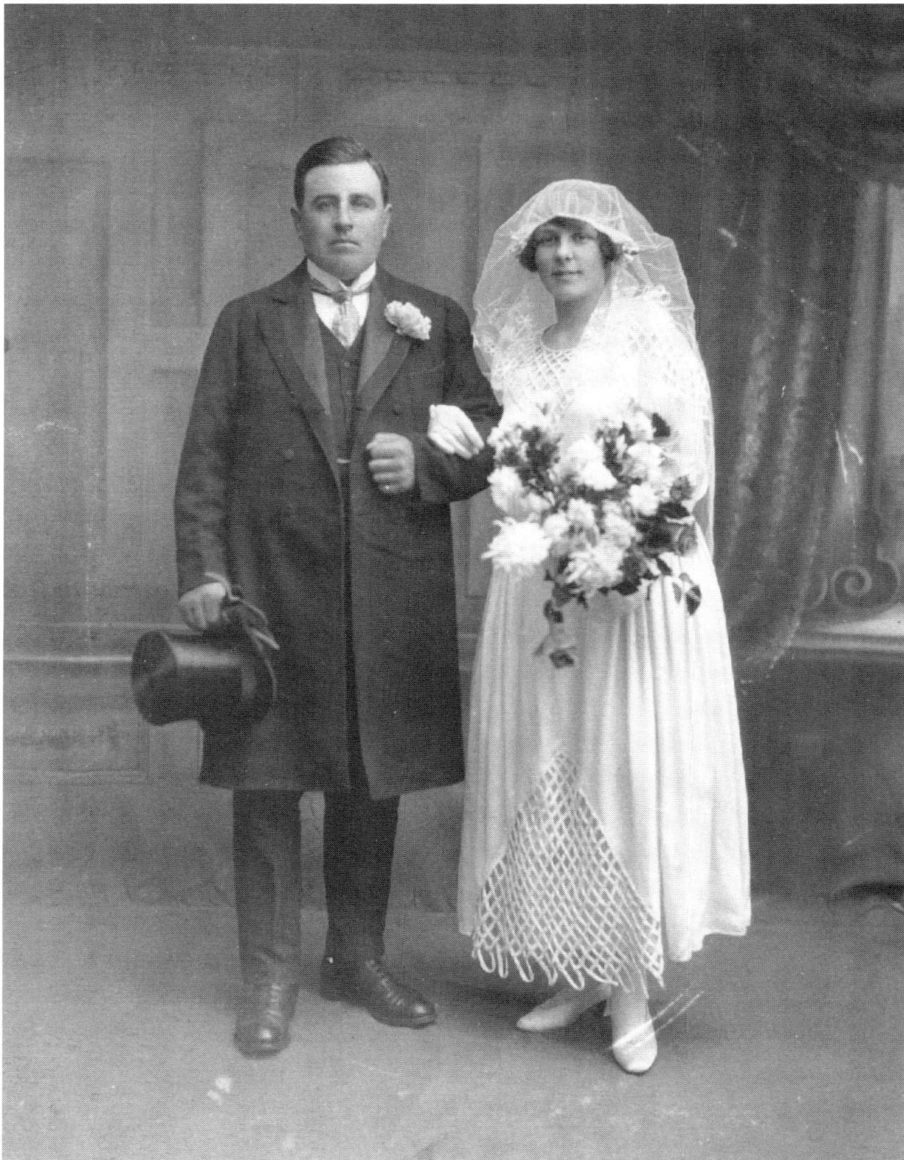

This wedding photograph of beautiful Hannah Edwards and Jack Wynn was actually taken two weeks after the wedding at the photographer's studio, as was the practice at that time. Jack was a well-respected farmer in Hadley and people for miles around still remember him today with great affection.

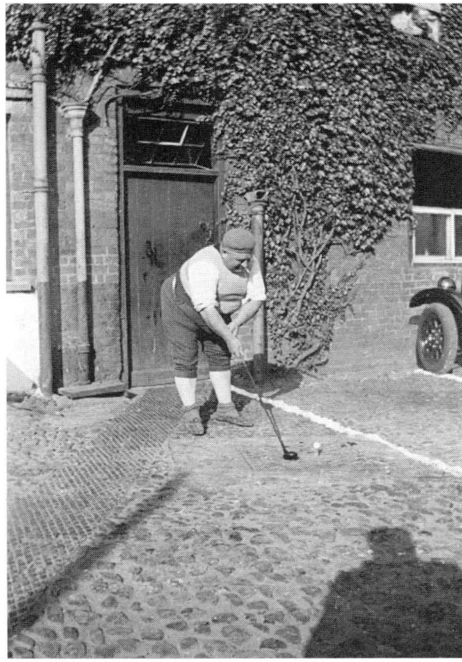

Jack Wynn playing golf outside the Swan Hotel in Whitchurch. This former coaching house was built between the fourteenth and fifteenth centuries and was pulled down in 1970 to make way for the Tesco supermarket. At the time of this photograph in 1933 the proprietor was Tommy Thomas, much liked by the locals for his sense of humour and for his ability to reduce his own profit.

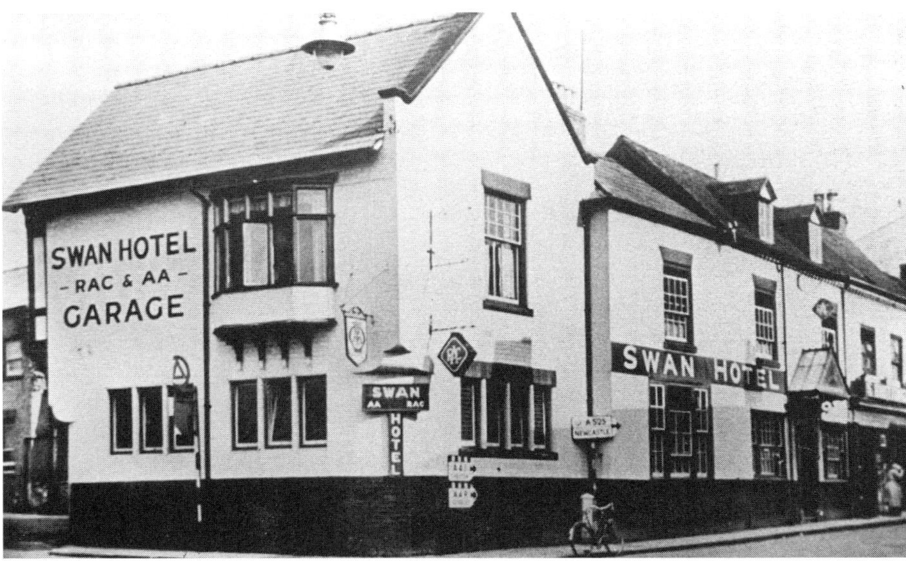

The Swan Hotel in the early 1930s.

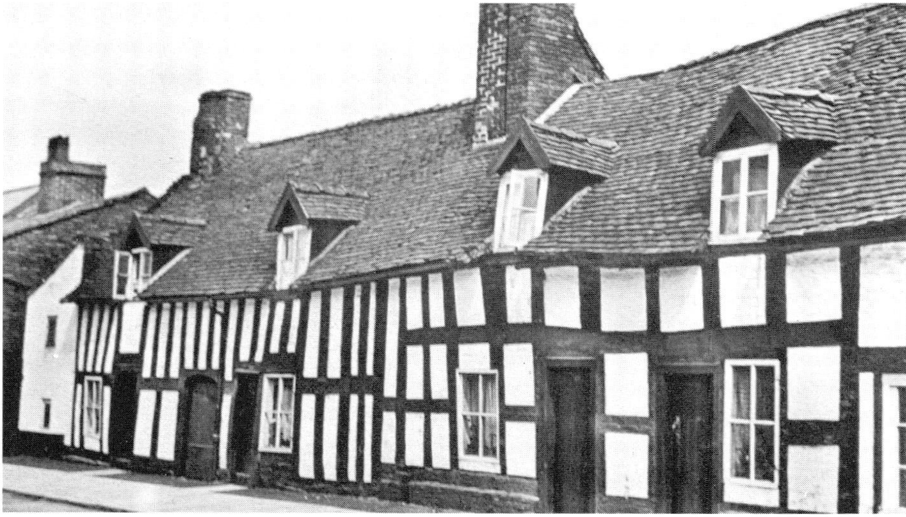

These beautiful sixteenth-century cottages in Station Road have now been demolished. Mrs Sarginson, whose family has lived in the town for many generations, wrote twenty years ago: 'Gradually these old houses are being demolished and the quiet narrow roads widened to take the rapid pace of the motor car. Soon the whole town will have changed and the quaintness and cosiness of the past will die.'

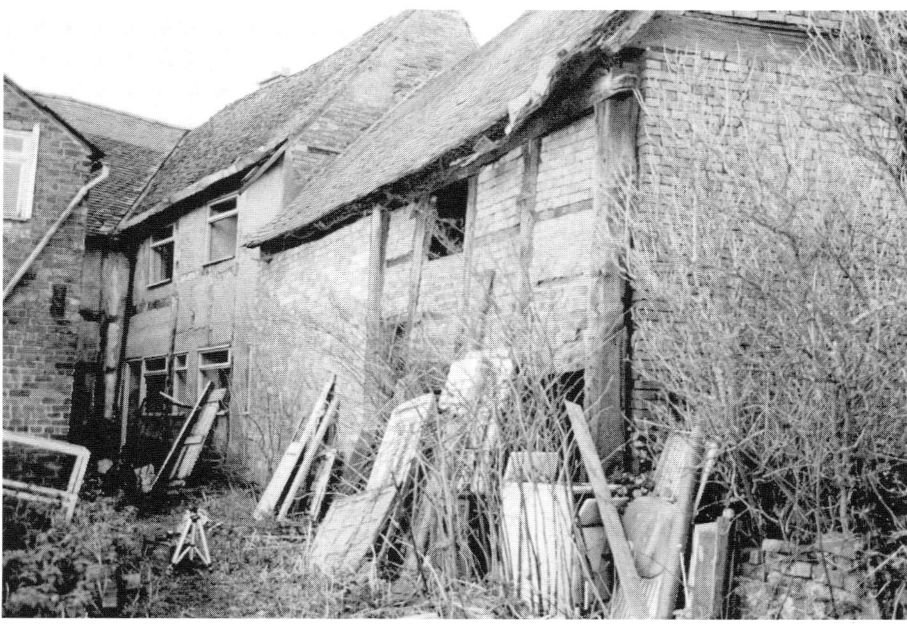

Fifteenth-century cottages in Piccadilly, photographed here in 1978. After the indiscriminate destruction of so many old properties these have survived and are now up for sale in the hope that somebody will preserve them for posterity.

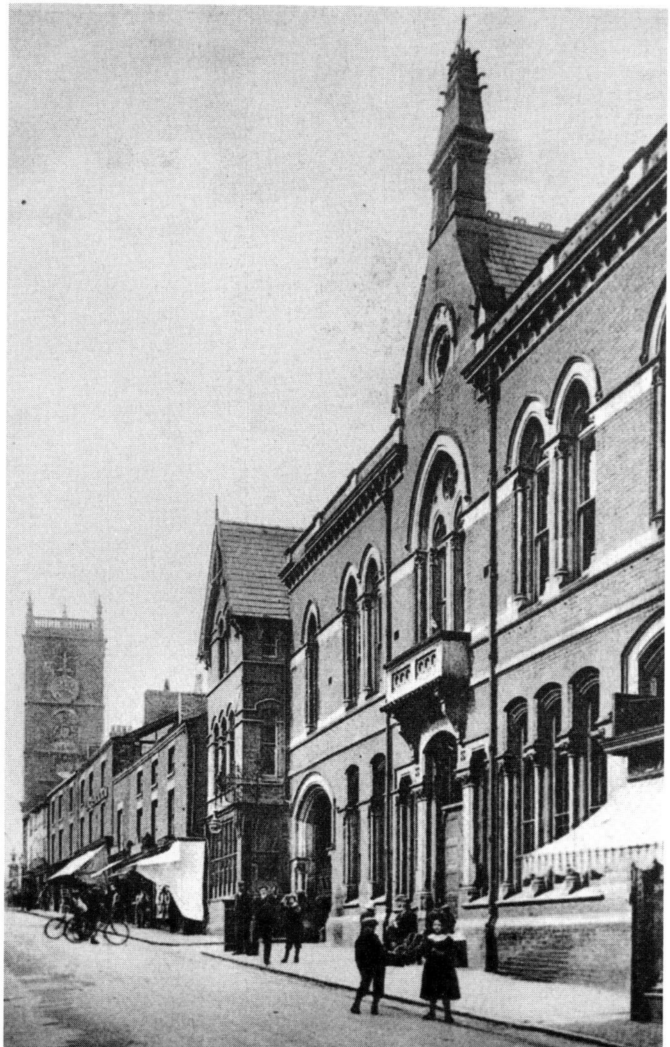

The Town Hall, now demolished, was officially opened in 1872 and was enlarged considerably in 1902 to house the library, the art gallery, with a collection of paintings by Randolph Caldecott, a reading room and a billiard room. Among the possessions of the library is the original charter, dating from 3 November 1362, granting the town a market on three days in every year. The Branks, which was used for 'the purpose of punishing those disorderly women who scold their husbands', is one of the more controversial pieces housed in the museum. It was an iron bridle or head-piece that encircled the neck and head and was closed by a padlock at the back. An iron pin with a notched wheel at the end projected inwards, pressed on the tongue and formed an effective gag. The Branks was used as late as the nineteenth century.

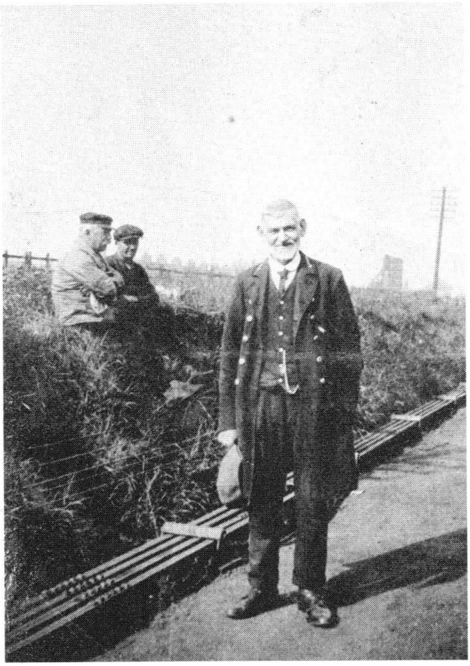

Employees of the Cambrian Railway, *c.* 1920. Left to right: Joseph Parker of Stockton, Dick Hentley and Charles Newbrook (guard).

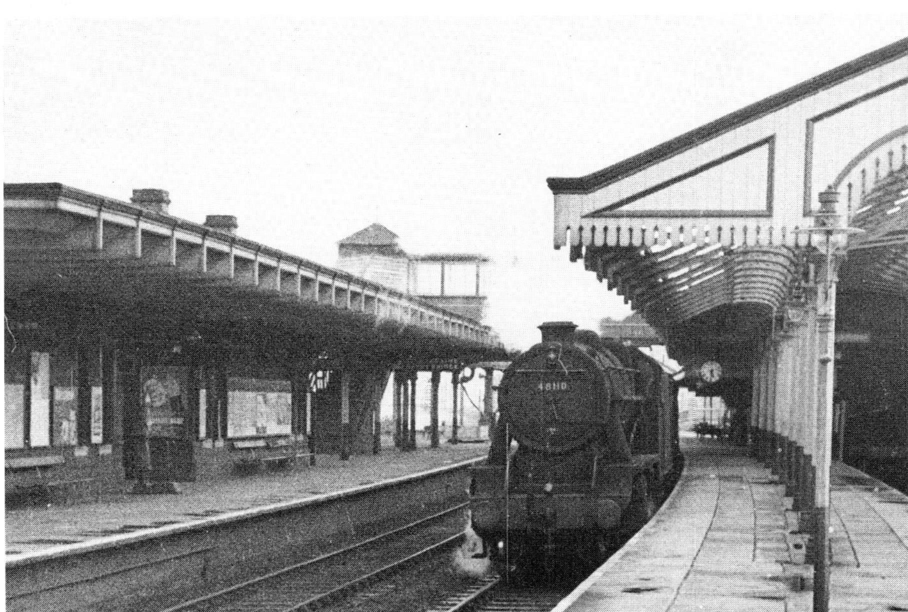

Engine 8F 48110 passing through Whitchurch station in 1953.

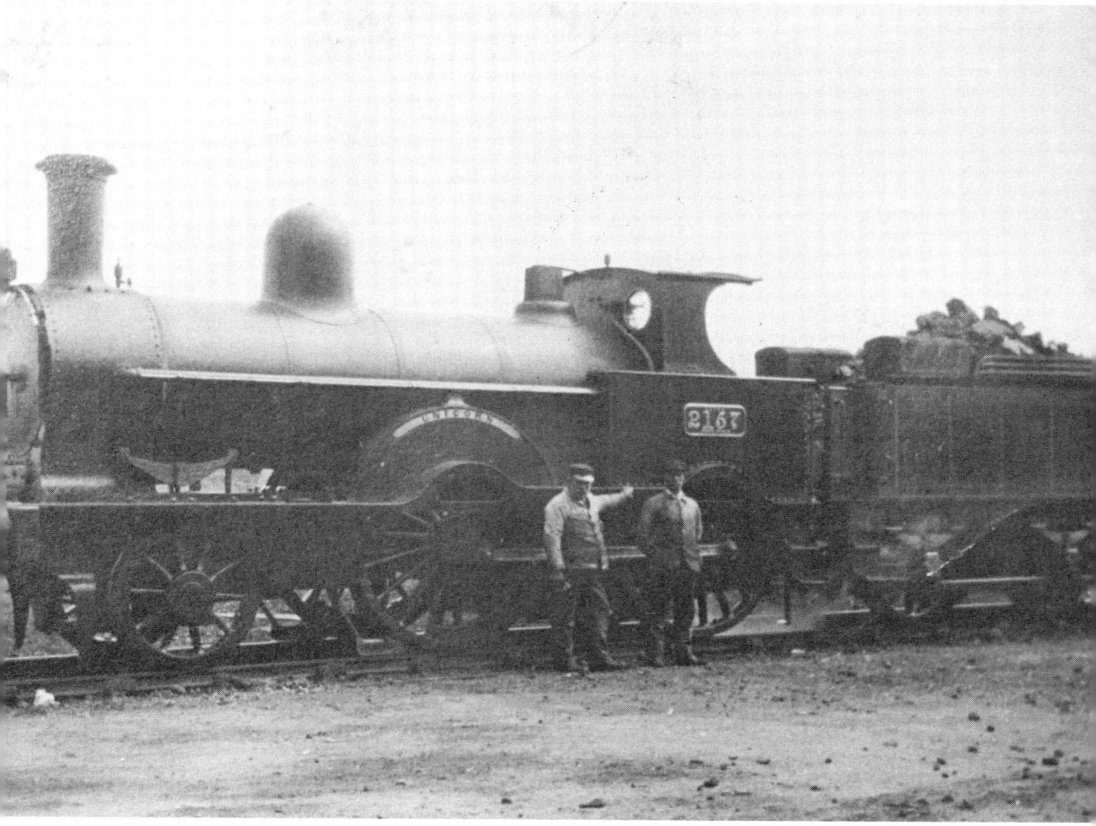

The locomotive 'Samson' class 2–4–0 No. 2157 *Unicorn* was built in 1874 and withdrawn in 1922. It is shown here with the driver, Joseph Parker of Stockton. Whitchurch was an important junction during Victorian times where the Cumbrian line met with the LNWR line to Chester and Crewe. The section between Whitchurch and Ellesmere was opened to goods traffic in April 1863 and for passengers in May of that year. The line to Oswestry, which became the main depot between Whitchurch and Welshpool, was delayed until 1864. The double track to Crewe opened in 1882. The line between Whitchurch and Wales was closed in 1965. For those not considering themselves railway buffs, the following information may be of more interest: the word 'navvies', used to describe men who travelled about the country building railways, actually derived from the gangs that had built the canals years before – nicknamed 'navigators'. One never thinks about the hard labour that went into the building of these tracks. Huge amounts of equipment and thousands of men were required. Tens of thousands of tons of earth had to be moved by the individual shovel. With the decline of the railway many of those closed tracks are now slowly merging back into the scenery.

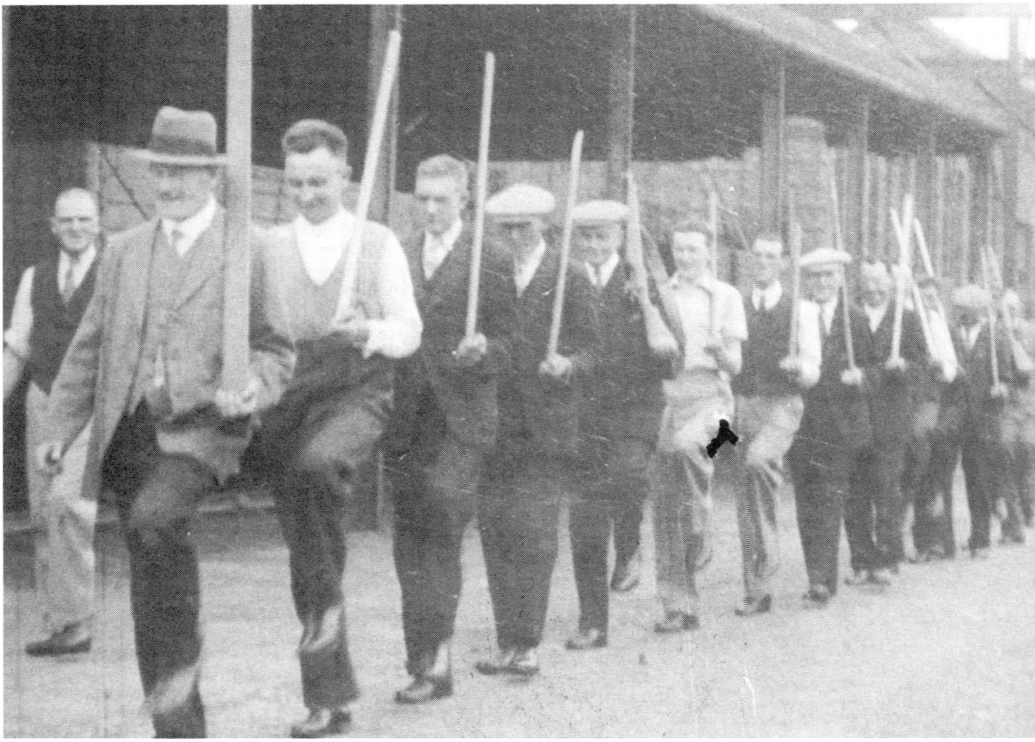

Whitchurch railway station staff as part of the Local Defence Volunteers (later the Home Guard) drilling in the station yard in 1940. Mr C. Harding, the station master, is at the front. Anything was used to simulate rifles.

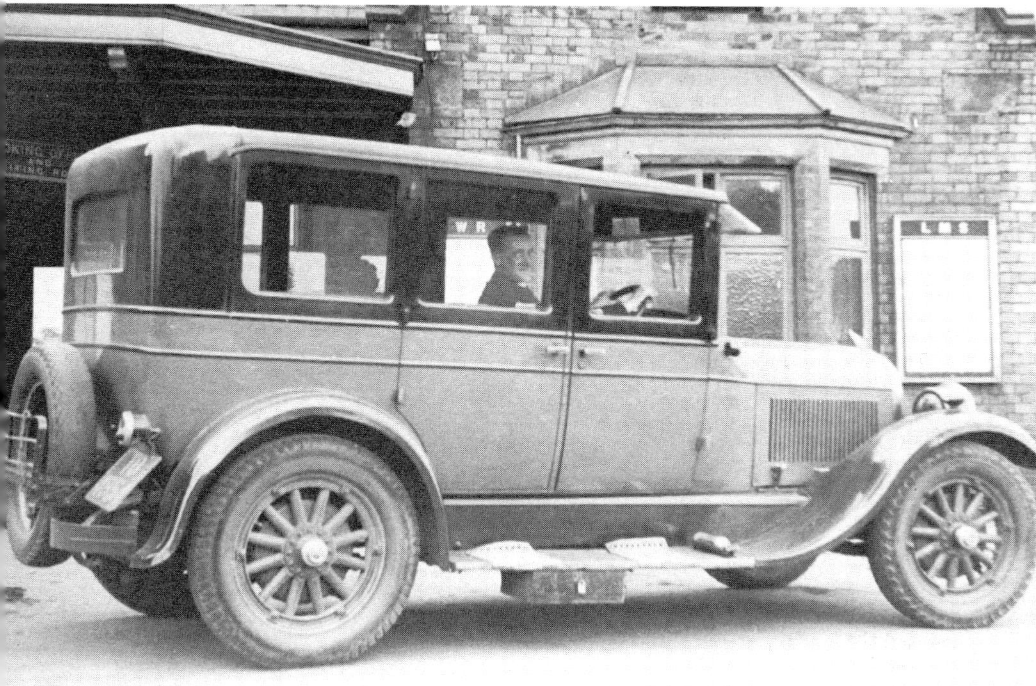

Mr Mountford and his taxi in 1922. For many years it was the only taxi service in Whitchurch. In the background stands the station with a new canopy over the entrance.

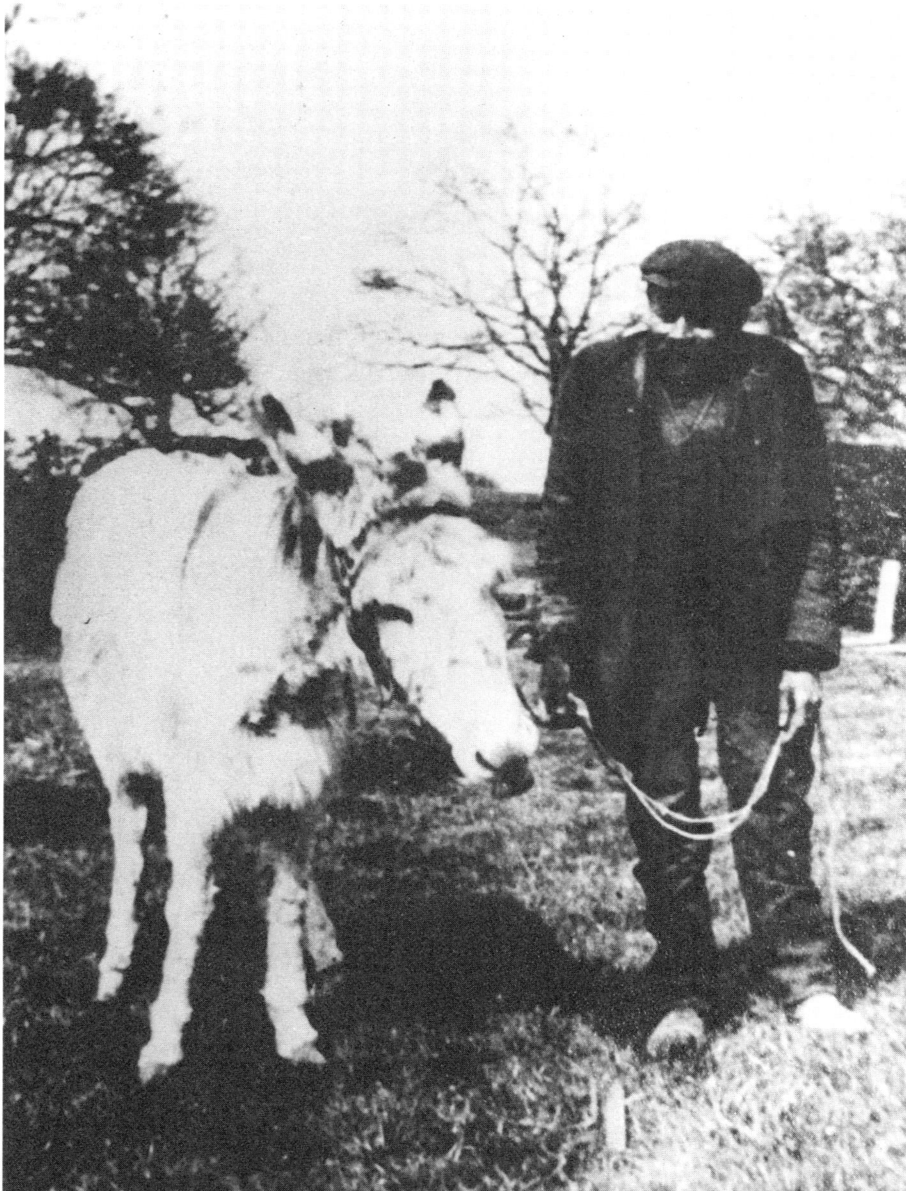

This is the only photograph in existence of Joey and his donkey, a well-known figure in the streets of Whitchurch around 1910. He eked out a living by trundling his donkey cart round the big houses collecting and delivering laundry. In between he used the same cart to fetch coke from the gasworks to sell door to door. Joey is still remembered by many of the senior citizens of Whitchurch.

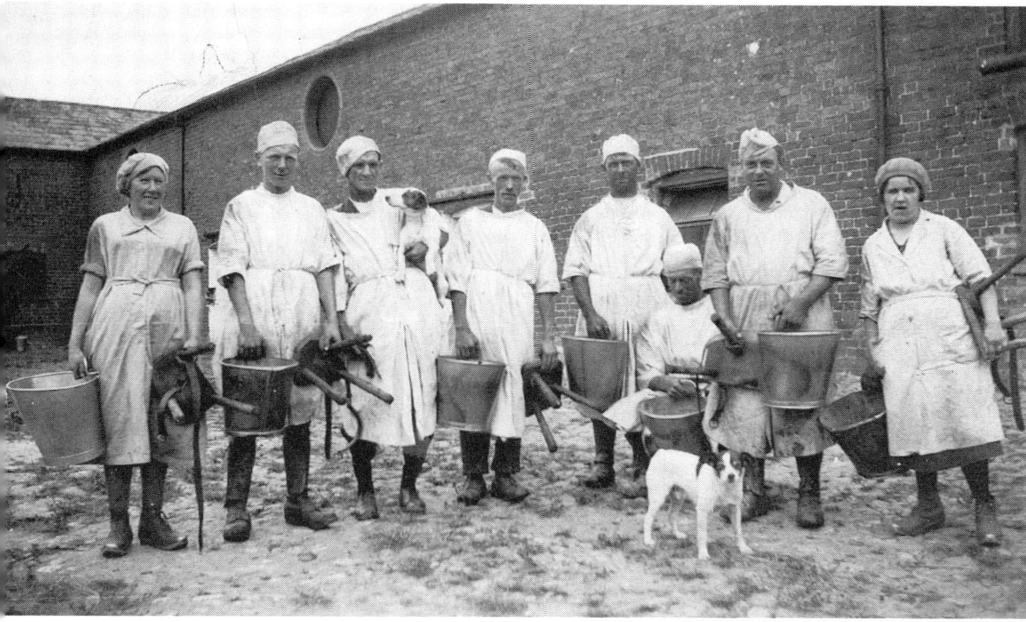

The milking brigade at Hadley Farm in 1935. Everybody would lend a hand to milk the ninety-strong herd. In the photograph are Harry Brown, who received a service medal, Bill Griffith and his two sons and wife, George and Wynni Harding, plus two canine helpers without names. The milking was done in the shippon (cattleshed) with two cows to a stall, fastened with a chain. The milker sat on a stool with the bucket firmly held between his or her knees. The milk was poured into large containers through a sieve, and later, when dairies collected the milk, churns were used.

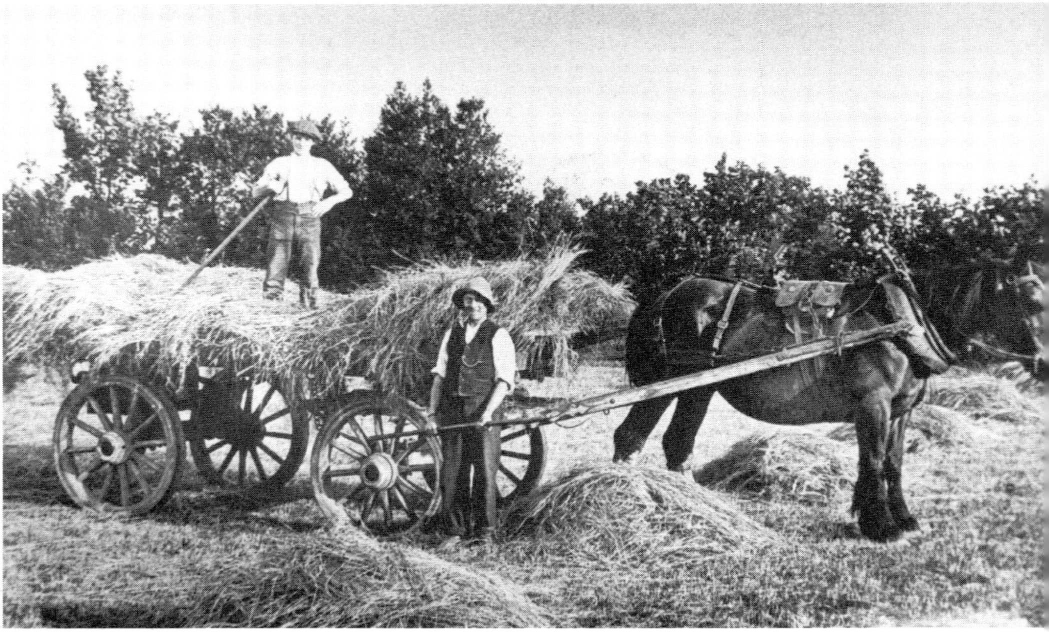

Before the arrival of the horse-drawn hay raker, the grass was cut by hand scythes and then collected with a wooden hay raker. Gangs of navvies would travel through the countryside and offer their services at the bigger farms and estates. During and after the First World War women had to take on many of these farming jobs as there was a great shortage of farm-workers. This photograph was taken in 1914.

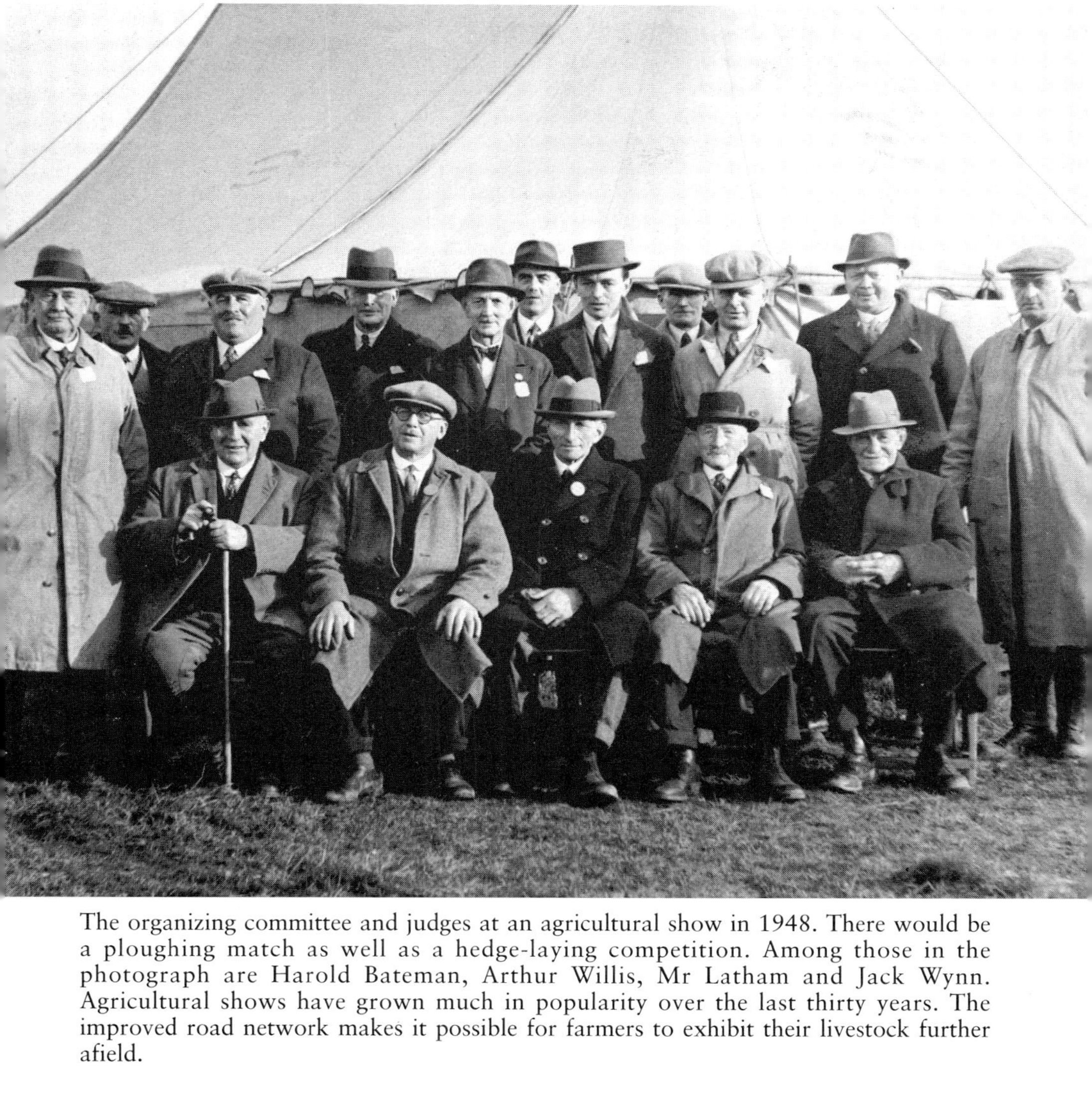

The organizing committee and judges at an agricultural show in 1948. There would be a ploughing match as well as a hedge-laying competition. Among those in the photograph are Harold Bateman, Arthur Willis, Mr Latham and Jack Wynn. Agricultural shows have grown much in popularity over the last thirty years. The improved road network makes it possible for farmers to exhibit their livestock further afield.

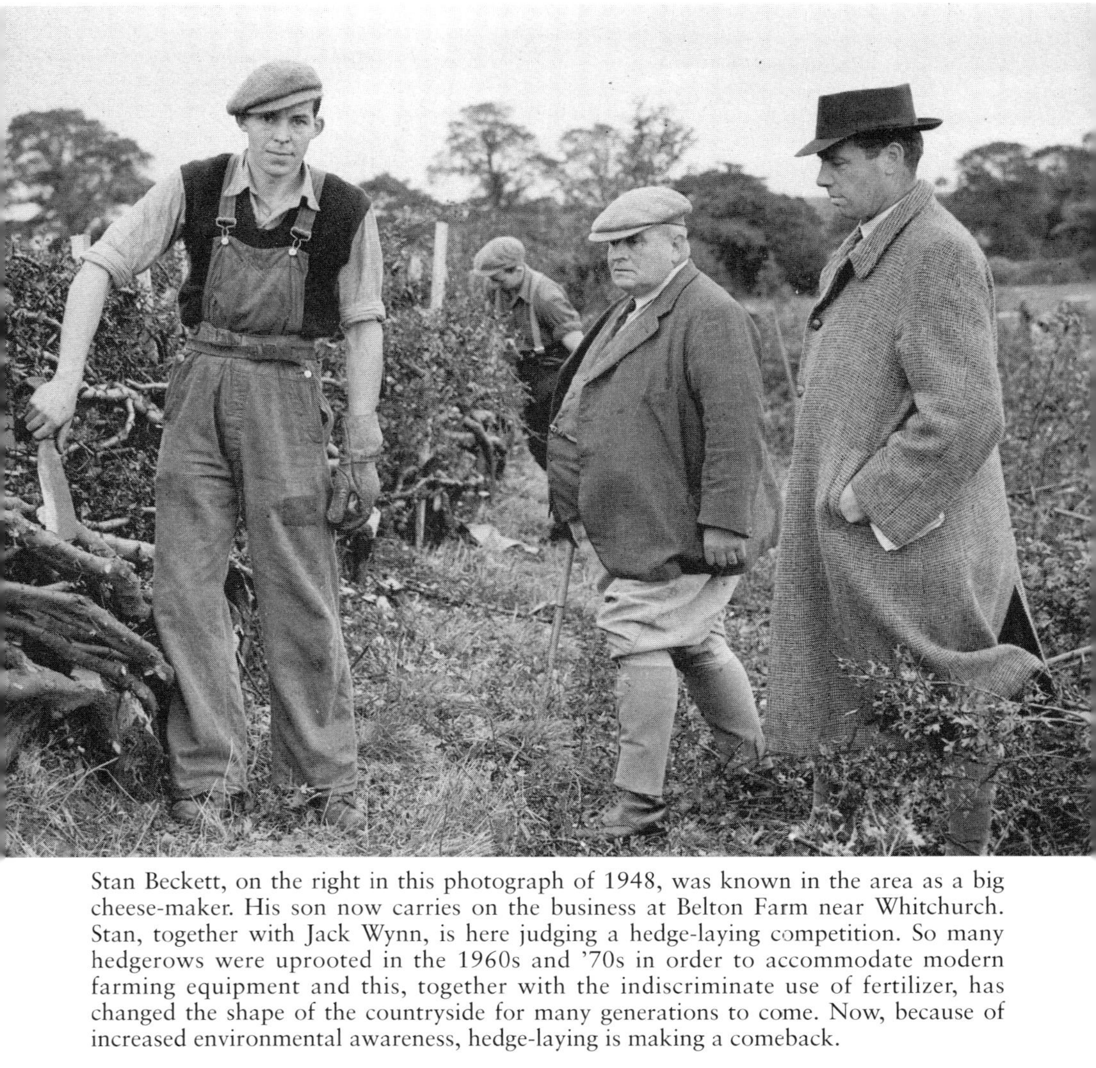

Stan Beckett, on the right in this photograph of 1948, was known in the area as a big cheese-maker. His son now carries on the business at Belton Farm near Whitchurch. Stan, together with Jack Wynn, is here judging a hedge-laying competition. So many hedgerows were uprooted in the 1960s and '70s in order to accommodate modern farming equipment and this, together with the indiscriminate use of fertilizer, has changed the shape of the countryside for many generations to come. Now, because of increased environmental awareness, hedge-laying is making a comeback.

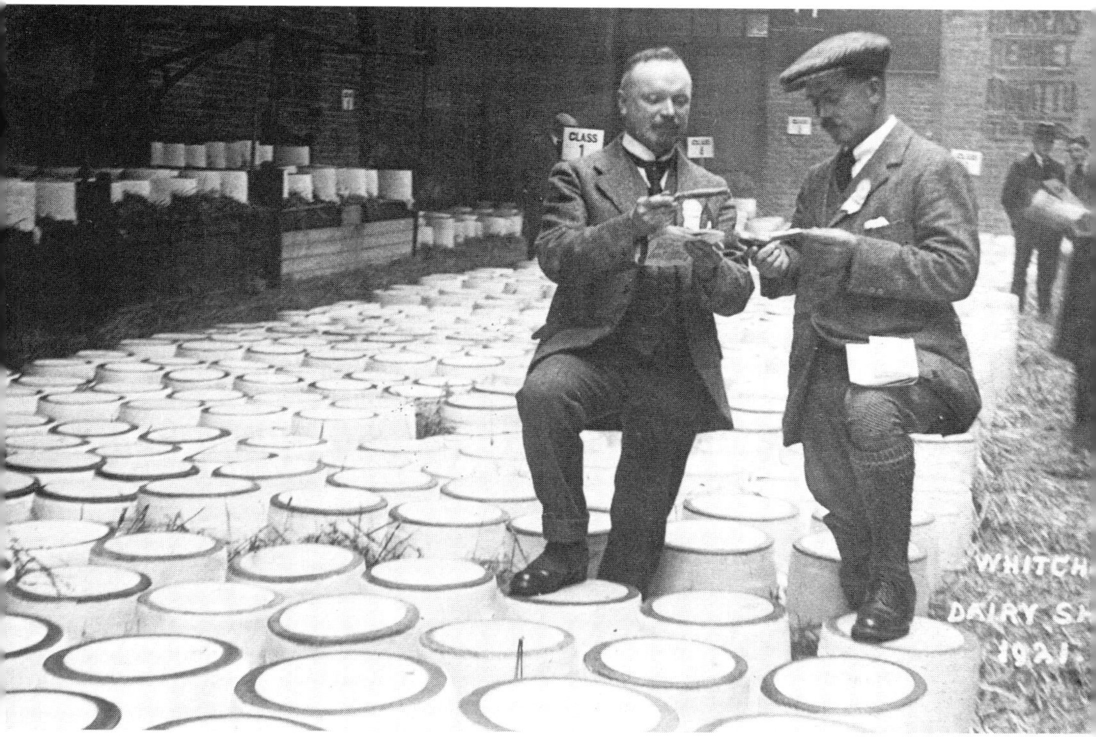

Two gentlemen from outside the town testing cheese at Whitchurch Dairy Show in 1921. Only cheese made from the milk of one herd was considered pure. When made with milk from different farms it was classified as factory cheese. Cheese-making was an important business for the farmers around Whitchurch. The dairy show and cheese market were held in the old Market Hall situated between the High Street and St Mary's Street. People would come from as far as Manchester to the market, which closed just before the outbreak of the Second World War. The old Market Hall burned down in 1941; the fire was started by a cigarette.

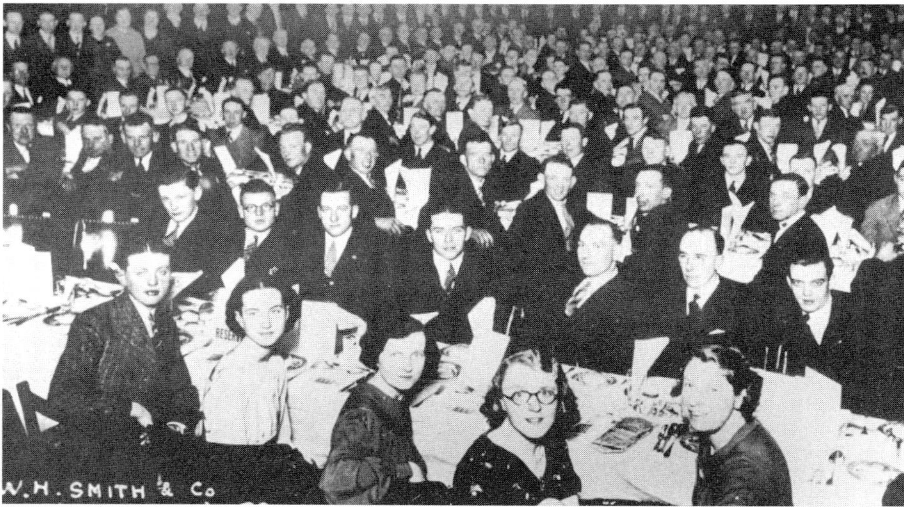

The centenary dinner at the Smith foundry in 1937 at which Bill Cliff received a service medal. Prefabricated haysheds and bandstands were the company's main produce; these were erected all over England by men from Whitchurch. During the war the workforce was exempt from joining the forces because of important government commissions. The company operated a 'tied cottage' system whereby the son had to follow the father into the factory as they would otherwise lose the cottage they lived in. Smith and Co., once one of the largest employers in the area, closed down in the 1980s.

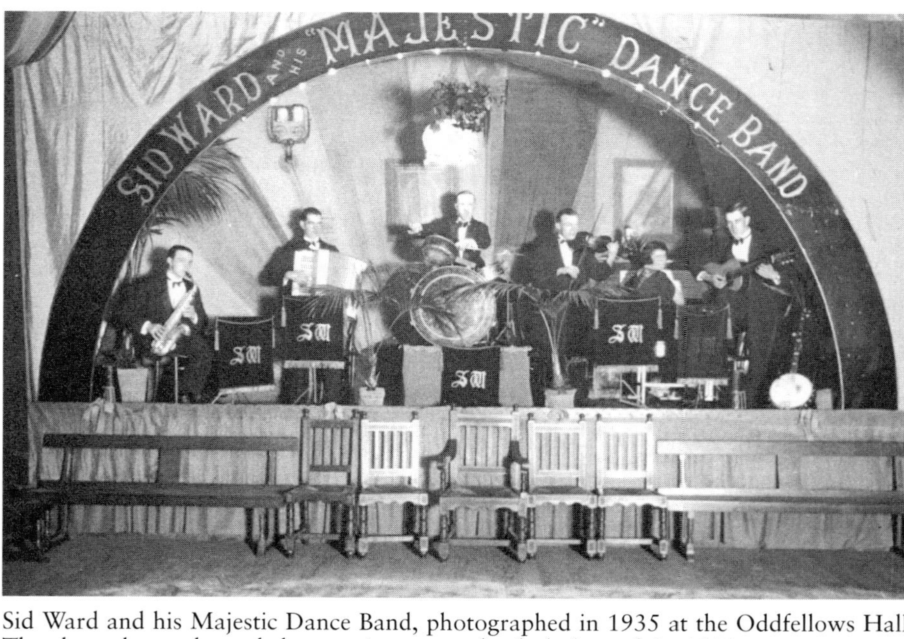

Sid Ward and his Majestic Dance Band, photographed in 1935 at the Oddfellows Hall. They brought much-needed entertainment to the dark days of the 1930s.

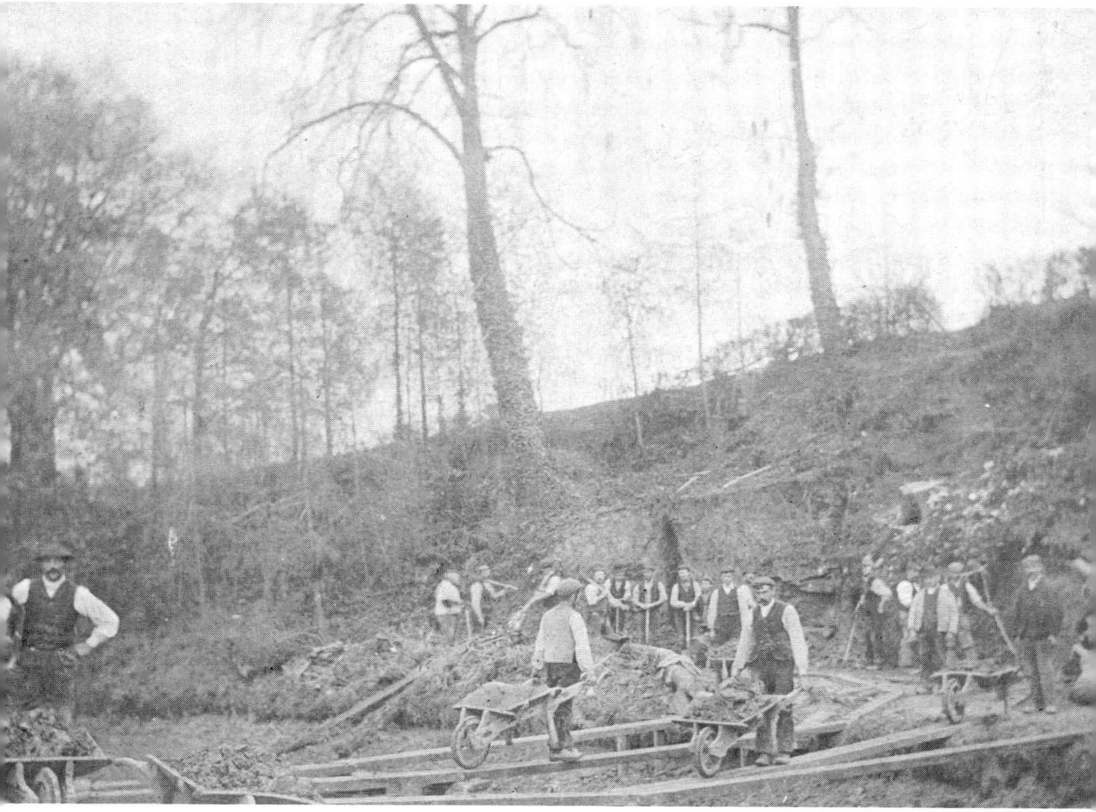

An unusual photograph, taken during the General Strike in 1926. These workers are repairing the banks of Staggs Brook. The material for the maintenance work was puddled clay from a clay pit near Prees. Pails loaded with clay were hauled by wire rope up to the wharf and loaded into the barges. You can see the men bringing the clay down to the brook in wheelbarrows.

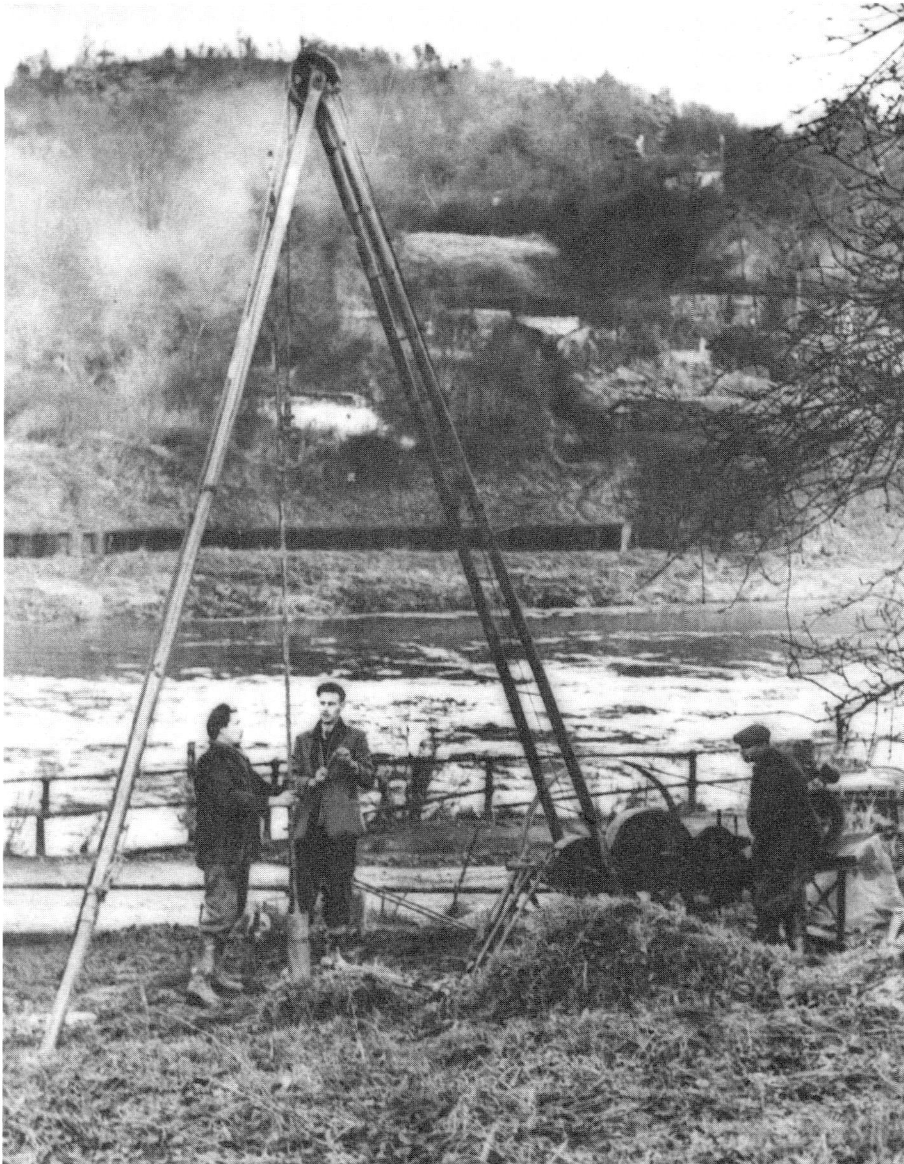

Drilling for water in the Prees area around 1924. The scheme to supply water to Whitchurch was finished in 1882 at a cost of £8,000. The sewerage system was installed two years later. The open irrigation main sewage works are located in Hadley and have changed little over the last one hundred years. Harold Jones is featured in this photograph. After returning from the First World War he moved to Ightfield and worked for Wyatt's the water engineers.

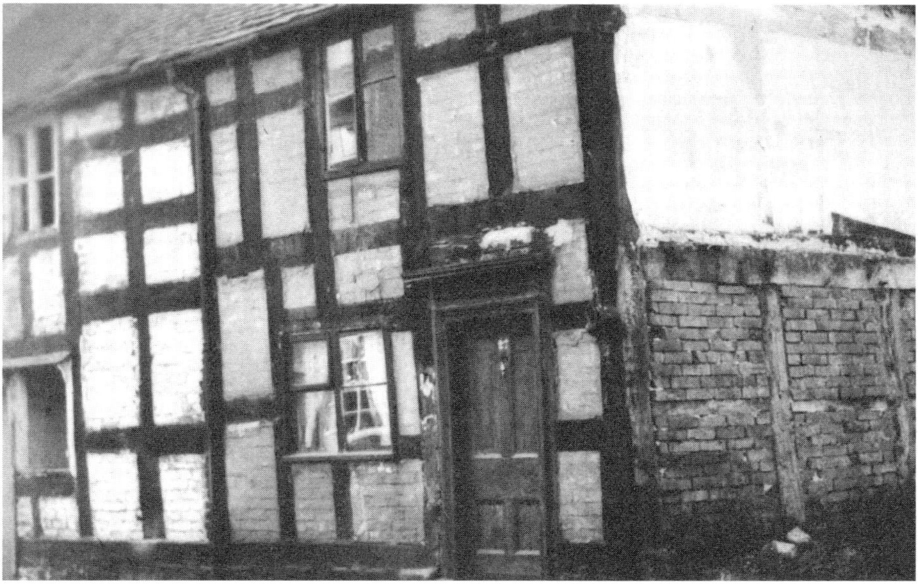

Hilda Cliff was born in one of the cottages in Newtown that have since been pulled down to make room for a car park. The rubble can still be seen. Nos 14 and 15 Newtown were supposed to be the oldest cottages in Whitchurch, dating back to the fifteenth century. Half-timbered houses were built in Shropshire later than anywhere else in England.

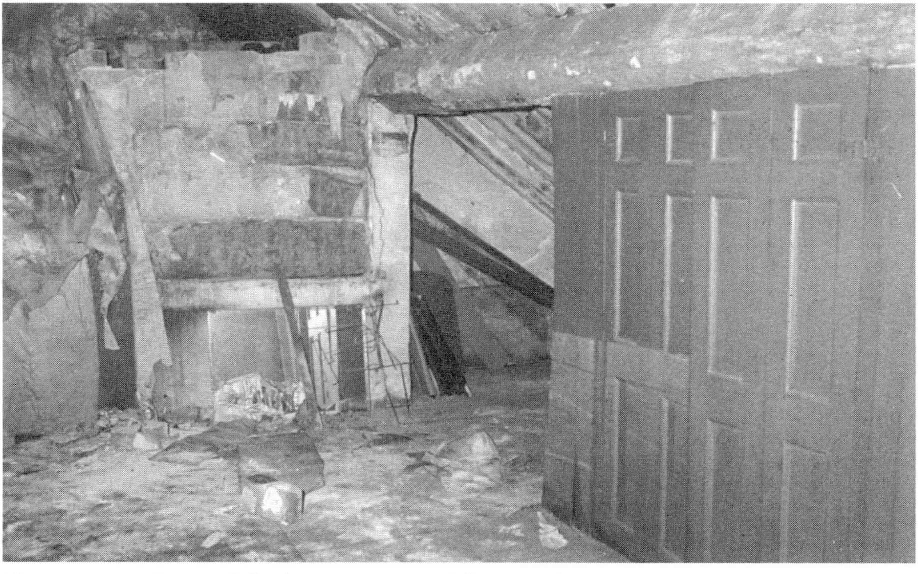

The interior of one of the houses in Piccadilly, revealing many interesting features that had been hidden by plaster and paint, such as oak panelling and fireplaces dating back hundreds of years.

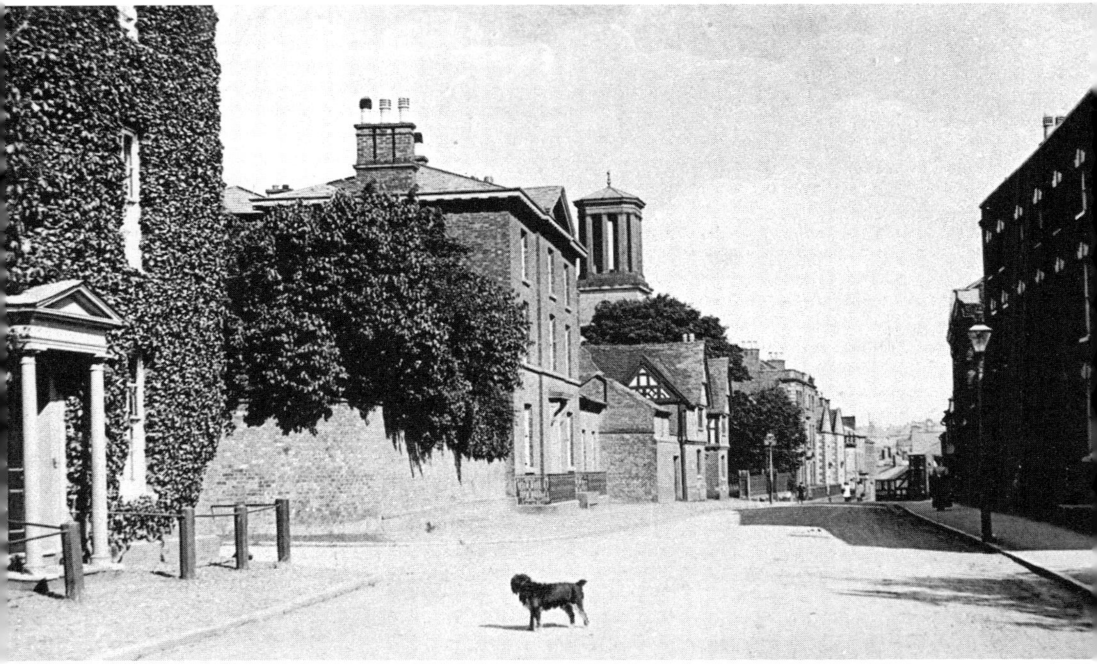

Dodington at the turn of the century. Once a separate manor, it is mentioned in the Domesday Book as 'Dodetune'. It is also stated that a stone was placed in the garden wall behind a house in Dodington that says: 'John Knight built this wall of profits made by a voyage with black cattle'. 'Black cattle' was the terminology for negro slaves.

SECTION TWO

Grindley Brook, Broughall

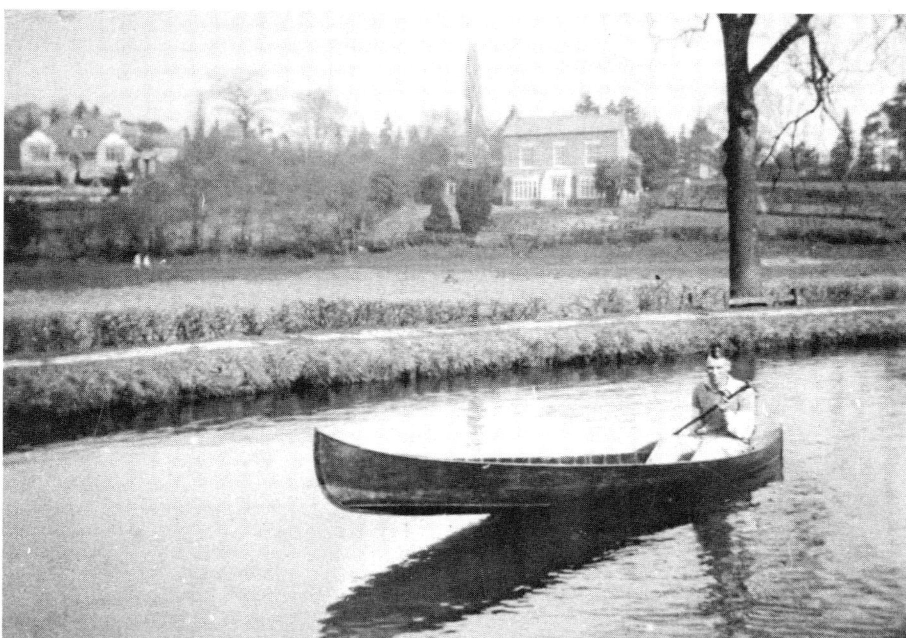

Punt on the Shropshire Union Canal, *c.* 1920.

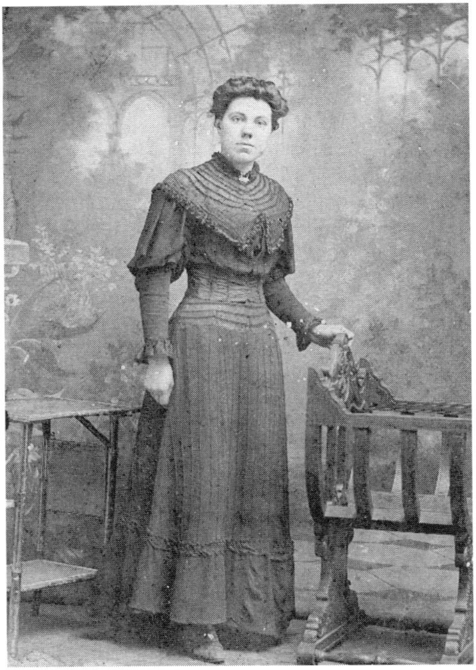

Frances Shaw, *c.* 1882. Before falling in love with the penniless canal boatman Thomas Shaw, Frances had already been married twice. Both previous husbands died very early on during the marriage, one drowning in the Shropshire Union Canal while being drunk. This proud and courageous woman followed Thomas Shaw on to the boat and was disinherited by her parents as a consequence. One of her jobs was to propel the boat through the tunnels. This was done either by pushing the feet against the tunnel walls or using the hands while lying on the back. The first of her children, Frances Mary, was born in 1912, followed by Thomas in 1915 and Albert in 1918. The children had to work on the boat from an early age. For a while she tried to carry on the business after her husband's death, but found it too difficult and had to sell the boat. With the money she bought a small cottage at Grindley Brook.

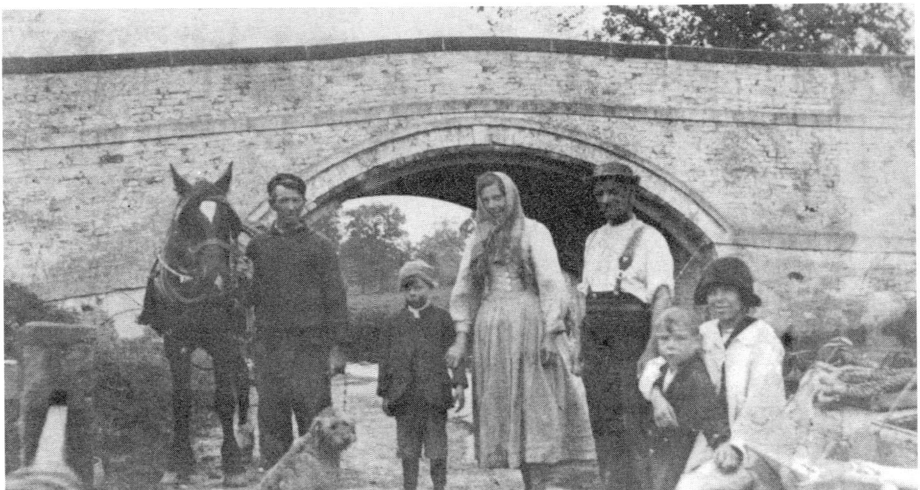

Frances Shaw in 1920 with her three children and two of her labourers next to the narrowboat by the Shropshire Union Canal.

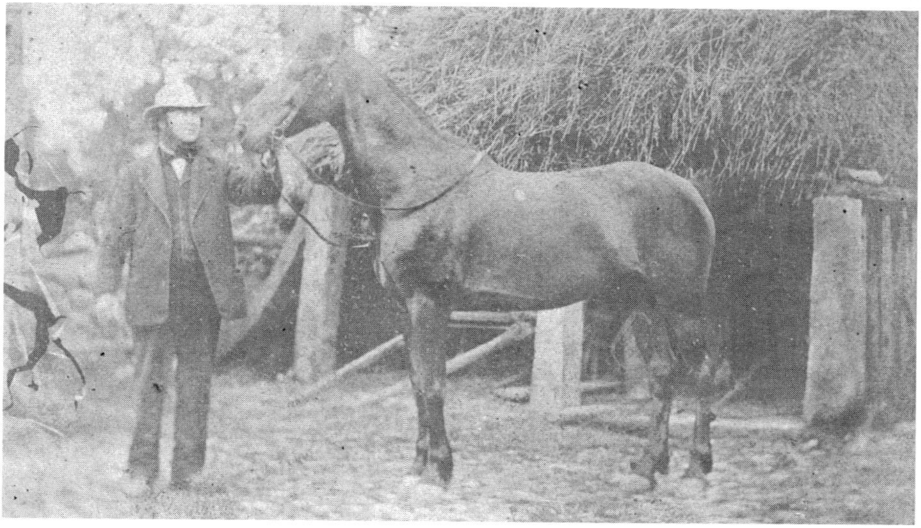

The only existing photograph of Thomas Shaw shows him with one of his boat horses, *c.* 1890. His love of horses was phenomenal. To supplement his income in the winter he would buy the mistreated, undernourished butchers' cart horses, fatten them up and then sell them back to the same butcher as different ones. Frances would always be around after these deals to make sure that the money was not spent immediately in one of the many inns Thomas liked to frequent. Ironically he died from a complication after being kicked by one of his own horses.

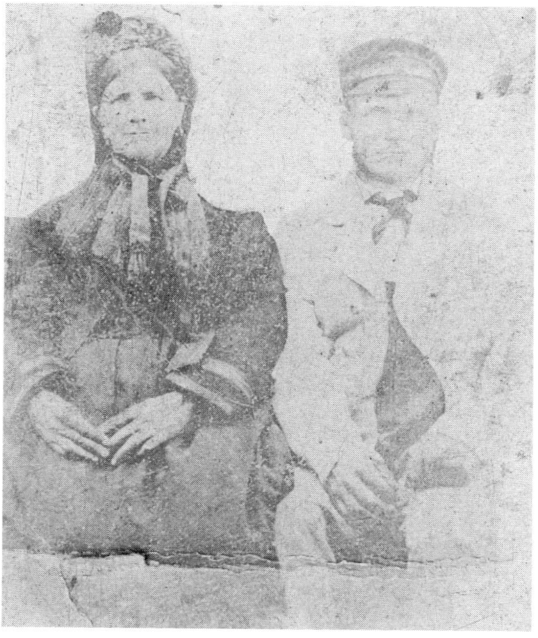

A copy of a daguerreotype (*c.* 1865) of the parents of Mr John Gibson who was the owner of the Red Lion Inn in Sandbach, Cheshire and the father of Frances. It was here that his daughter first met Thomas Shaw.

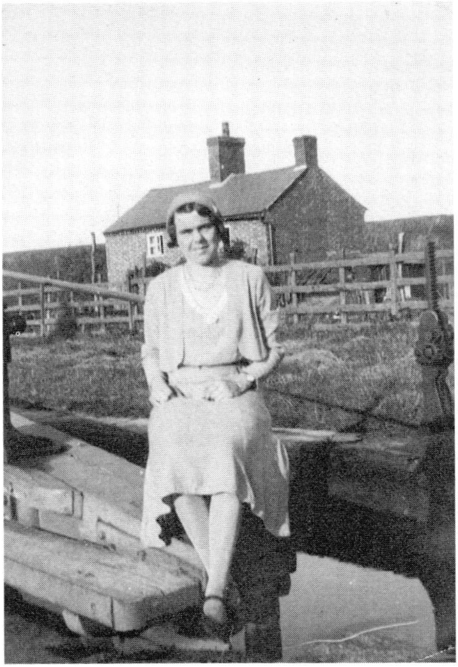

Frances Mary Shaw seated beside the canal.

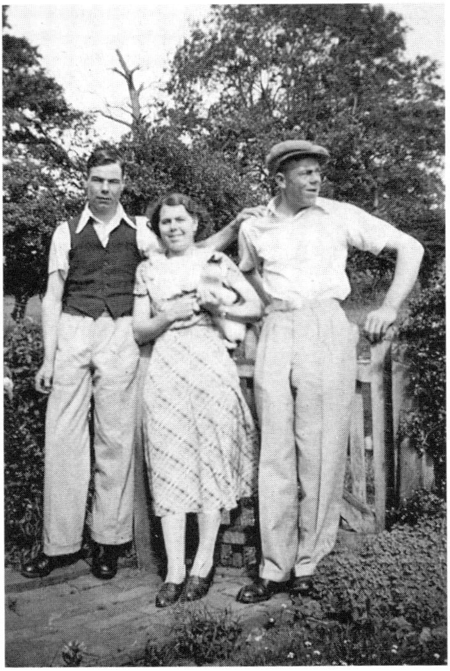

Not many families are fortunate enough to have six generations captured on film and also to have remained so close to each other. Frances Mary Shaw is shown with her two brothers, Albert and Tom, in the garden at Grindley Brook in 1930. Like so many girls early this century, Frances Mary went into service at the age of 13. She was lucky with the family that employed her. Being frightened of the big rooms after living on the boat, she was allowed to sleep in the same bedroom as the daughter of the house and also to attend school in her free time.

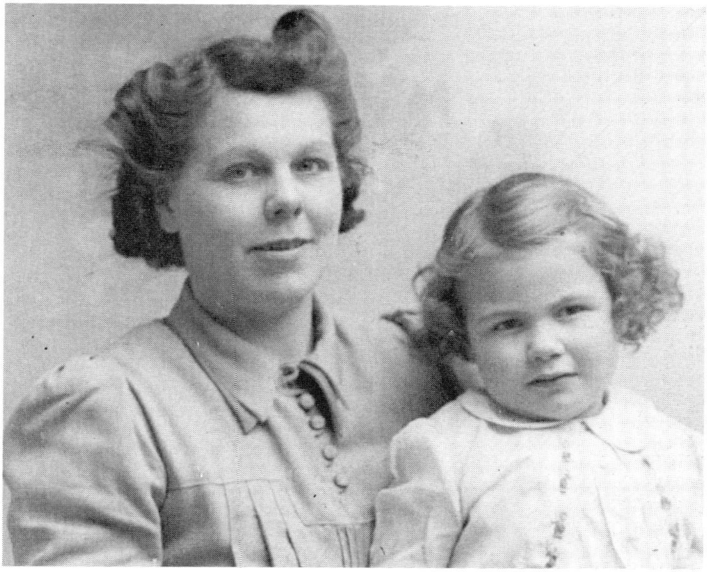

Frances Mary and her only child Marie in 1939. Her husband, Mr Chidlow, lost his life very early on in the Second World War.

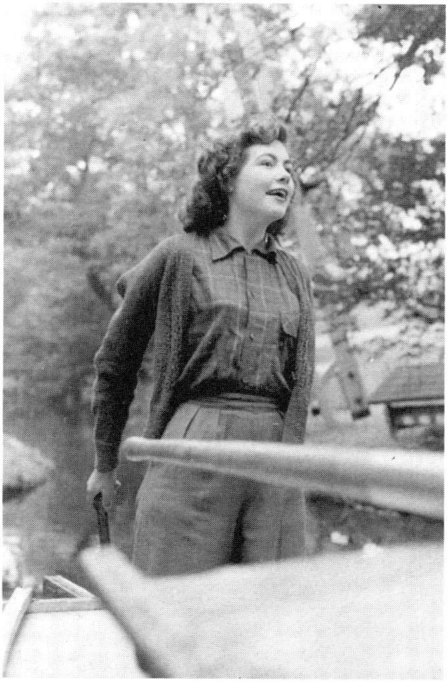

Marie Chidlow, now Marie Sarginson.

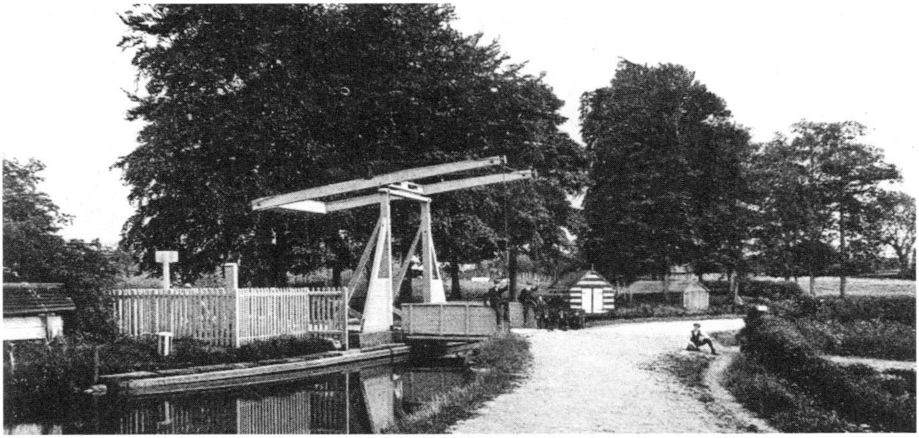

New Mills Bridge near Grindley Brook, date unknown. The Shropshire Union Canal was a lifeline to the town of Whitchurch as all goods were transported on the boats, from coal to clay, from bricks to pottery and livestock. The arrival of the railway to Whitchurch in 1832 slowly drained away the business from the canal boatmen. The arm of the canal from Grindley Brook into the town was finally filled in in 1950. Now it is being reopened to attract tourism. Unfortunately for the townplanners, houses have been built on top of part of it.

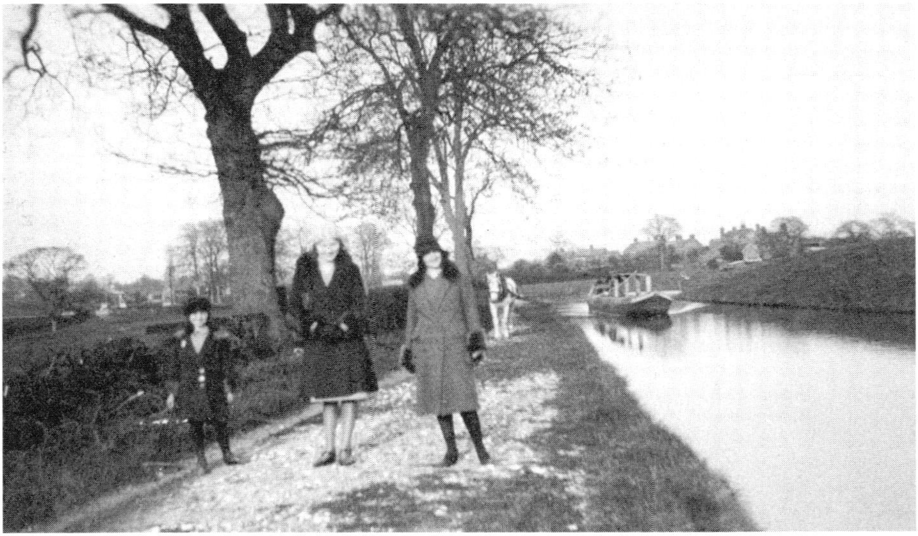

Sometimes two donkeys were substituted for a horse to pull the narrowboats. Travelling in the dark winter months was dangerous for the boats; there was no knowing what obstacles, human or otherwise, lurked on the towpath. Those operating the flyboats usually carried a loaded gun. The group in this photograph of the Shropshire Union Canal around 1928, however, means no harm. Pictured on the left is Vera Mountford.

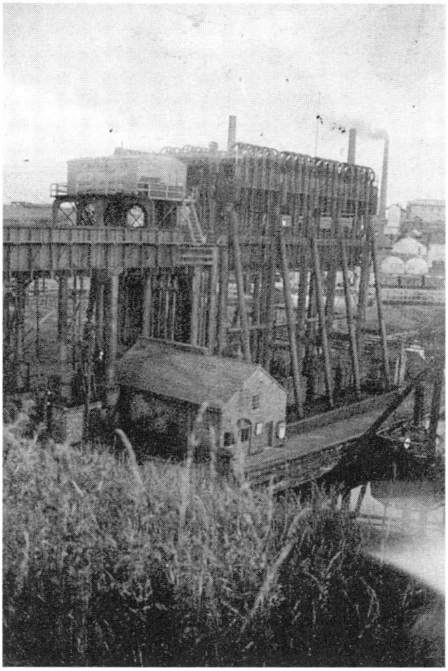

A canal lift, called the Anderton lift, situated at the junction of the Shropshire Union Canal and the River Wever, *c*. 1908.

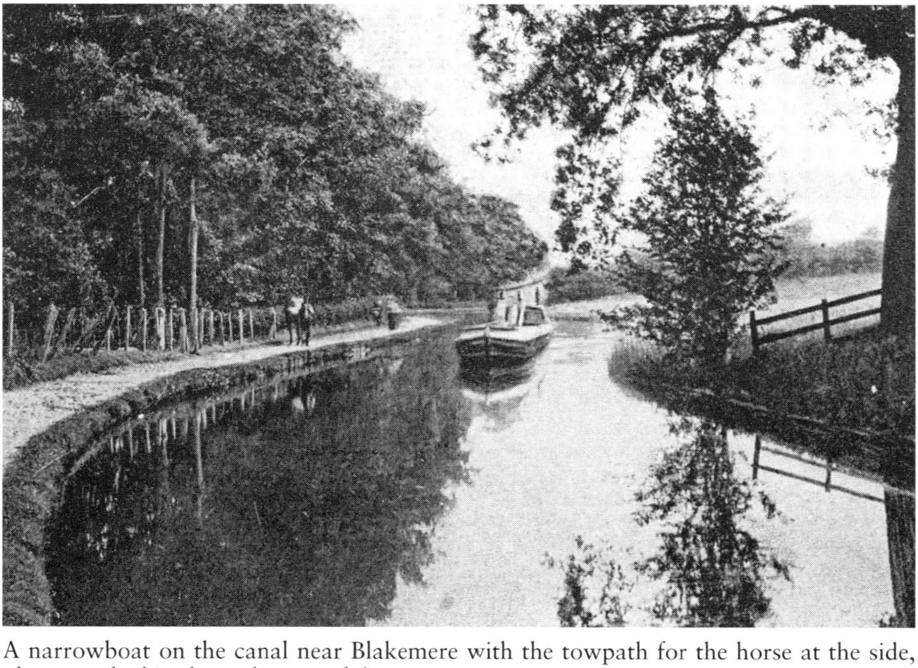

A narrowboat on the canal near Blakemere with the towpath for the horse at the side, photographed in the early part of the century.

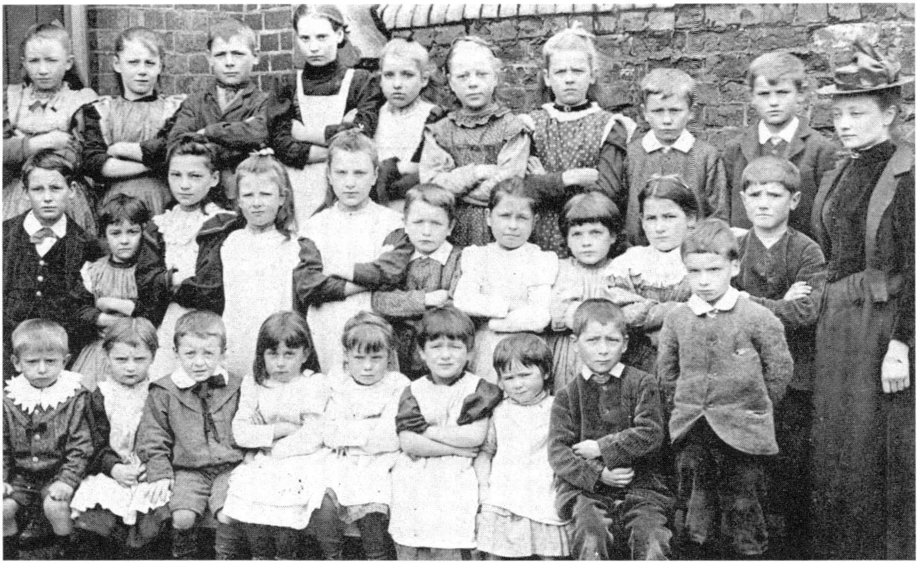

Class at Grindley Brook School, *c.* 1914. Among the children are Bill Cliff of Grindley Brook, and Albert and Thomas Shaw. The school also served as a chapel. It is said that the schoolmistress was very stern and that she used the cane quite freely. The school is now a private home.

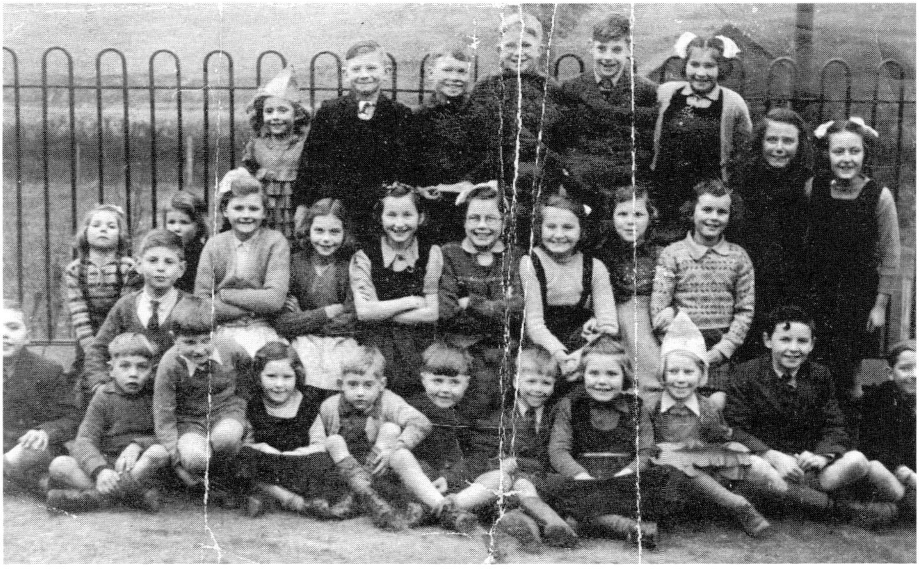

A new generation at Grindley Brook School. Featured in the photograph are Eric Cliff, Eileen Jones, Neville Fox, Marie Chidlow, Harry Dotten, David Oliver, Marjorie Pace, Kathleen Evans, Josephine Ackerley, Brenda Fox, Margaret Fox, John Cliff, Georgina Dawson, Nancy Edge, Winnifred Pierson and Anna Lewis.

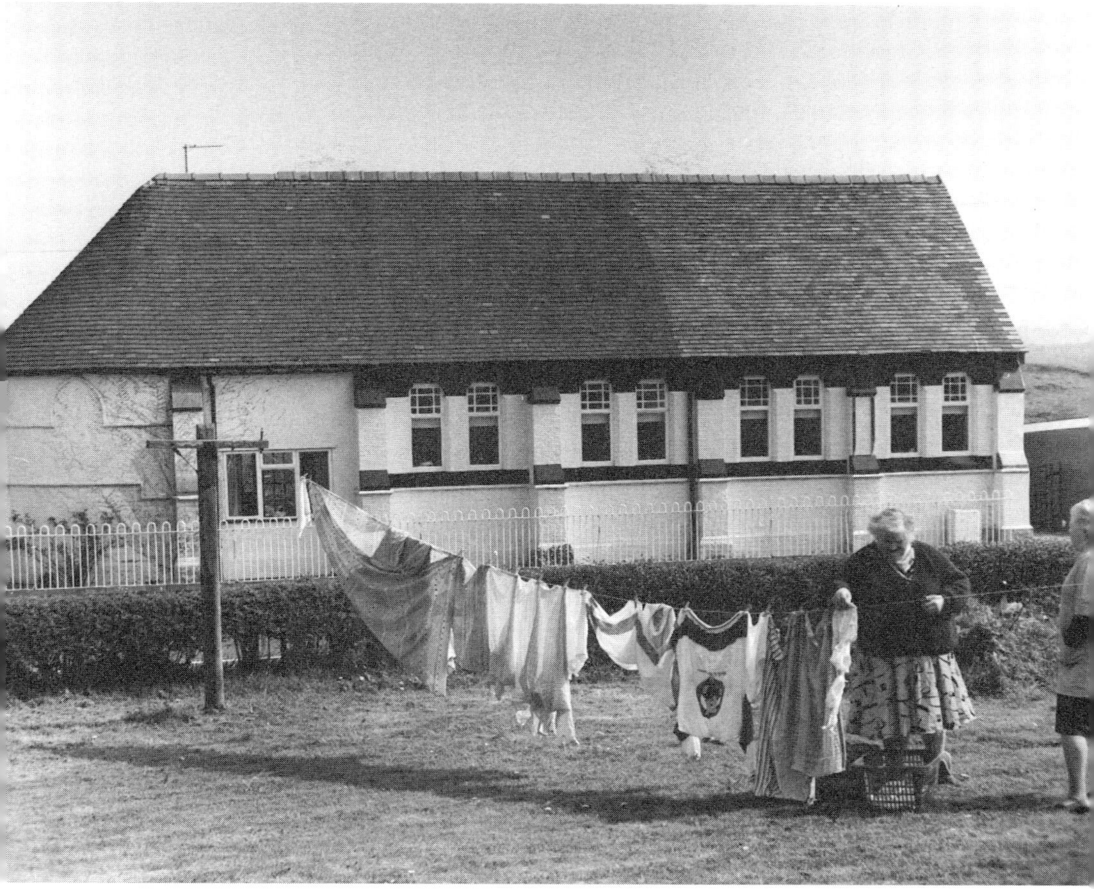

Grindley Brook School as it is today. It has been a private home for a number of years now but luckily the new owners have kept the building more or less as it used to be.

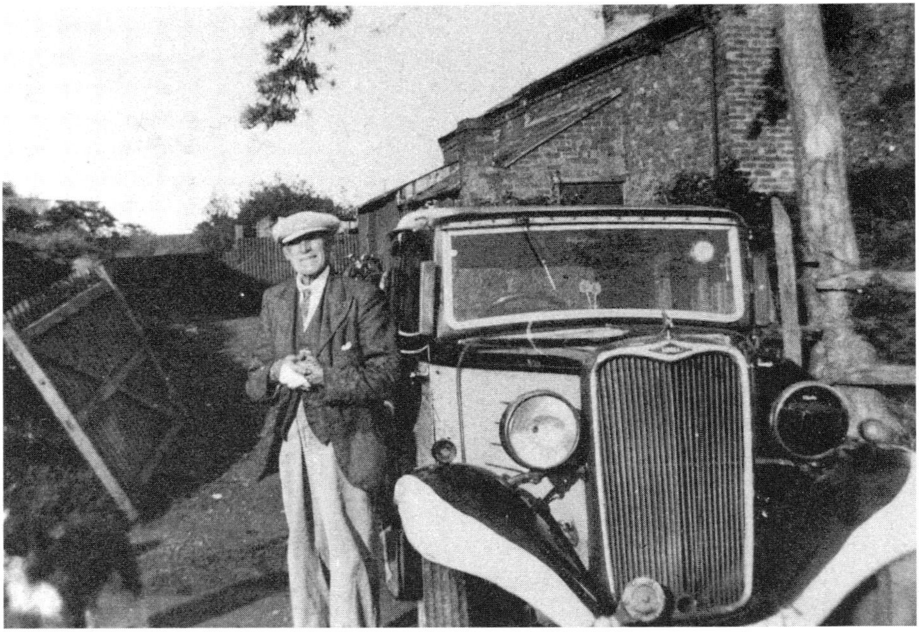

Bill Cliff, featured here with his new car in front of his cottage in Grindley Brook around 1949. Like his grandparents before him, who ran The Bridge tavern, Bill remained a resident of Grindley Brook all through his life. That tradition is now being followed by his son. At 13 he became a 'bound apprentice tinsmith' for the Smith foundry and in his free time Bill made a name for himself as a successful road runner.

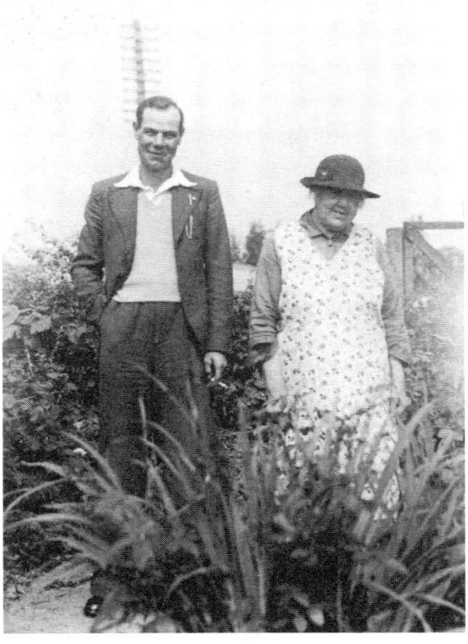

Albert with his mother Frances Shaw at the cottage garden in Grindley Brook in 1930. The Cliffs and Shaws are still neighbours now, in 1994.

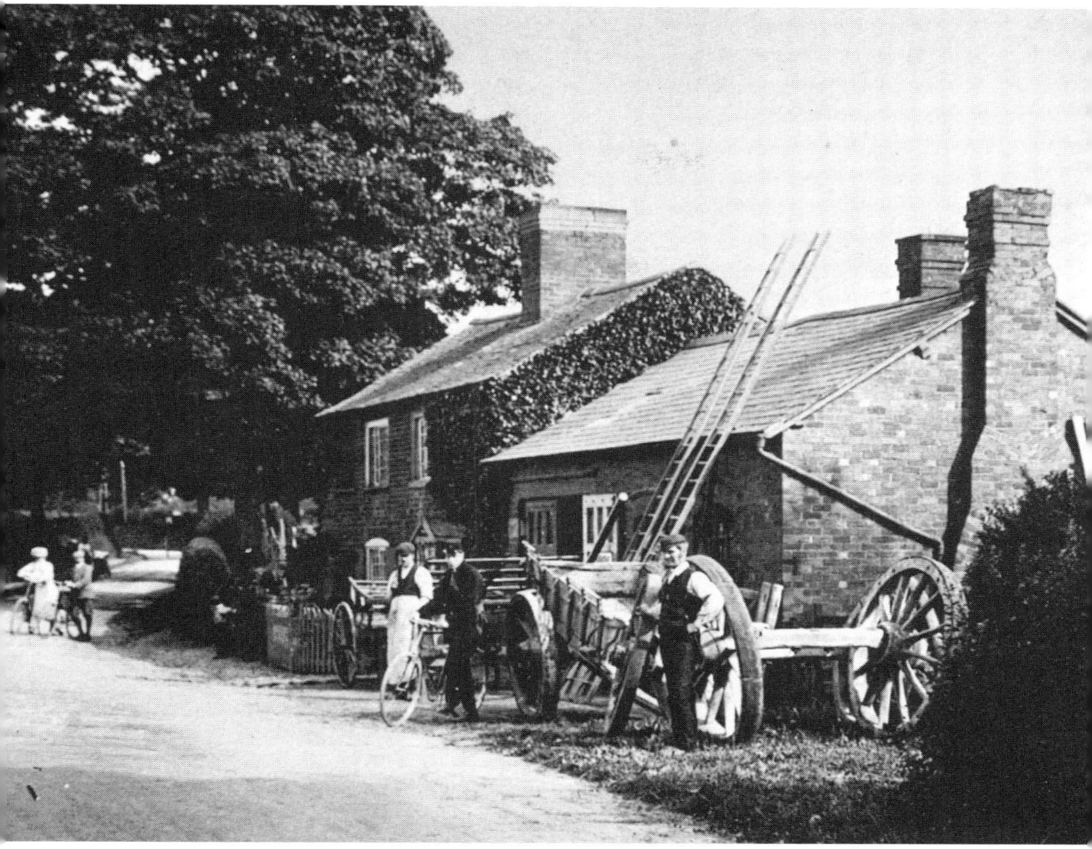

The prefabricated horseshoe came into existence at the turn of the century and was not liked by many blacksmiths. With the arrival of the railway, carriage-horses became a thing of the past and business was restricted to the farm animal. The blacksmith then turned his hand to the repair of bicycles and some, later on, to the repair of the motor car. Many businesses closed down or the blacksmith would come for just a few days from a neighbouring village. This photograph of the smithy in Broughall dates from around 1910. Notice the lady on the bicycle.

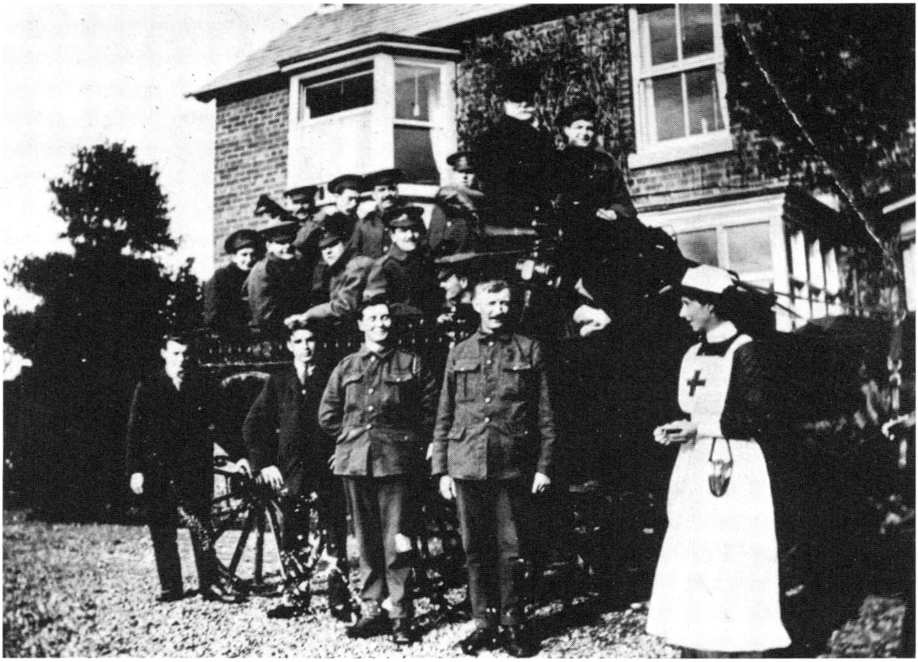

Broughall House as a Red Cross hospital during the First World War. The nurse is probably Miss Lambert, who was well known in the Whitchurch area for her kindness and courage.

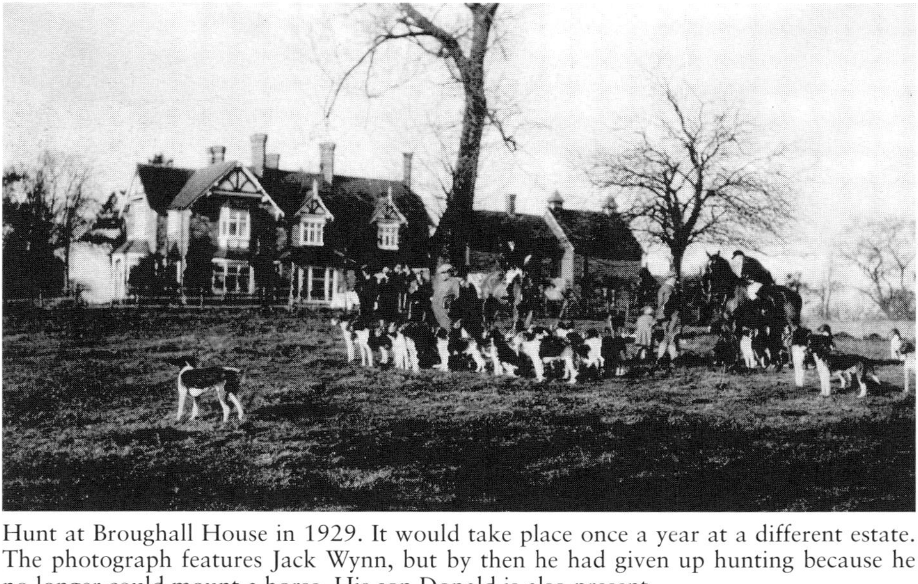

Hunt at Broughall House in 1929. It would take place once a year at a different estate. The photograph features Jack Wynn, but by then he had given up hunting because he no longer could mount a horse. His son Donald is also present.

SECTION THREE

Prees, Lower Heath, Fauls

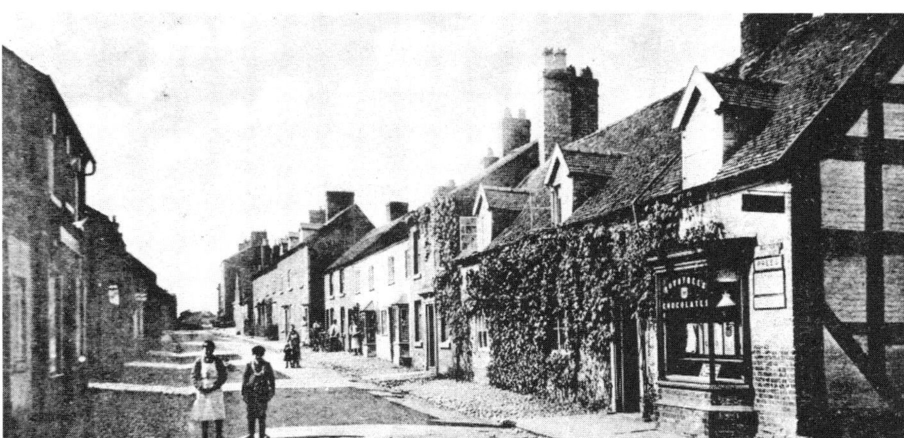

Shrewsbury Road, Prees, *c.* 1900.

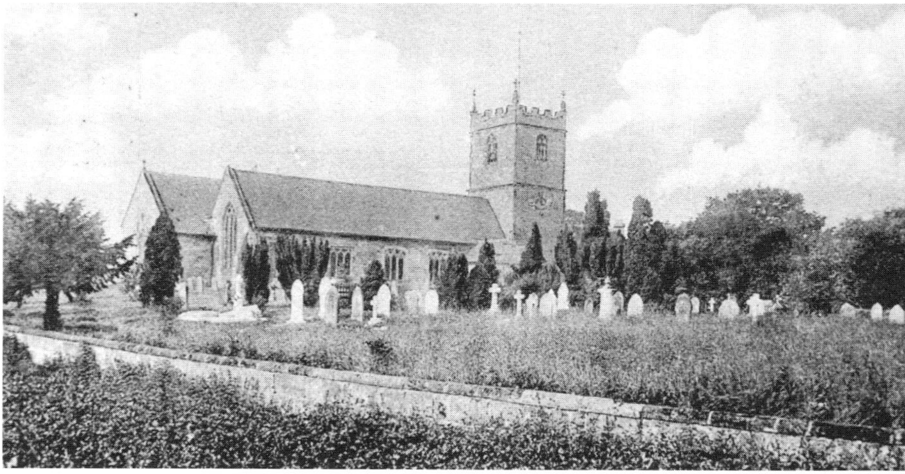

Most of St Chad's Church, Prees is over six hundred years old but the tower dates from the eighteenth century. Many treasures found in the church are said to have been built for Richard Sandford, who died at the battle of Shrewsbury in 1403. John Allen, vicar of St Chad's from early in 1846, completely renovated the church, uncovering the beautiful ceiling; one old beam in the roof is dated 1610. He also added most of the stained-glass windows. A modern window dedicated to Sarah Sandford has pictures of St Elizabeth of Hungary. Among many memorials to the Hill family is a relief showing the funeral of Sir John Hill in 1824. His son was Wellington's right-hand man.

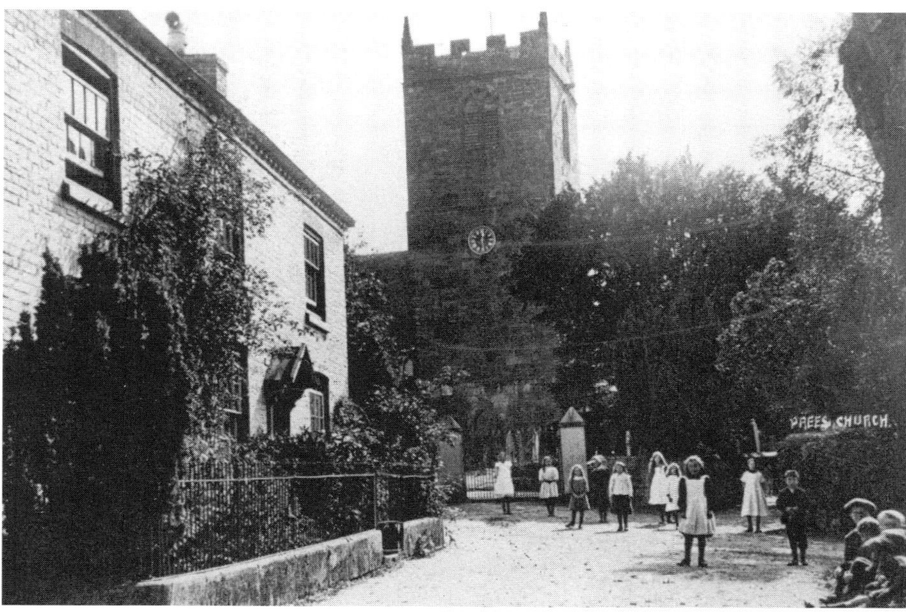

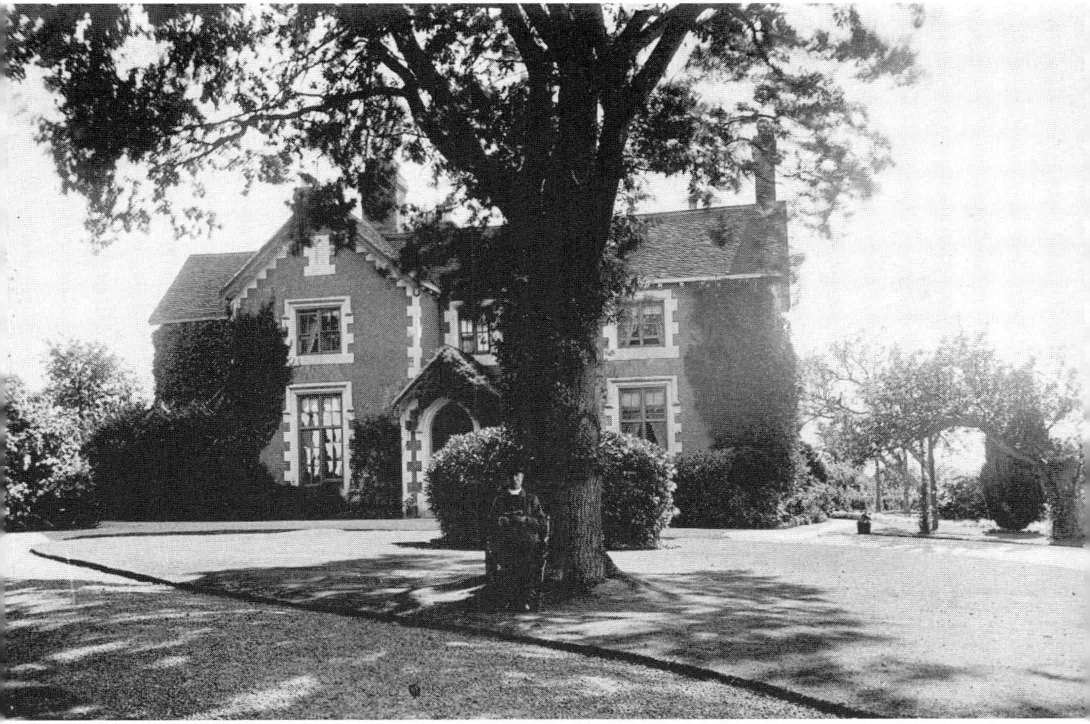

Revd Fitzgerald posing outside the Vicarage in Press, *c.* 1900. The Vicarage was built by John Allen, who later became Archdeacon of Lichfield. He said that the old Vicarage, built in Tudor times, was 'Not fit to live in'. A driving force in the affairs of Prees, he also instigated the building of a church in Fauls and the complete renovation of St Chad's Church. Many illustrious friends from his Cambridge days visited him at the twenty-two-bedroom house in Prees: Tennyson gave a reading of his poetry in the schoolroom and Thackeray made John Allen the model for Captain Dobbin in *Vanity Fair*.

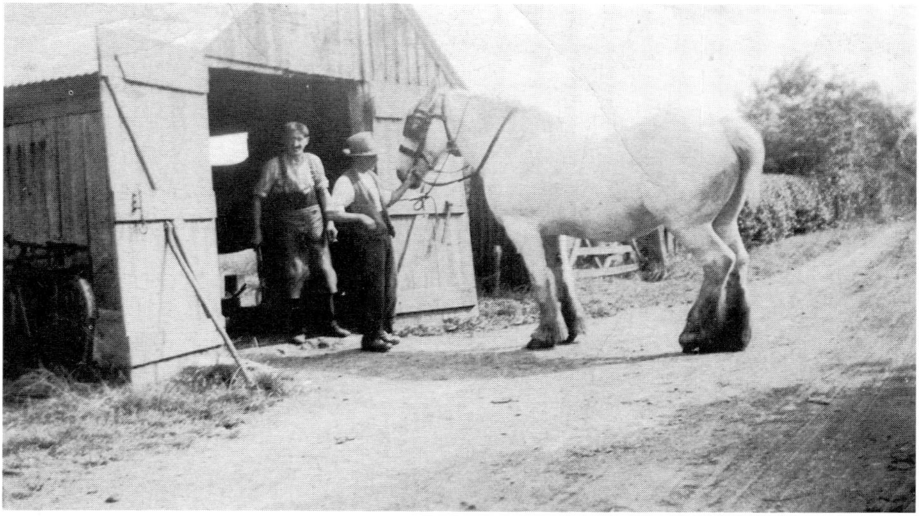

The original smithy in Prees was turned into a café, and this tin shed at the back became the new smithy. Frank Williams, featured here, came to Prees twice a week. The date of this photograph is not known.

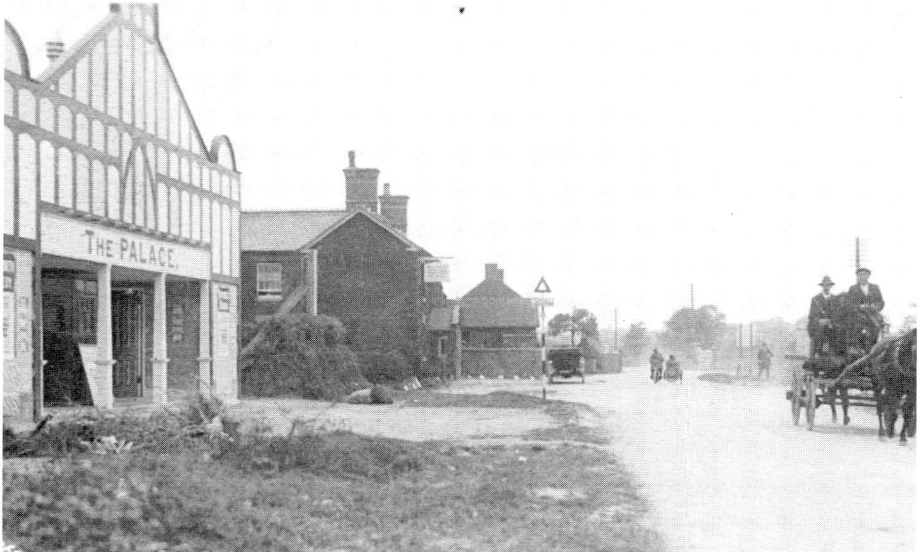

The Palace camp cinema at Prees Heath was much frequented by the soldiers stationed here during the First World War, as well as by local people. In the background is the level-crossing of the camp's light railway, which joined the main Cumbrian line near Steele Heath. The cinema building was demolished in the 1980s.

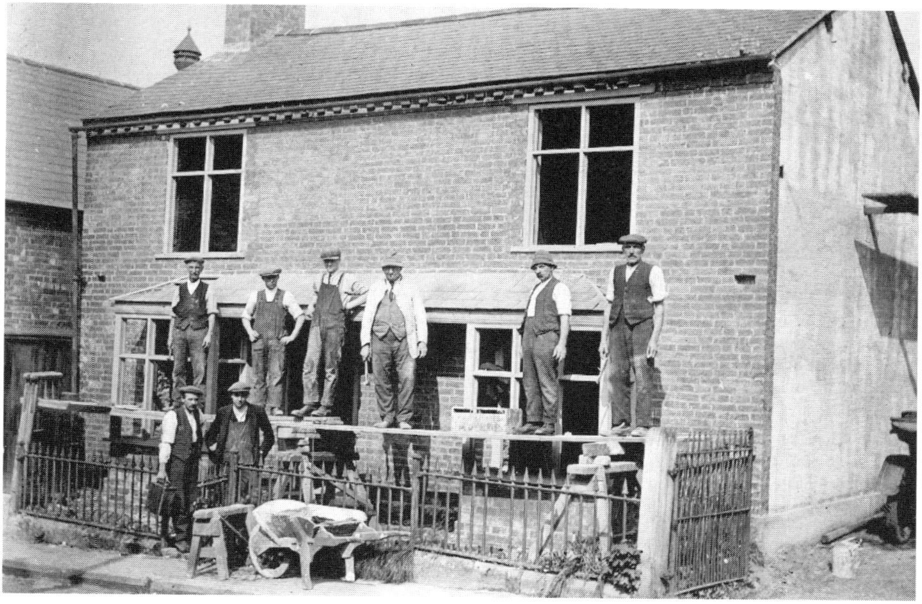

The first Oddfellows Hall was built in Prees in 1883 and the society existed here for fifty years. The new hall was built in 1920 by Mr Ford from Fauls. The hall was purchased in 1956 by the Parish Council for use as a village hall.

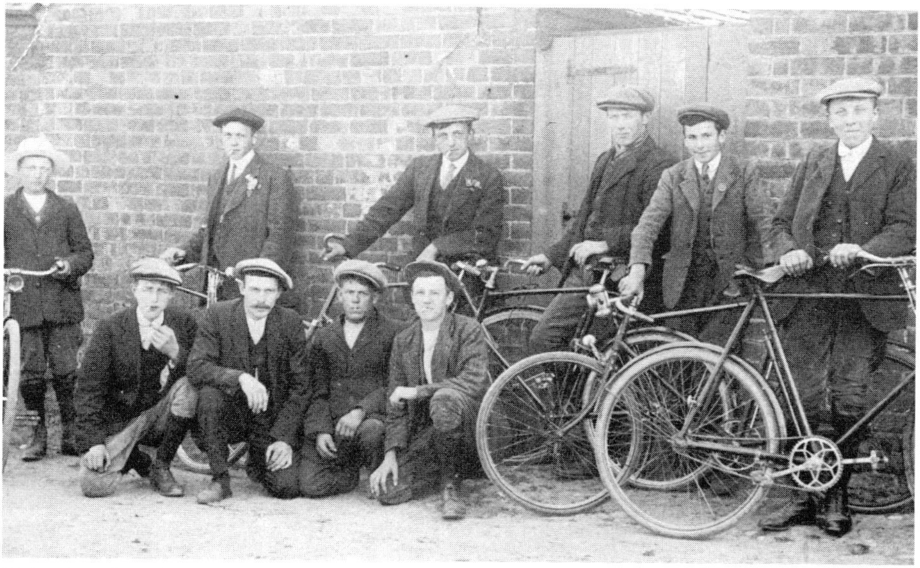

Enjoying their leisure time in front of the Oddfellows Hall in the 1920s, this group includes William Dutton, Percy Dowler and Percy Davies. The friendly society of Oddfellows is still in existence today. In the days before welfare it would provide members with small amounts of money for emergencies. Membership fees varied.

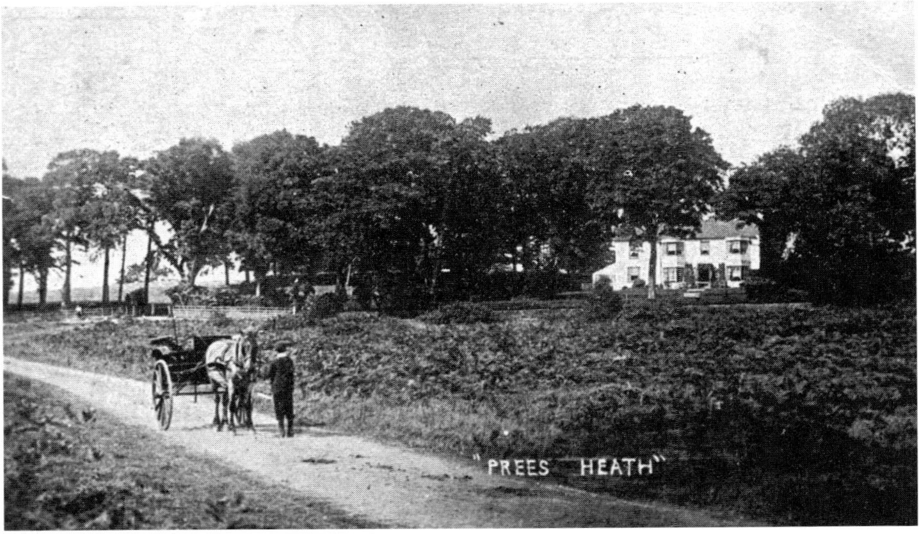

Site of the future camp at Prees Heath, photographed *c*. 1900.

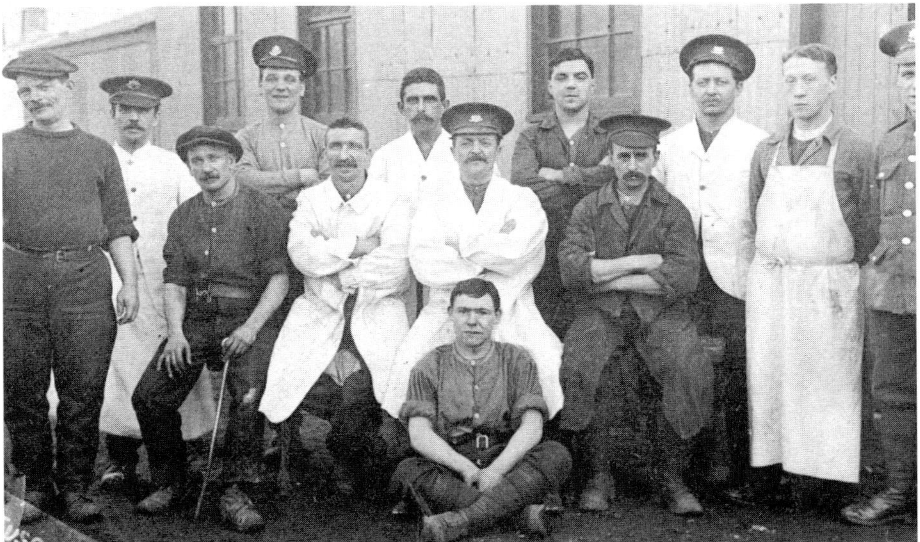

Cooks of the 17th Cheshire Regiment stationed at Prees Heath Camp during the First World War.

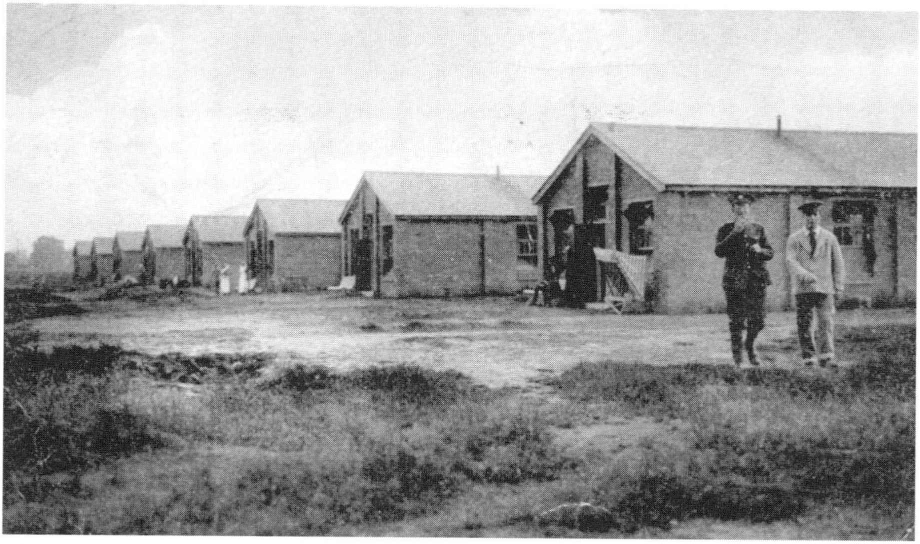

The military hospital and the camp at Prees Heath during the First World War. At one time more than 30,000 men were encamped in these prefabricated huts. During the Second World War a landing-strip for light aircraft was added. POWs, mainly from Poland, occupied part of the camp during the war. Behind these dry statistics are hidden human tragedies, particularly from the First World War: young girls with no prospect of marriage and family, fathers robbed of their sons to take over the business or the farm, villages empty and silent.

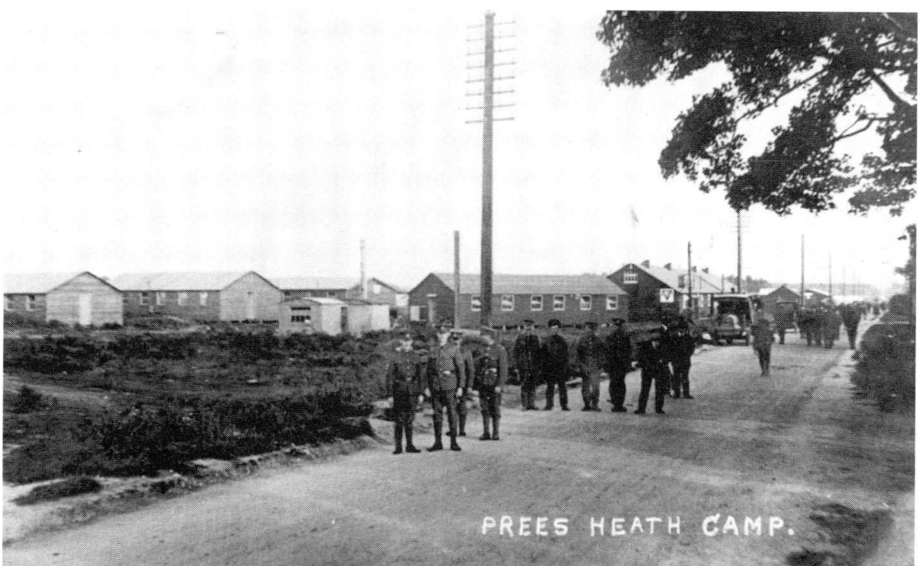

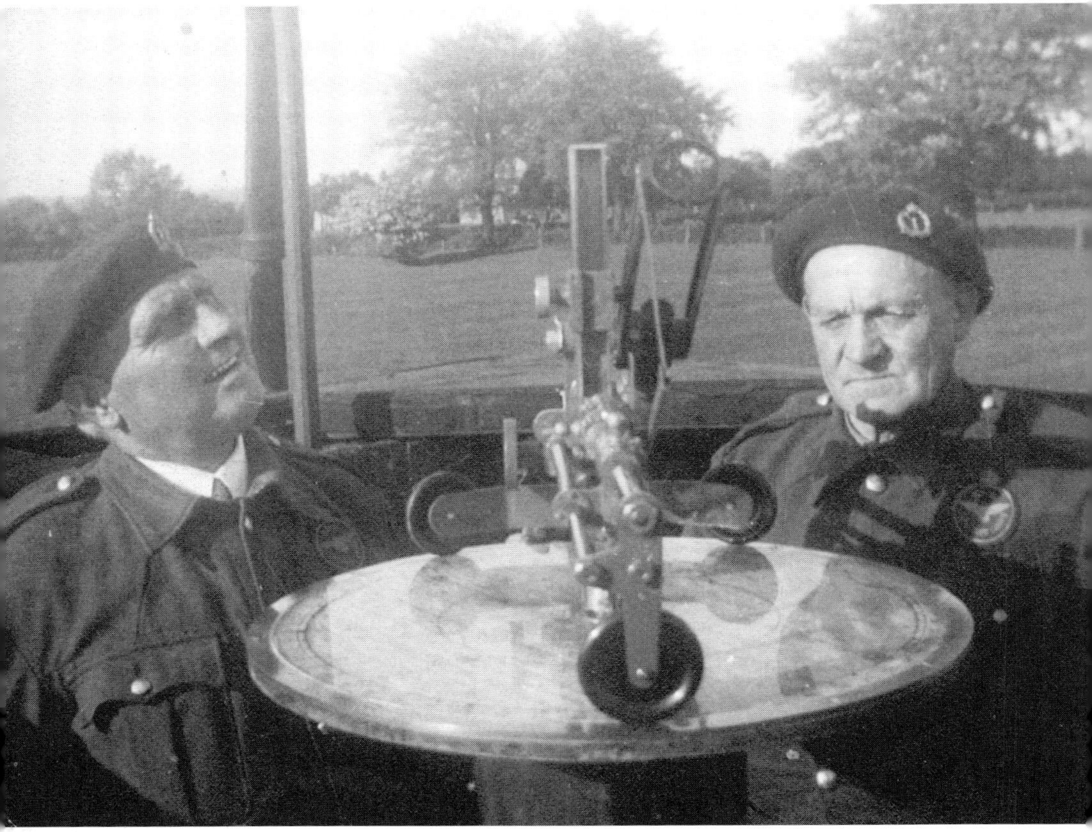

An observation post during the Second World War. These were located either on top of a building or in an area with views all around. The instrument had a 360° scale on the edge to track aircraft spotted through the top part. Mr Forrester and Mr Hatch of the Royal Observer Corps are on watch for incoming enemy planes. Even after all this time very little information has been released about the activities at Prees Heath Camp during both wars.

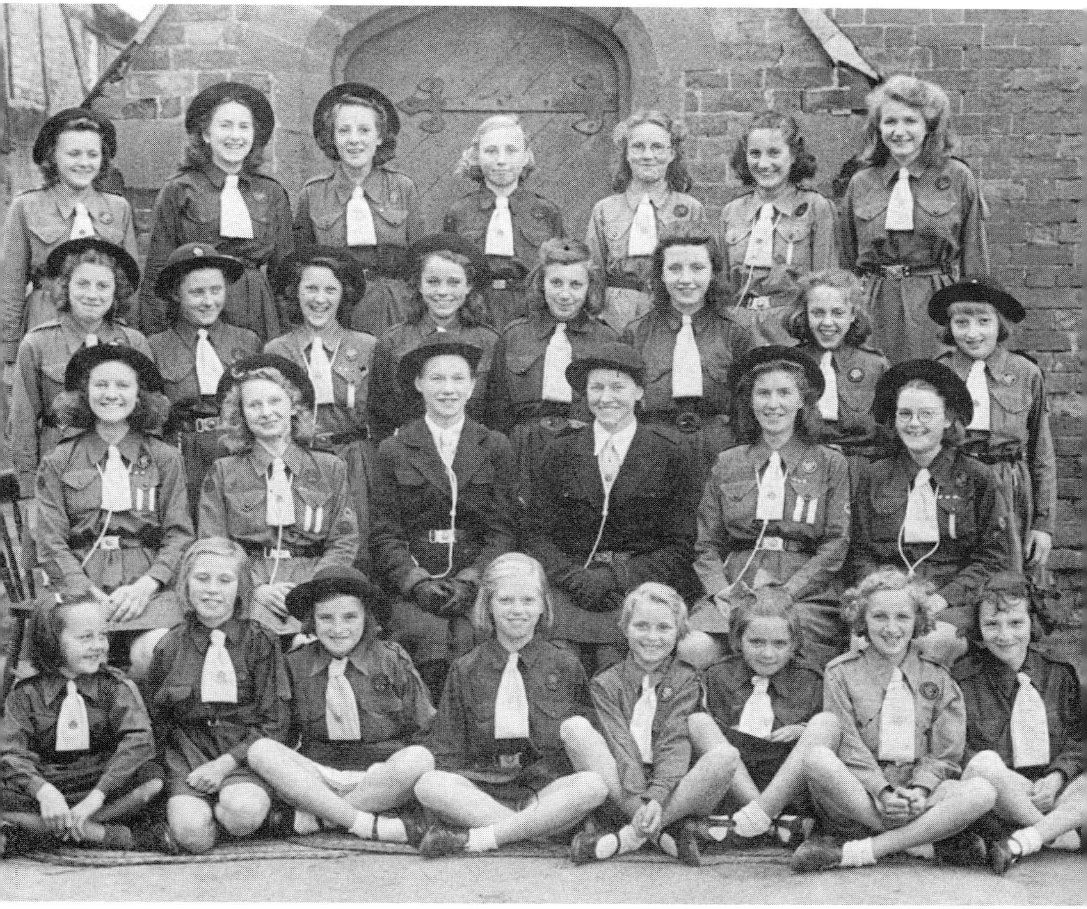

The Girl Guides were formed in 1924. The leader in this 1940 photograph taken in Prees, Mrs Patrick, later became head of physical education at Shropshire County Council. Some of the girls featured here are: Rose Dutton, Olive Green, Tessa Williams, Mary Heyward, Lena Edwards, Nora Barns, Edna Hopwood and Mary Ray.

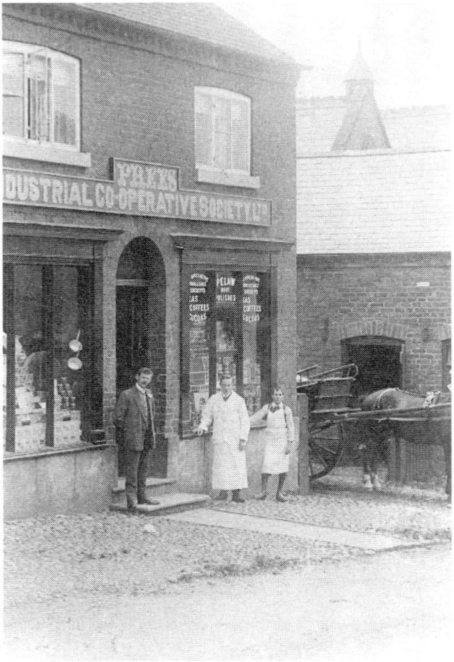

Prees Co-op, Shrewsbury Street. For many people in a small community the Co-op, better known as the 'Co', was the most important shop. Members were allowed a quarter credit but accounts had to be settled on the last day before you could start running up the bill again. The Co-op would be run by a local committee and would also be involved in many of the social activities of the community. Money was lent to the Co-op by the wealthier families of that area. Groceries, including freshly baked bread and cakes, would be delivered daily, packed in brown paper parcels. The date of the photograph is not known.

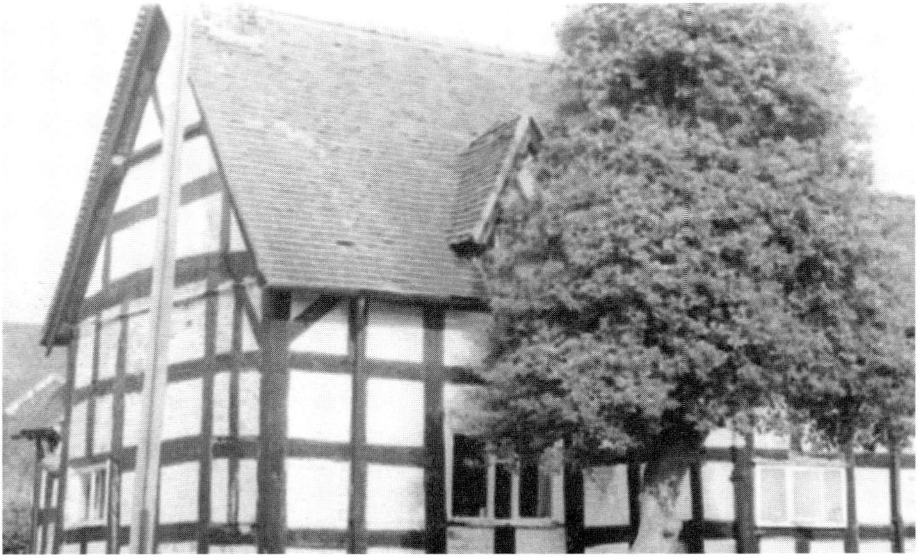

One of the half-timbered houses in Ightfield, photographed in 1975.

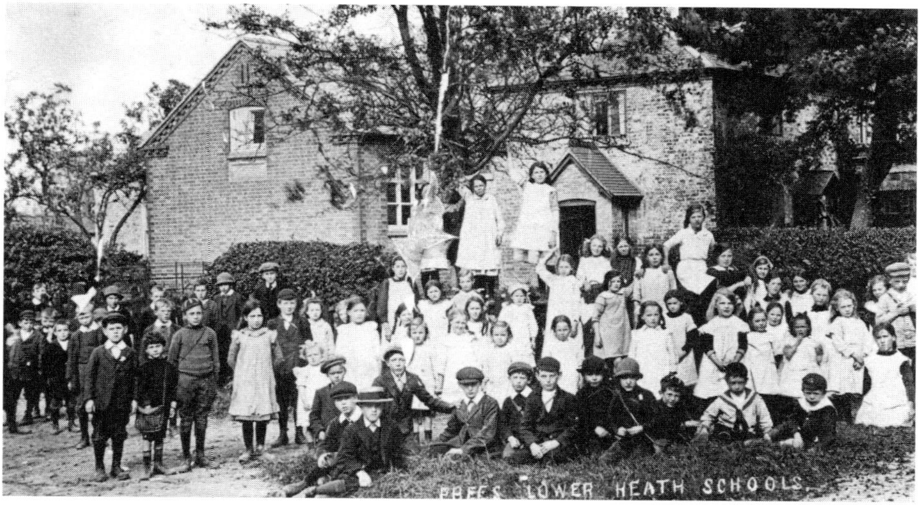

Lower Heath School in 1914. Industry Hall (as it was originally called) was erected by Sir Richard Hill in 1799. According to a pamphlet found among the papers of Lower Heath School and sent to Archdeacon Allen in 1878: 'The school was opened to admit ten boys and thirty girls, to instruct them to procure a livelihood and fit them to be good and useful servants.' The school is situated 2 miles from Hawkstone Park, then the seat of the Hill family. The children were summoned to the school by a bell, which was rung a quarter of an hour before the time school would start. The principal work in which the children were instructed was the processing of wool. This was brought to the school in fleeces, where it was picked by one group, carded by another and spun by a third, and at last turned into stockings. A small compensation was given for the children's labour.

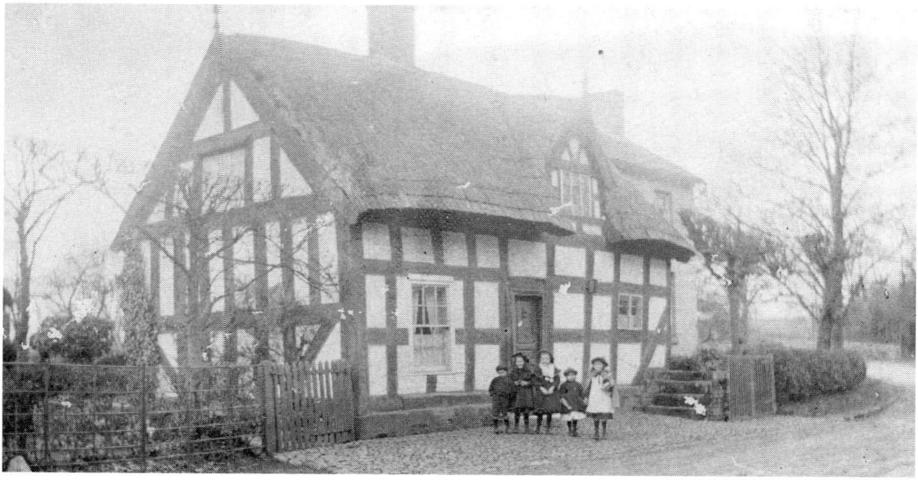

This cottage in Sandford, seen here *c.* 1900, was once a public house. It was later occupied as a private home by the miller whose last resting place is Fauls churchyard. The mill has long ago fallen into ruin. The children in front of the cottage are waiting for the teacher to take them to school.

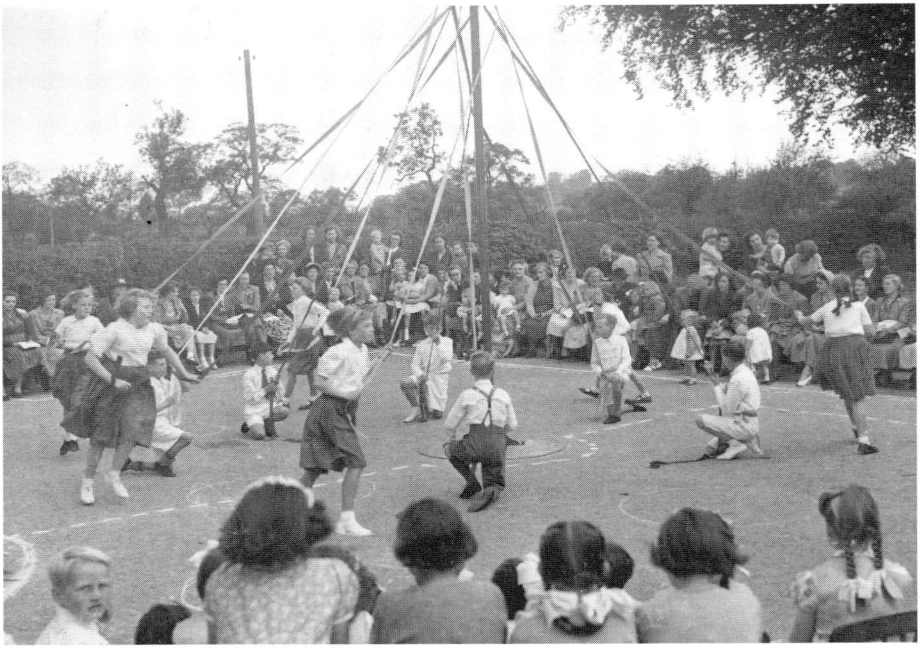
Maypole dancing at Lower Heath School in the 1940s.

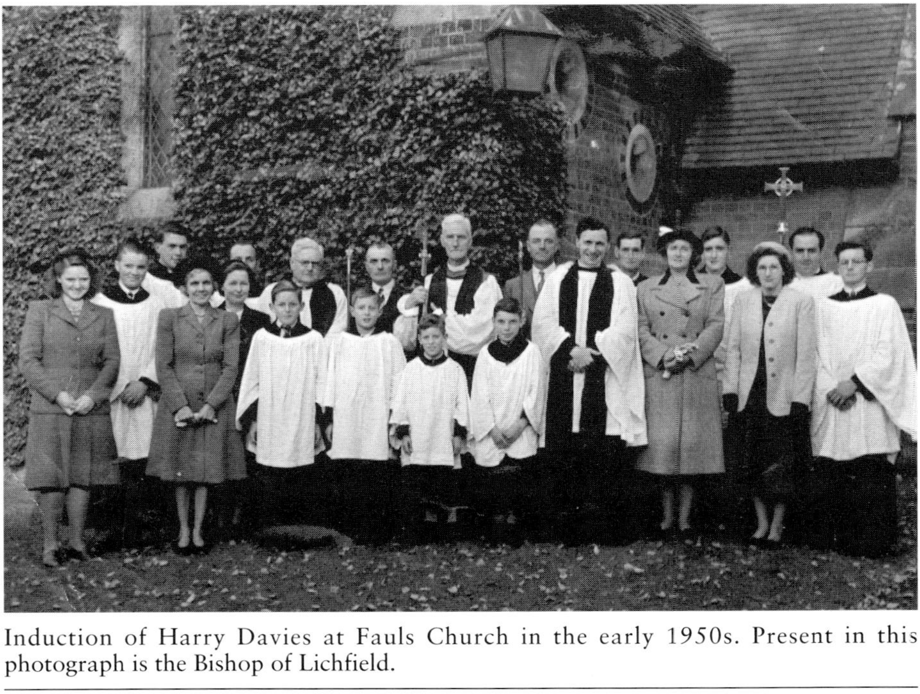
Induction of Harry Davies at Fauls Church in the early 1950s. Present in this photograph is the Bishop of Lichfield.

SECTION FOUR

Hawkstone Park, Marchamley, Ightfield

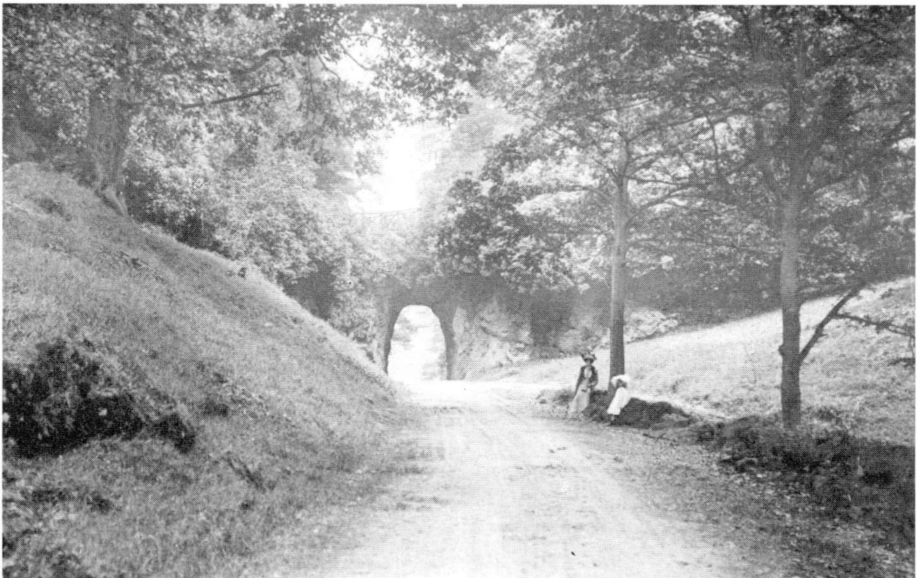

Hawkstone Park, *c.* 1910.

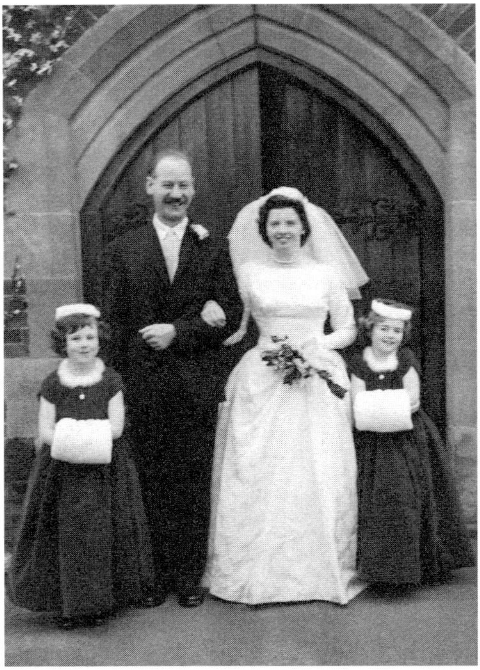

The wedding of Penelope (Penny) Sheldon, (to whom this book is dedicated), to John Dickerson at Fauls Church near Prees. The bridesmaids were Lindsey Cross and Melanie Corbishley. John had by then retired as a pilot with the RAF and Penny was a teacher. Penny came from Marchamley.

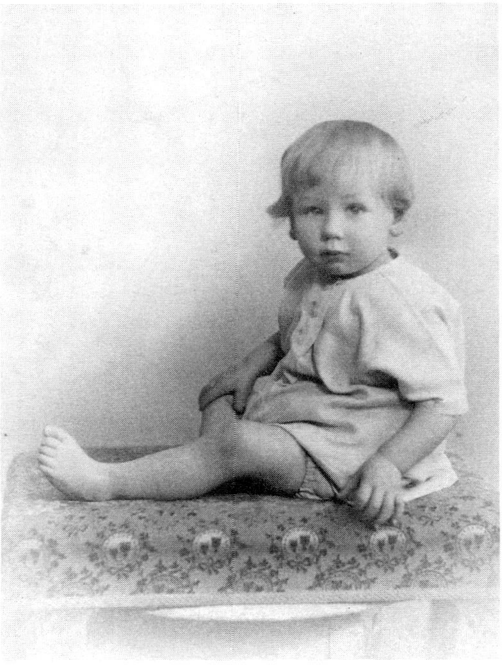

John Dickerson, son of Frederick George Dickerson, thatcher to the Corbet estate, at about 2 years of age, in the late 1920s. There is,as yet, little indication of his thirst for knowledge and his great love of classical music.

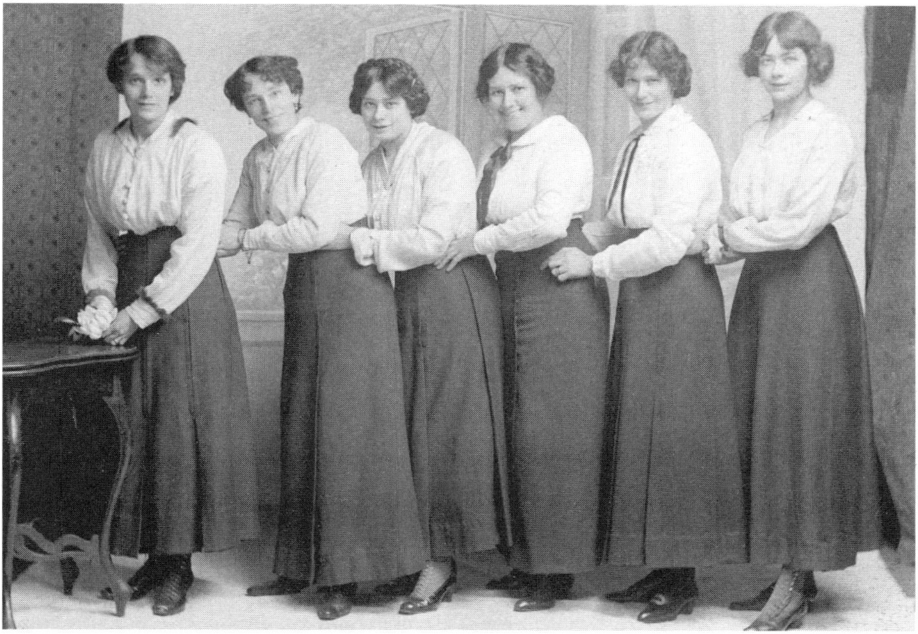

Jessi May Williams, mother of John Dickerson, featured here with her sisters Daisy, Flori, Sally, Dolly and Ethel in a photographer's studio in London, *c.* 1920. Domestic agencies had sprung up around that time all over the country. Then as now, London was the mecca for many young girls. It is rather ironic that today, when more women than ever before make up the country's workforce, nannies and servants are one of the biggest growth industries.

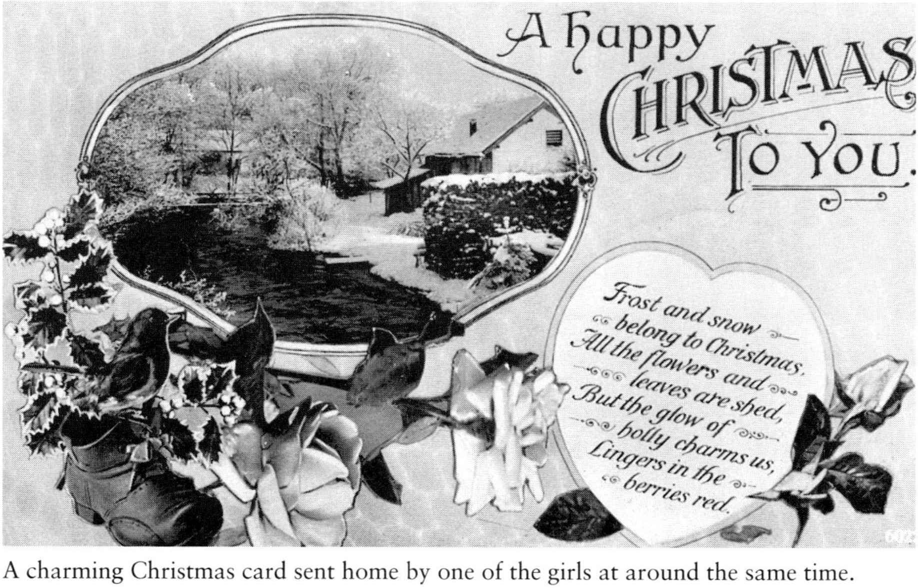

A charming Christmas card sent home by one of the girls at around the same time.

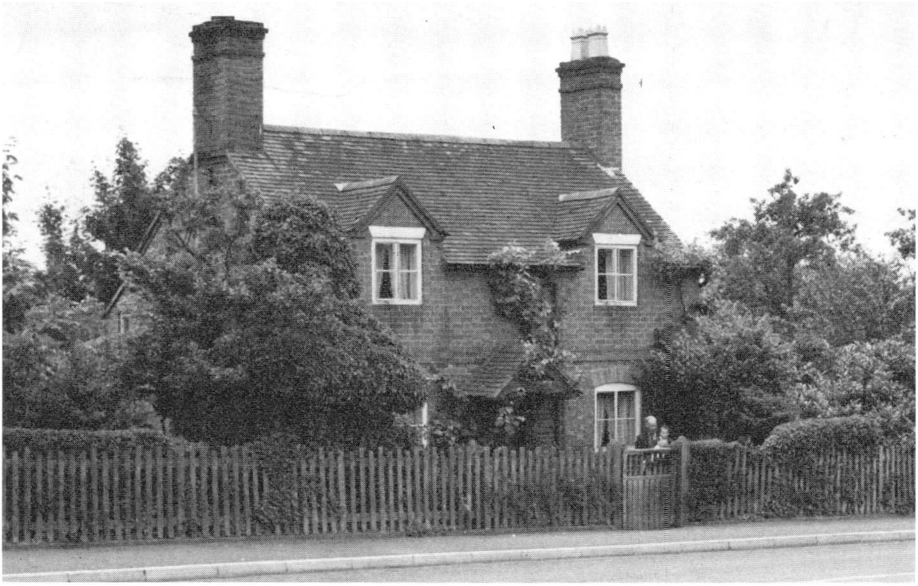

Frederick George Dickerson was regarded as the best thatcher in Shropshire. Originally from Norfolk, he settled in Shawbury at the turn of the century. He worked on the many cottages in the area that belonged to the Corbet estate. He is featured in this photograph in front of his cottage in Shawbury with one of his grandchildren. The cottage has changed very little over the years. Because of death duties the Corbet estate was sold off in the 1950s.

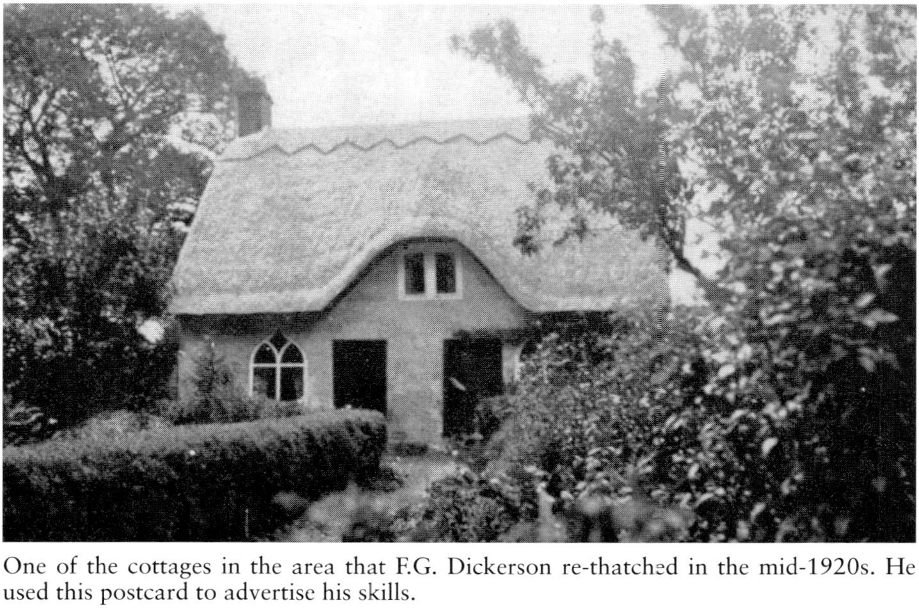

One of the cottages in the area that F.G. Dickerson re-thatched in the mid-1920s. He used this postcard to advertise his skills.

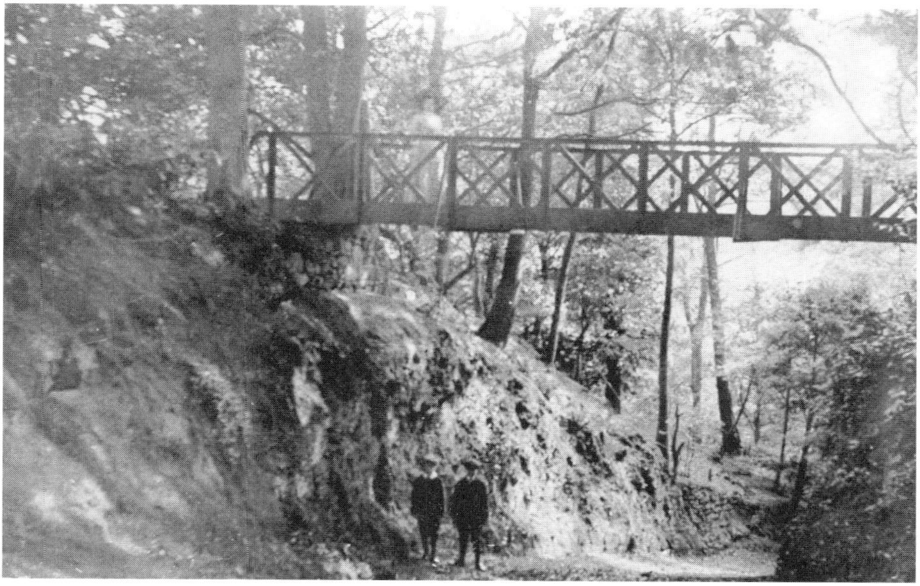

Terrace Bridge in Marchamley in 1912 and (below) a walk close by, photographed in 1930. The bridge no longer exists. Coming originally from a farming family, Penny Dickerson lived in Marchamley until she married John. This pretty hamlet is situated near Hawkstone and has changed very little.

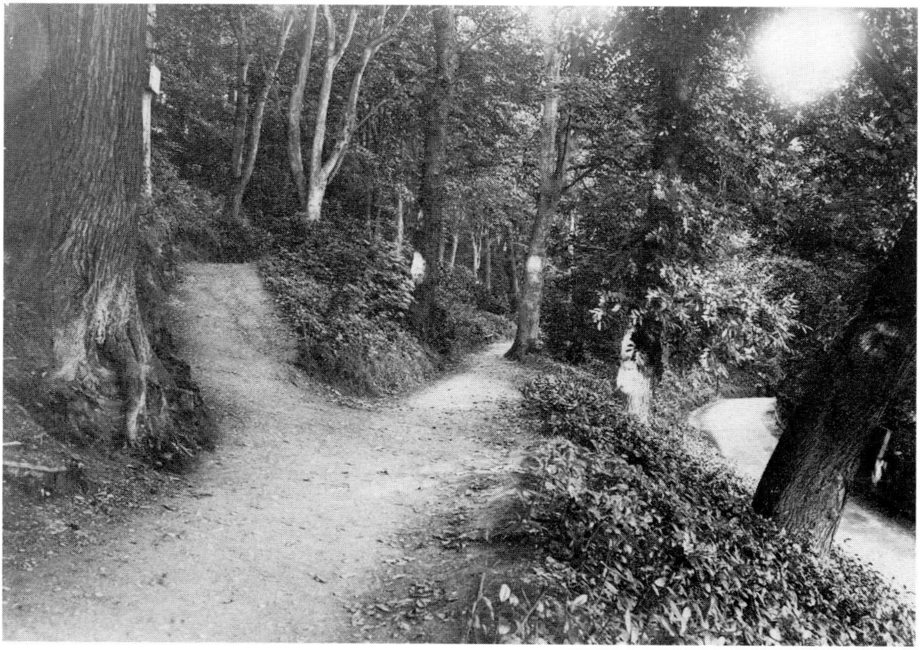

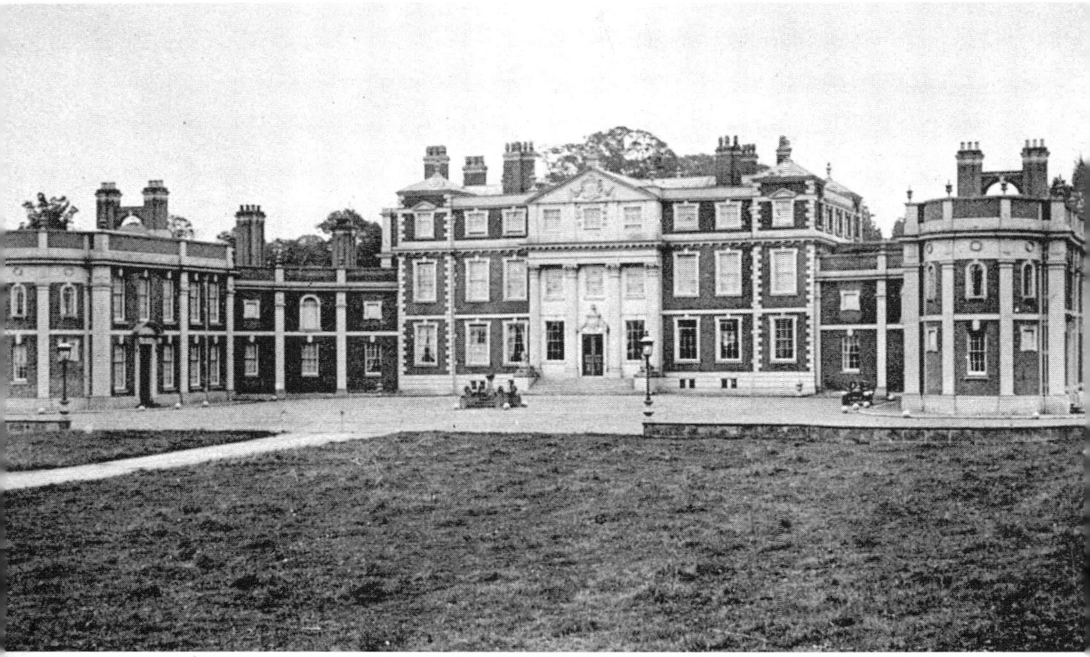

Hawkstone Hall, near Wem. The Hill family have dominated the history of Shropshire for over four hundred years. It was Sir Rowland Hill who founded the Hawkstone estate in the fifteenth century by purchasing the two neighbouring manors of Hodnet and Soulton. A house at the site was either erected or restored. His descendant, Richard, became known as the 'Great Hill', and amassed a fortune. His nephew, Sir Rowland Hill, made the house into what it is today. Once standing in over 300 acres of land, it is one of the most extraordinary places in the country. By the time the 3rd Viscount Rowland Clegg Hill succeeded his father in the late nineteenth century, he was ill and in dire financial difficulties. Suffering from rheumatism, he drove around the estate in an invalid carriage. He was declared bankrupt in 1894. After his death in 1895, the contents of the hall were sold by public auction and the hall itself stood empty until 1906, when the 4th Viscount Hill sold the estate to George Whiteley MP, who was later created Baron of Marchamley. In 1924 the house was bought by the Redemptorists and the park was divided. Hawkstone Park Hotel became the major owner of the land around, including the golf course. The park was reopened for the public in 1993.

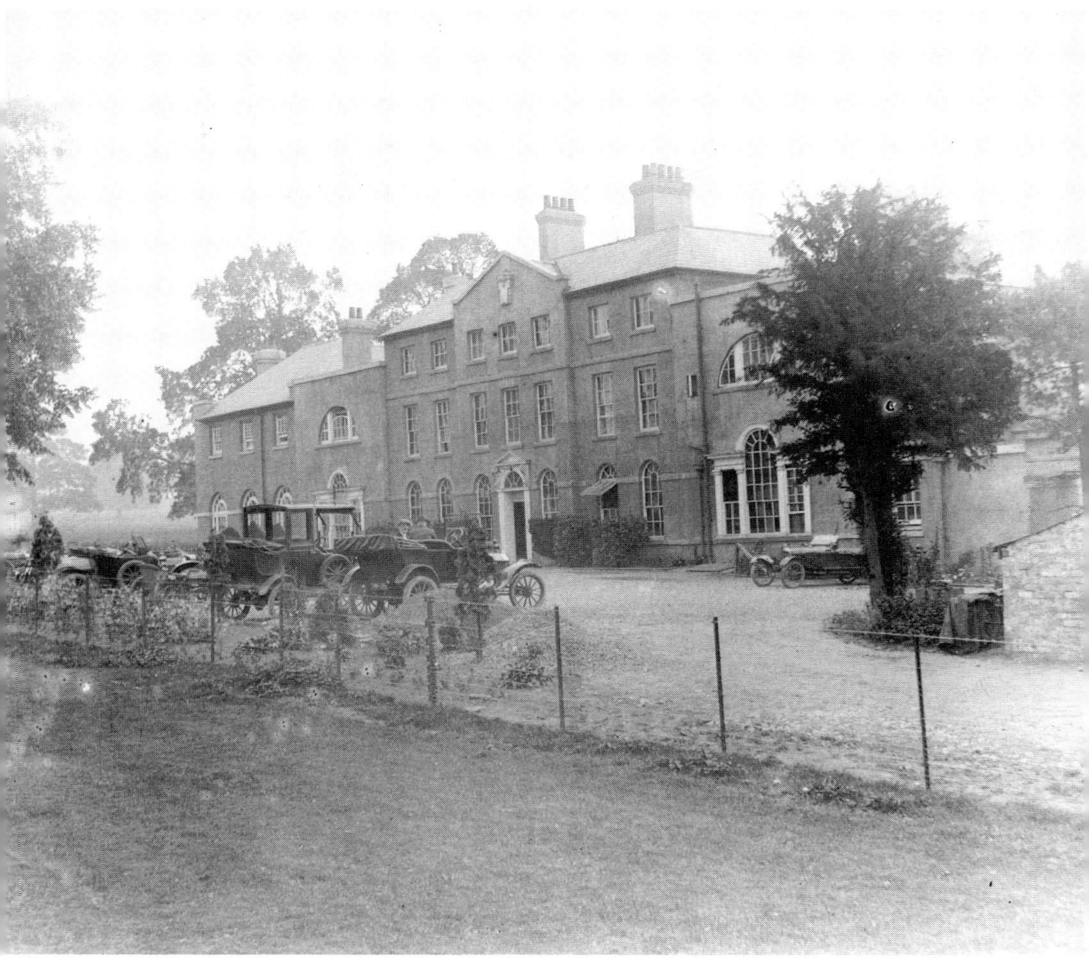

The Hawkstone Park Hotel, c. 1910, was built in 1774 by the Hill family to accommodate the many visitors to the p.ark. It had one of the earliest golf courses in England, now much enlarged.

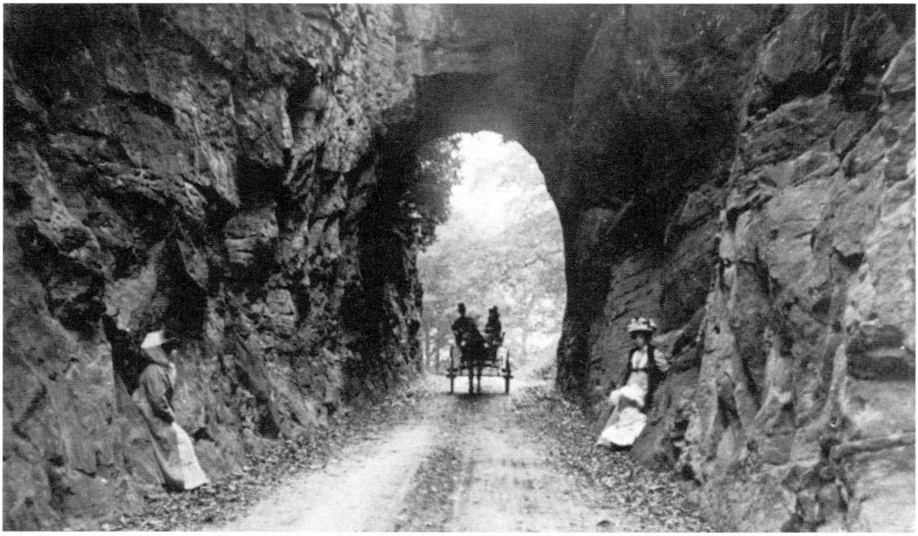

Thackeray, visiting Hawkstone Park during his stay at Prees Vicarage, described the park and the grotto as 'sinister'. Thought to be old Roman copper mineshafts, the grotto is an eerie place. Subterranean passages with the greenish streak of copper lead to a large cavern that was occupied by a hermit during the late 1800s. During that time the Hills transformed the grotto into a place of delicate beauty, covering the walls with a rich assortment of sea-shells and objects brought back from all over the world. Sadly, however, twentieth-century vandals have stripped the walls bare. The photographs of the archway and the grotto date from the turn of the last century.

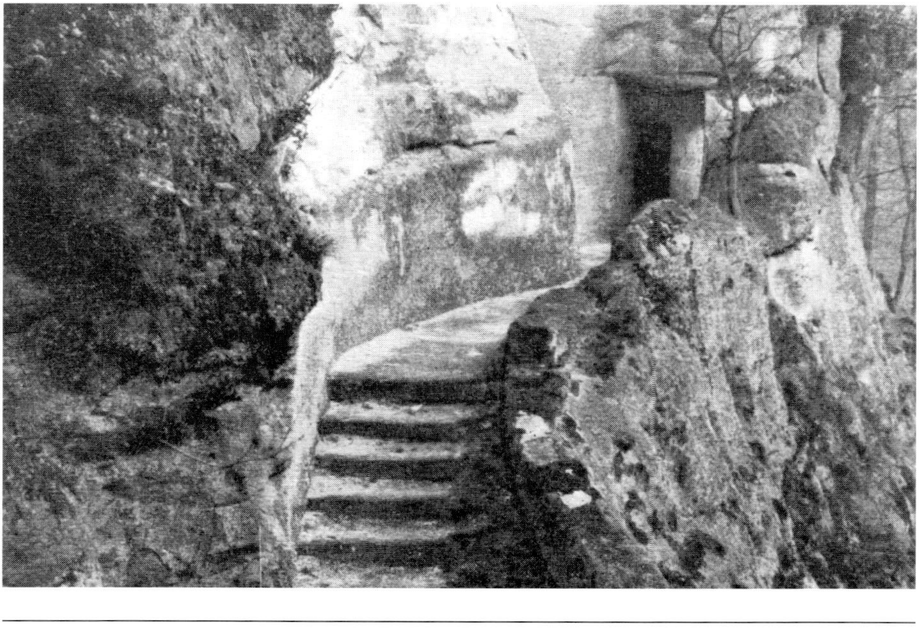

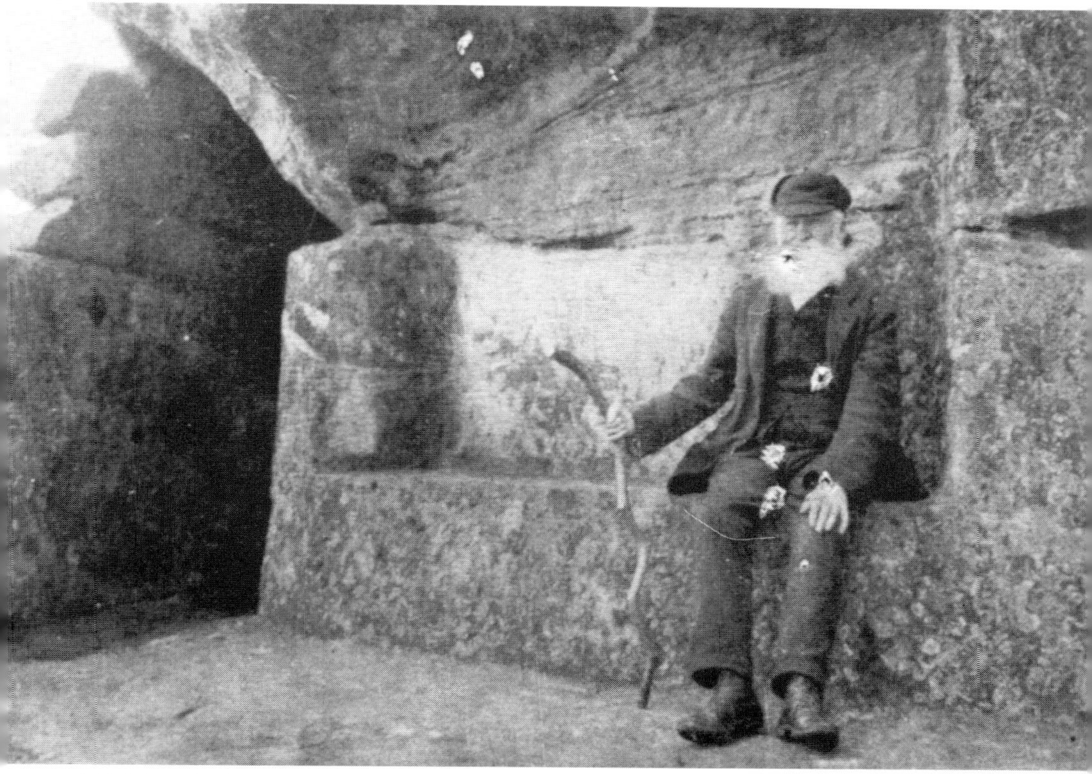

Official guided tours were provided through Hawkstone Park. The Jones family acted as guides for four generations. This photograph of 'Old Jones', taken around 1890, is actually the son of the first Jones to be employed by the Hills and provided with a cottage on the estate.

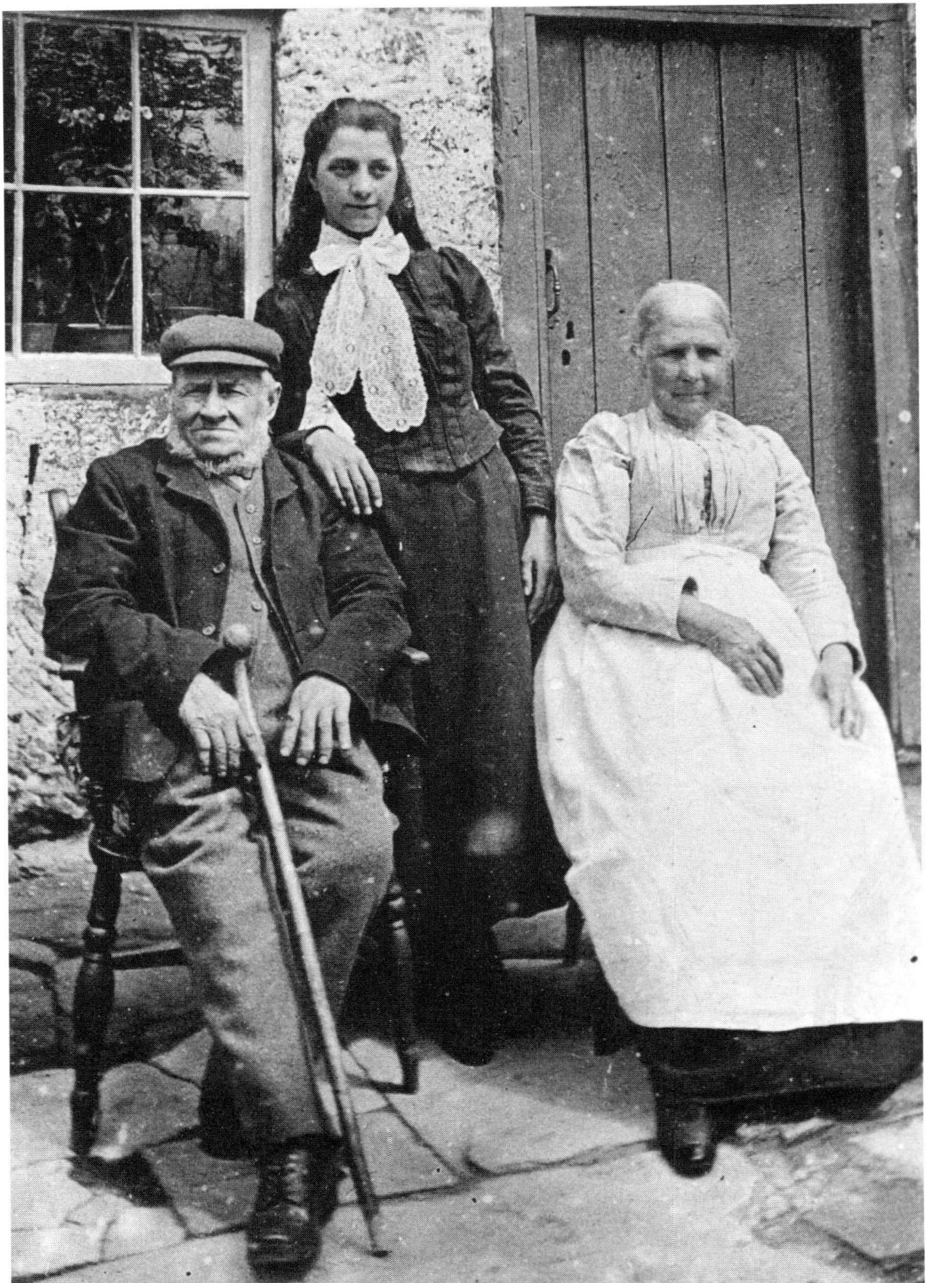

James and Sarah Jackson with their granddaughter Alice at No. 7 Weston Heath, Hawkstone, 1902.

The obelisk, photographed here in 1912, was built in 1785 by Sir Richard Hill. Built of local white stone it stands 112 ft high. It was dedicated to General Lord Hill, who served with his six sons under the Duke of Wellington. He was born at Prees Hall and later moved to the Citadel at Hawkstone. The original sculpture fell off in a storm and has now been replaced by one made of fibreglass. The Barclay brothers have now taken over the park and it has become a major tourist attraction.

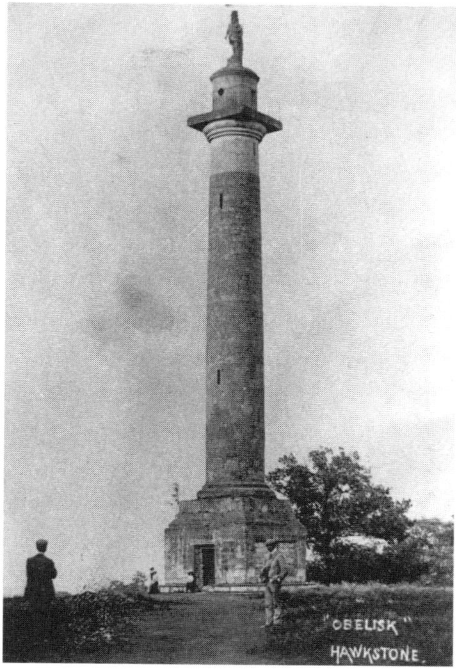

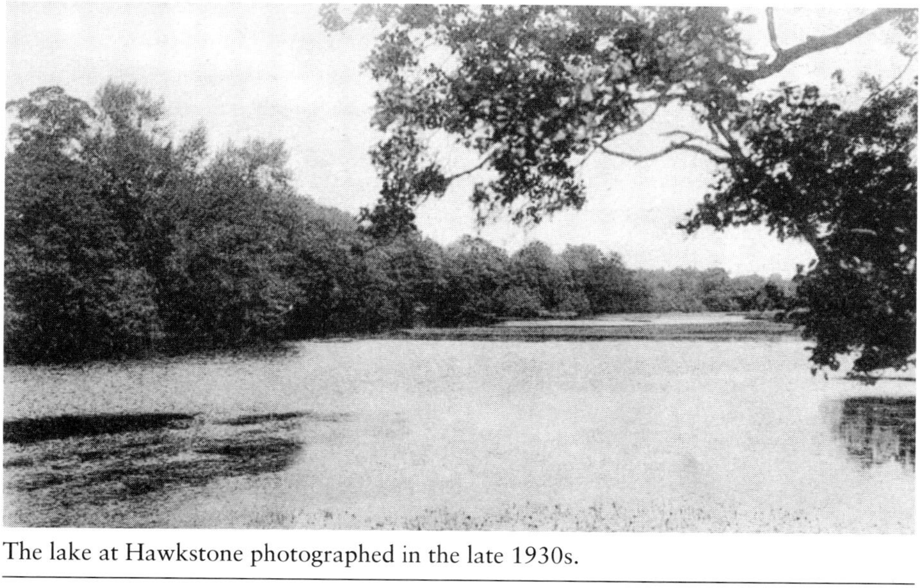

The lake at Hawkstone photographed in the late 1930s.

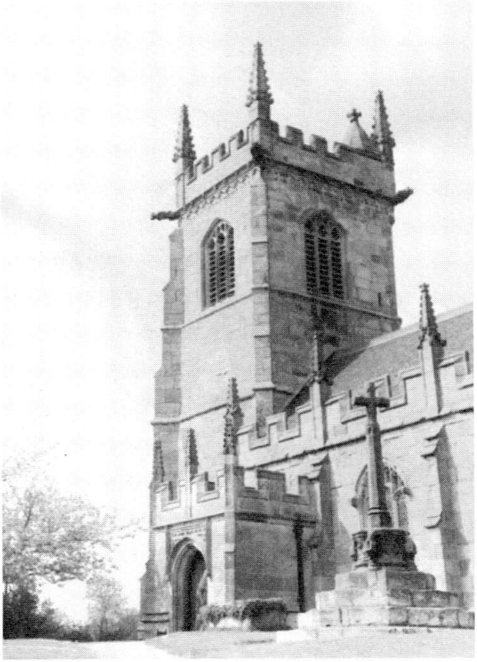

Looking out over beautiful countryside, the fifteenth-century tower of Ightfield Church watches over the churchyard, with its old cross. The poet Arthur Mainwaring was born in Ightfield and is best remembered as editor of *The Medley*. The first issue of the *Tatler* was dedicated to him. The church has a fine brass of his ancestor William Maynwaring, who was a benefactor of the church. This photograph was taken around 1950.

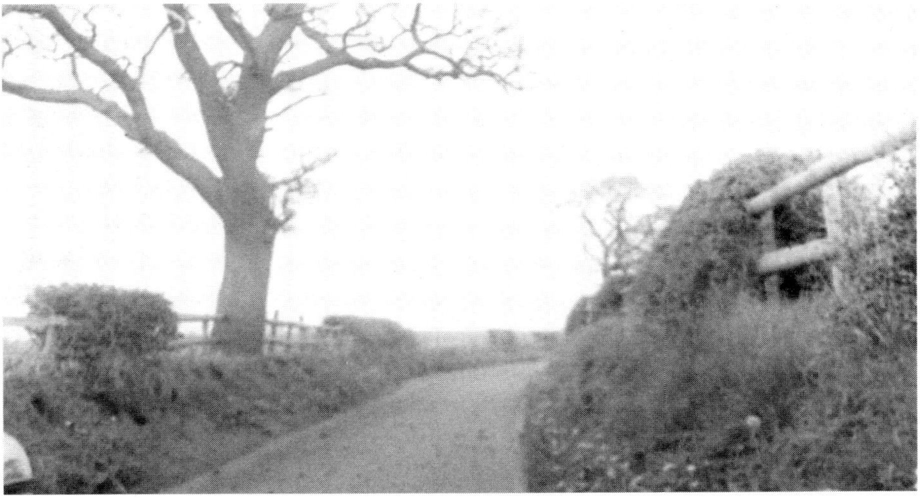

A country lane to Ightfield, photographed in 1975. It is easy to transport yourself back in time when driving through these beautiful lanes with their ancient oak trees.

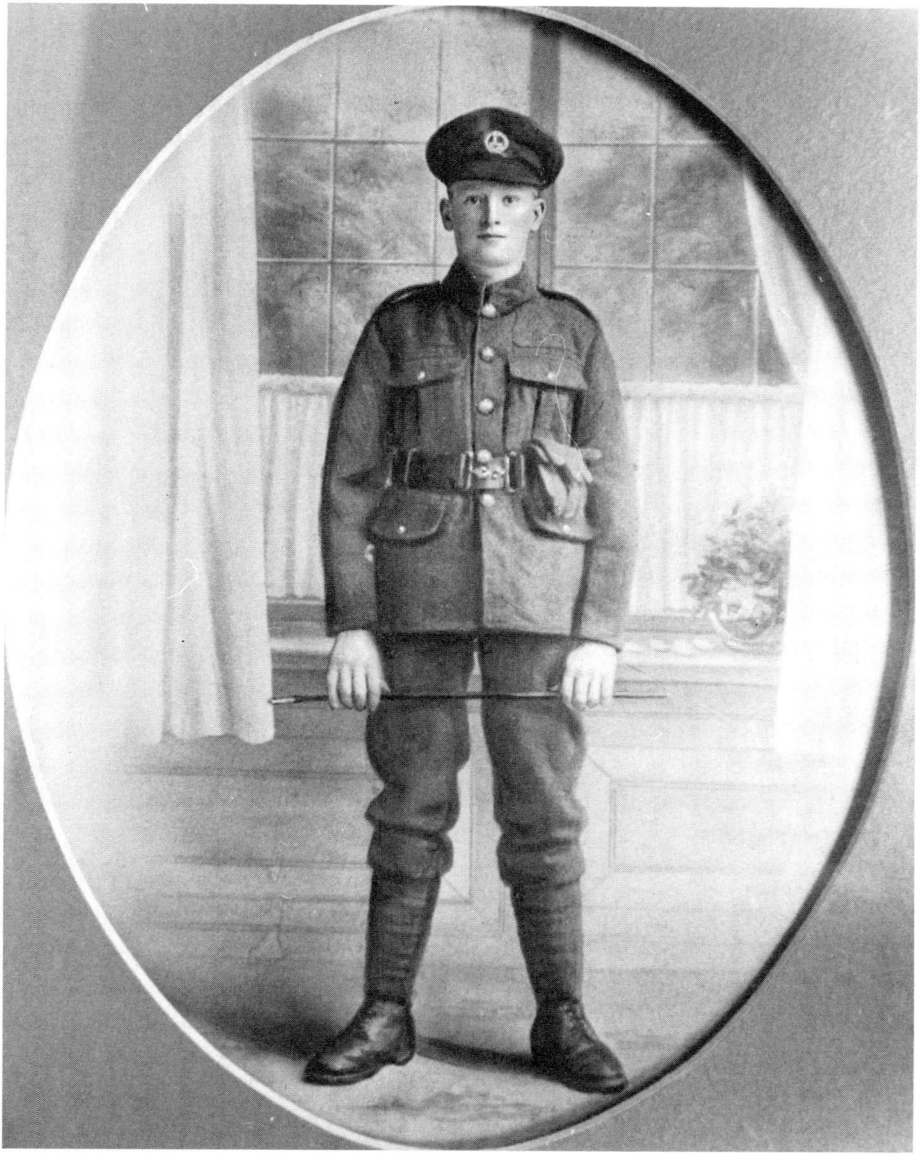

Harold Jones was born in the first month of this century in Stanton-upon-Hyne-Heath near Hodnet. He joined the Army at the age of 17 and fought for his country in the First World War. He took part in the battle of the Somme but throughout his long and happy life he would never talk about that experience. With the money he received for joining up, he bought an antique cup and saucer for his mother. Harold loved the countryside around Ightfield and knew every tree and every house in the area. A happy man, he would burst into song even at the ripe old age of 80. After the war Harold moved to Ightfield and lived there for the rest of his life. He is photographed here in 1917.

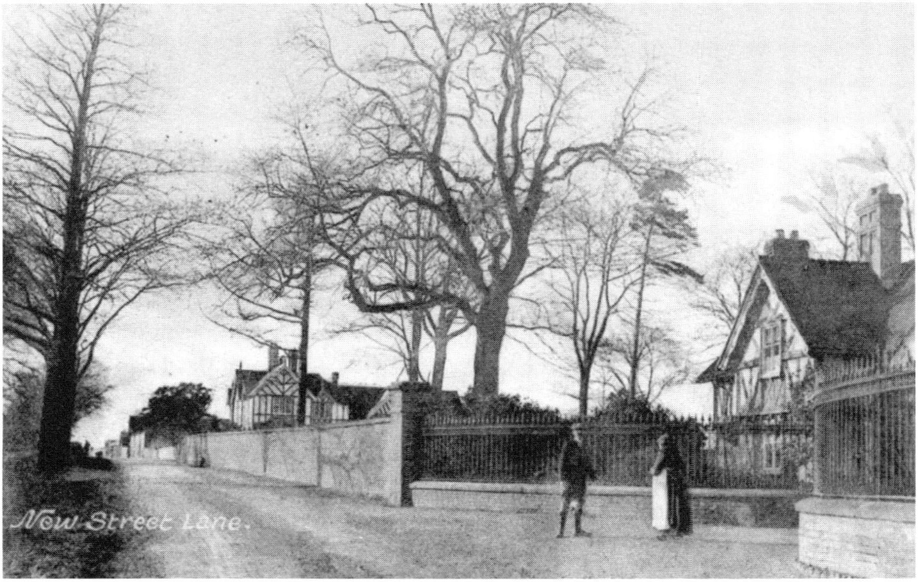

New Street Lane in Ightfield at the beginning of this century.

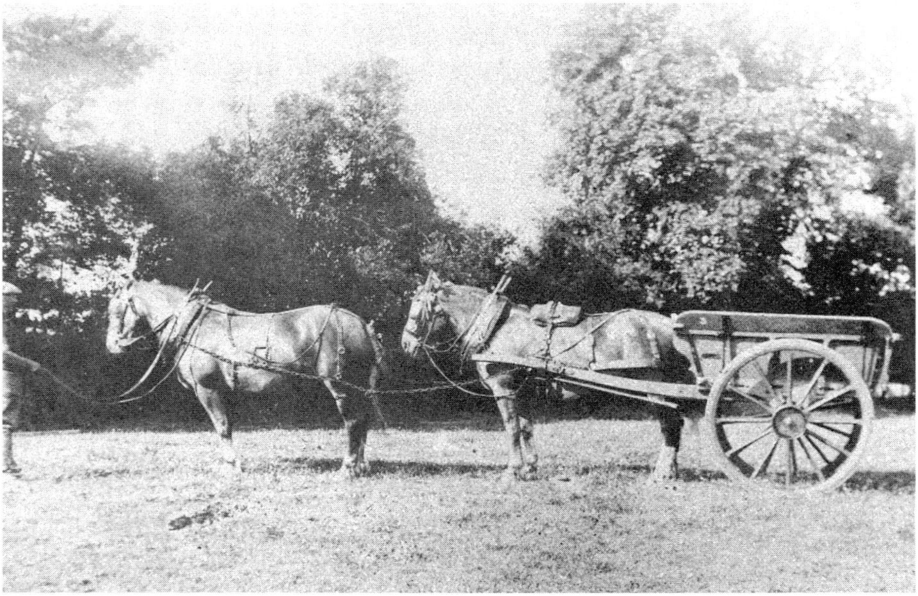
The wagoner's job on the estate or farm was to look after the horses' harnesses and repair the carriages and wagons. It was a skilled job, usually passed on from father to son. This photograph was taken in 1922 on an estate in Stanton-upon-Hyne-Heath, where Harold Jones started his working life as an apprentice. Harold's father would work from six in the morning until dark.

SECTION FIVE

Moreton Say, Market Drayton

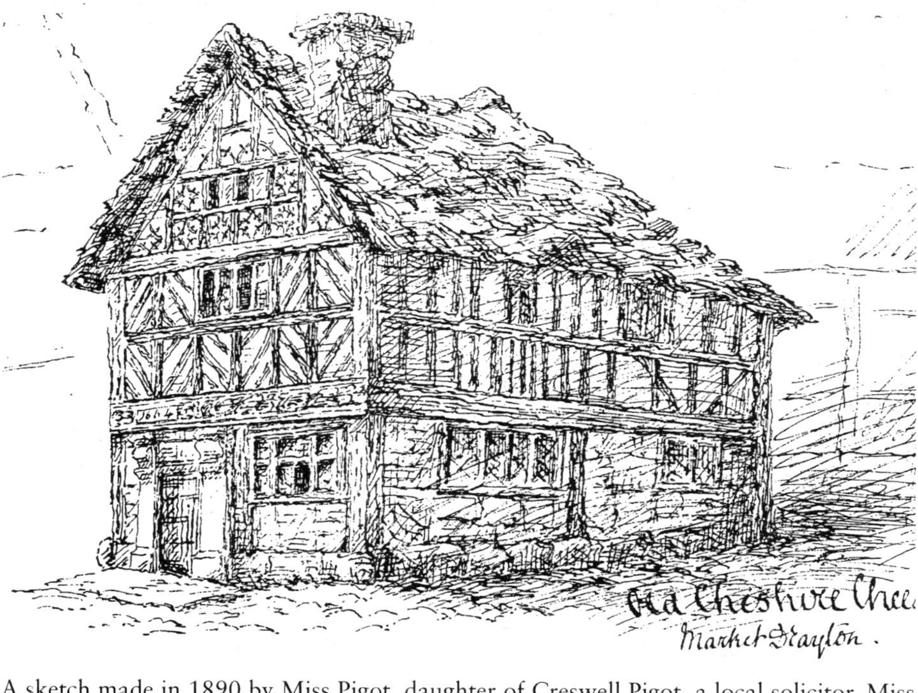

A sketch made in 1890 by Miss Pigot, daughter of Creswell Pigot, a local solicitor. Miss Pigot had a passion for half-timbered houses. This tudor building, known as the Old Cheshire Cheese House was bought by the Billingtons, whose gingerbread was sold all over the world.

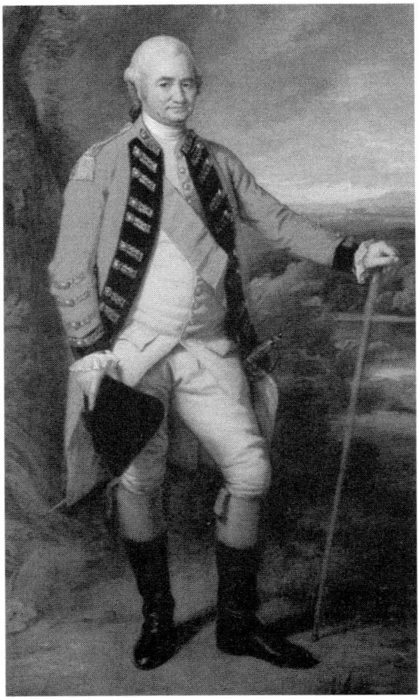

Robert Clive remains an enigma, a man of opposites. Supposed to be stupid and with just an elementary education, he had a brilliant, if somewhat unorthodox, career, and won an empire for his country. Born in 1725, he was the eldest son of Richard Clive, a lawyer. The household with twelve children was not well off and because of this his mother arranged for Robert to be fostered by an uncle and aunt in Manchester. Returning home to Styche he displayed a fierce temper and could not be disciplined. Robert was expelled from three schools, including the Market Drayton Grammar School. This earned him the nickname 'the first Shropshire hooligan'. His battles in India for the East India Company are well documented and it is known that he brought back a fortune. The King received him and the Queen became godmother to his child. He became MP for Shrewsbury but was already in poor health and mentally exhausted. There were rumours about corrupt trading in India and obtaining money by unjust means. In November 1774 Robert Clive committed suicide and his body was returned to Styche.

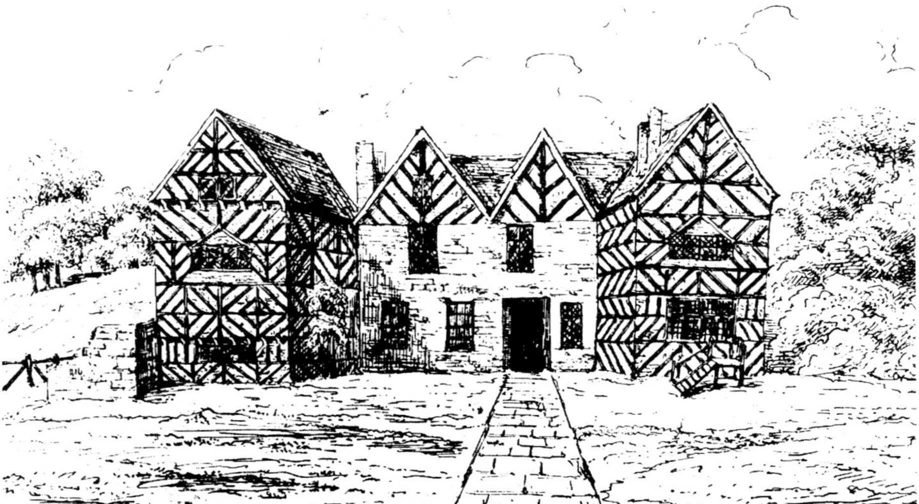

Old Styche, a tudor house, from a drawing made before it was demolished. Robert Clive, better known as Clive of India, built a new hall on the site as a gift to his father after returning from India.

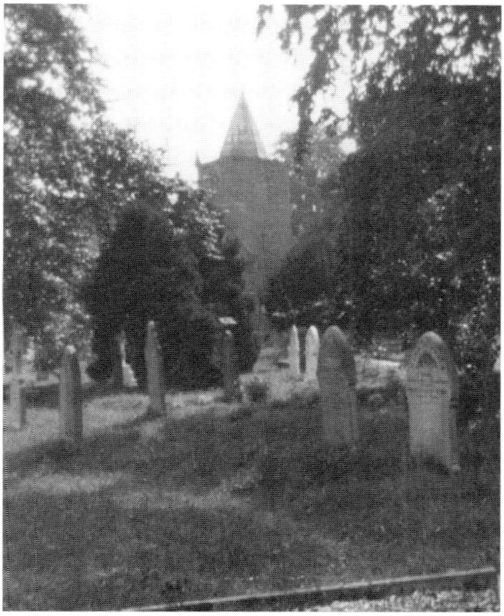

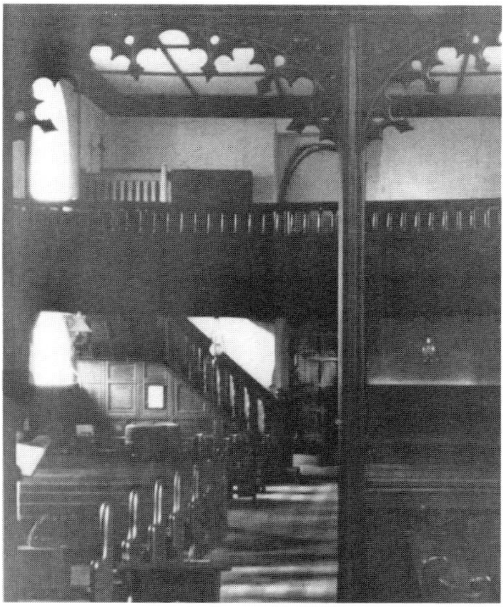

The parish church at Moreton Say owes its name to the township of Moreton – the town on the Moor – and the family of Say, who held the manor for many years until the thirteenth century. The Norman west doorway and the piscina for washing the holy vessels suggest that the church was built soon after the Norman conquest. The west gallery was erected in the time of King Charles I but the paintings it once displayed have been varnished over. The tower was built in 1769 and the roof erected in 1788. The spire, which can still be seen in this photograph of around 1900, was taken down in the 1950s when more restoration was carried out. It was in 1900 that the lead coffin with the remains of Robert Clive was found pushed half into the wall and half into the church. A small monument to the memory of Lord Clive is the only reminder of the area's most famous son.

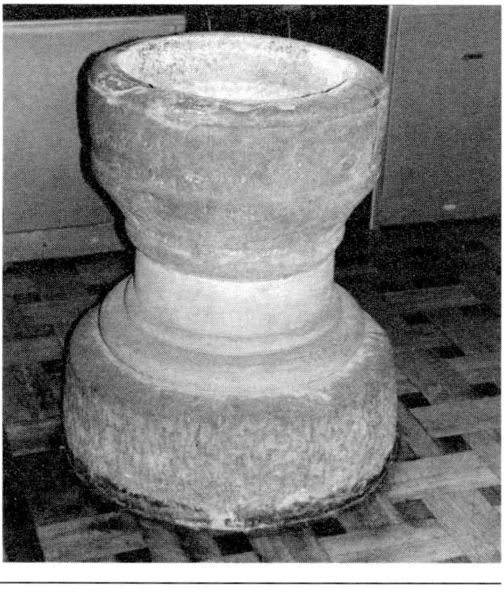

A fourteenth-century font, ejected from the church, was put to use in the farmhouse opposite the church but brought back by the direction of the archdeacon in 1872.

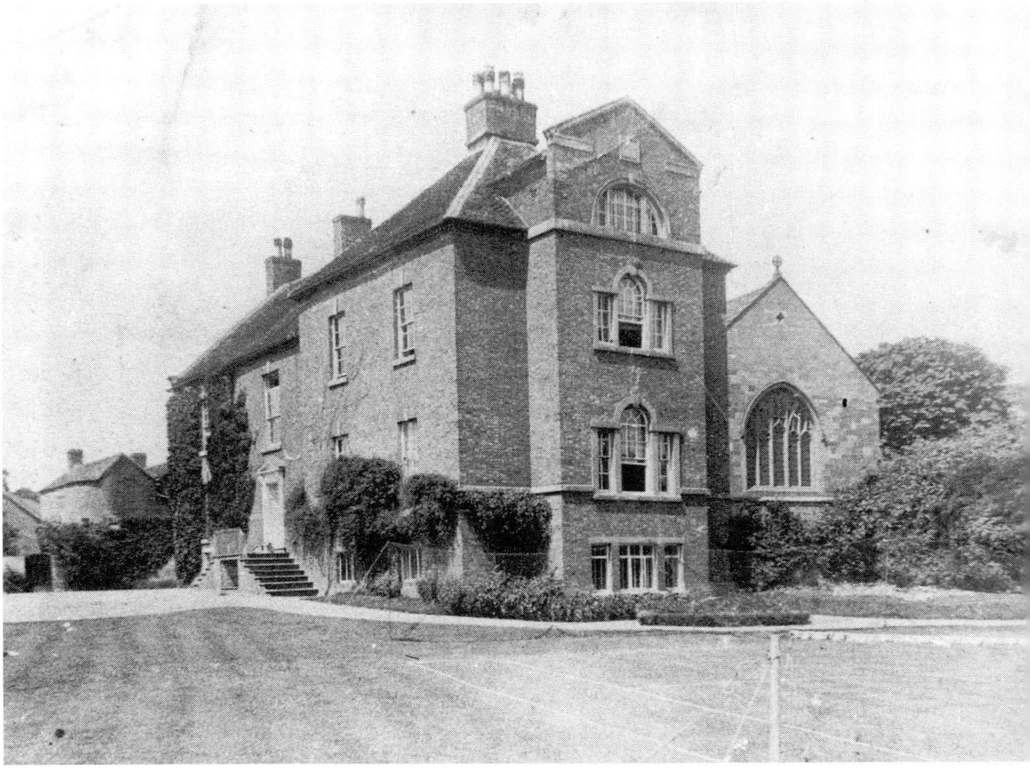

The central part of the Vicarage dates back to around 1680; the east end was built by Archdeacon Clive, who lived there as curate of Moreton in the last half of the eighteenth century. Robert Upton, vicar and rector, spent fifty-six years at Moreton Say, until 1874. The vicarage was pulled down in 1953 and a new one built on the site. The parish register has the signature of Reginald Heber, later to become Bishop of Calcutta, as well as an entry of £300 left in trust for the poor of the parish by Mr H.B. Clive. The baptism and burial of Lord Clive are also recorded. The photograph dates from around 1920.

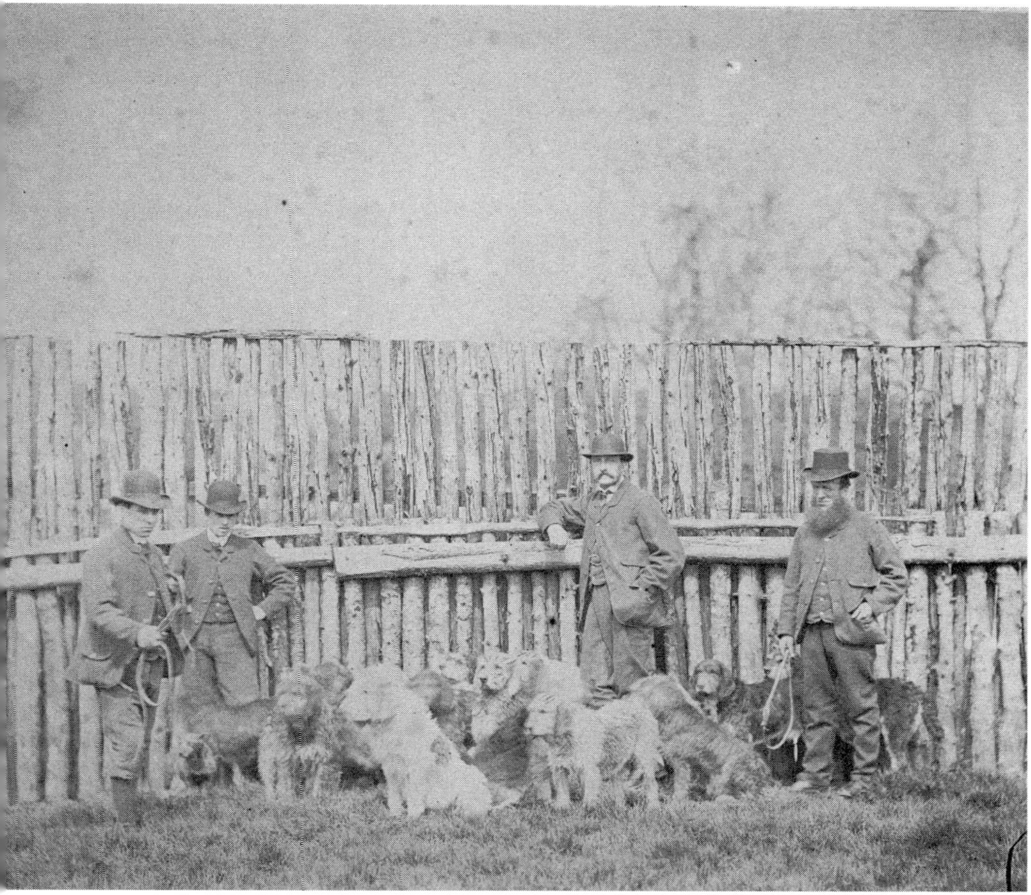

Sir Roland Hill, the first Master of the North Shropshire Hounds, hunted without subscription. He sold the hounds in 1841 to the North Shropshire Hunt. At the end of the nineteenth century the hunt's territory extended from Whitchurch in the north to All Stretton in the south. William Wynn of Wynnstay assumed direct control of the hounds in 1843 and held meets at Hawkstone, Cloverley and Styche. Similar hunts took place on farmland. The Wynn family (no relation to the William Wynns) kept hounds at their farm in Hadley. This photograph from around 1880 shows Donald Wynn's grandfather at Hadley. Donald can still remember his initiation ceremony: blood from the dead fox's tail was smeared on to his face. Fox hunting, now a very emotive issue, still remains part of this country's history.

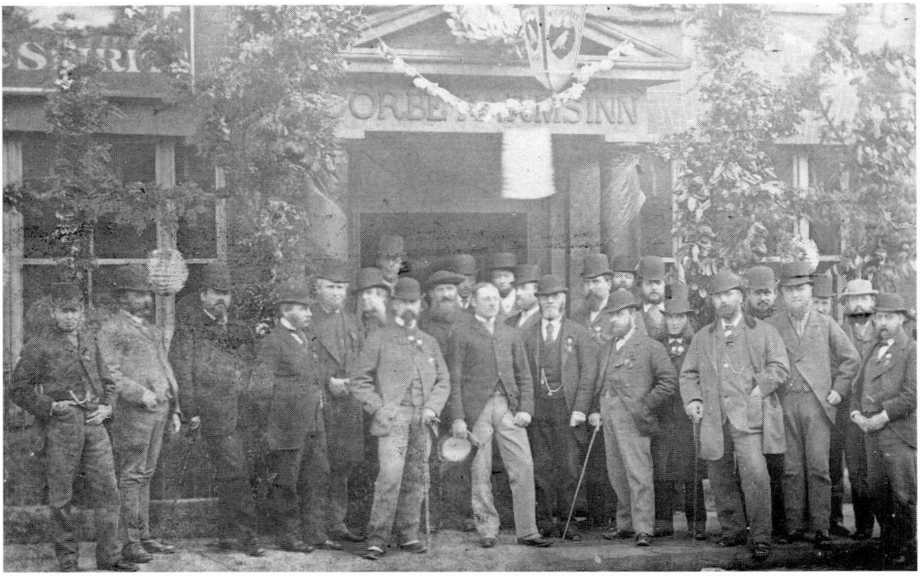

Reginald Corbet, Lord of the Manor of Market Drayton. Above, his 'coming of age' party in 1878; below, photographed on horseback in front of Adderley Hall at the age of 57. He was born in 1857 and like his father he became Master of the Cheshire Fox Hunt. Educated at Eton and Radley, he was made Justice of the Peace for the County of Salop and Captain of the Shropshire Yeomanry. In later life he did not involve himself very actively in the day-to-day affairs of the town. He died at the age of 88 and is buried at the church in Adderley.

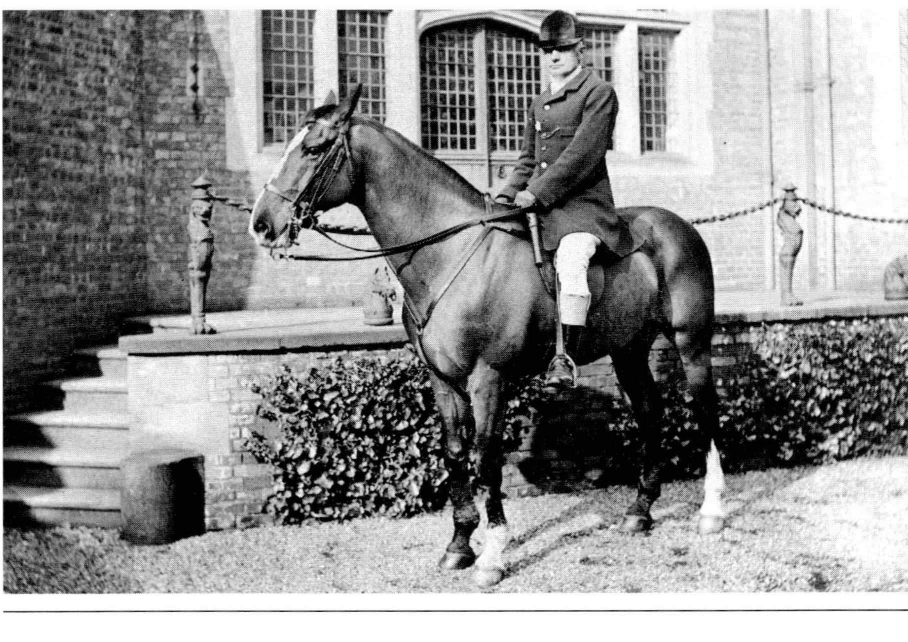

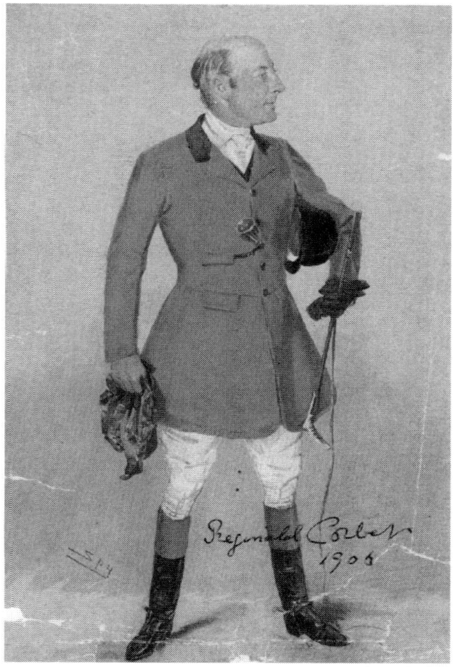

This cartoon from 1906, signed by Reginald Corbet, underlines his passion for horses. At some stage he tried to breed labradors but without much success.

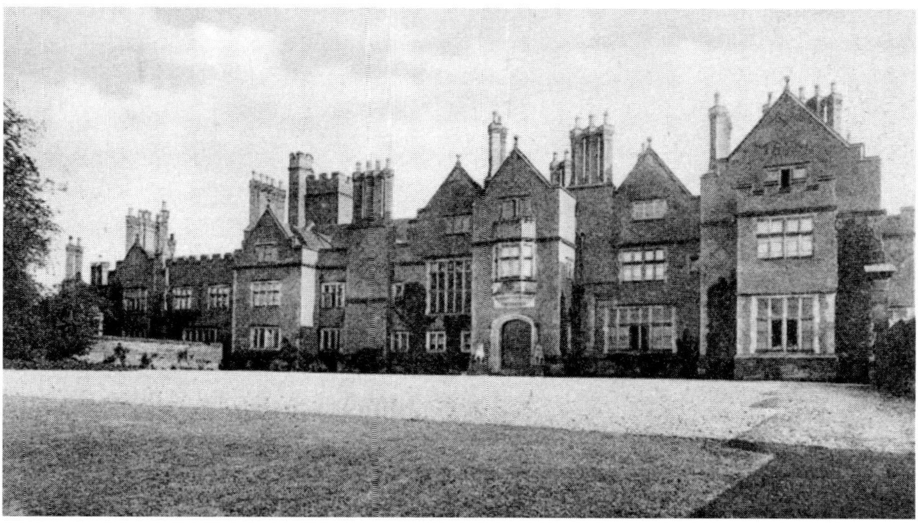

The Market Drayton branch of the Corbets, who came originally from Normandy during the Norman conquest, was established in Adderley and Stoke-on-Tern during the sixteenth century. Adderley Hall was erected on the site of an older building and work on the building was completed in 1878. At one stage it was taken over by the Shropshire Yeomanry and after that occupied by American troops. Before being pulled down in 1953 it also served as a hostel for displaced persons. This photograph dates from around 1910.

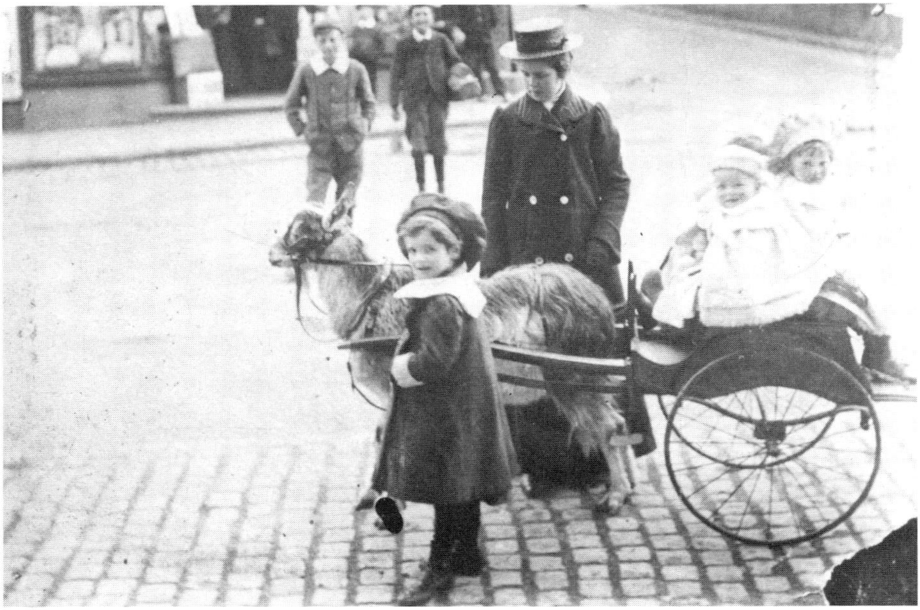

An unusual form of transport in the centre of Market Drayton. This rare goat cart is now in the possession of the Civic Society. It is not certain whether the children, photographed here with their nanny at the turn of the century, are those of the Clifford family.

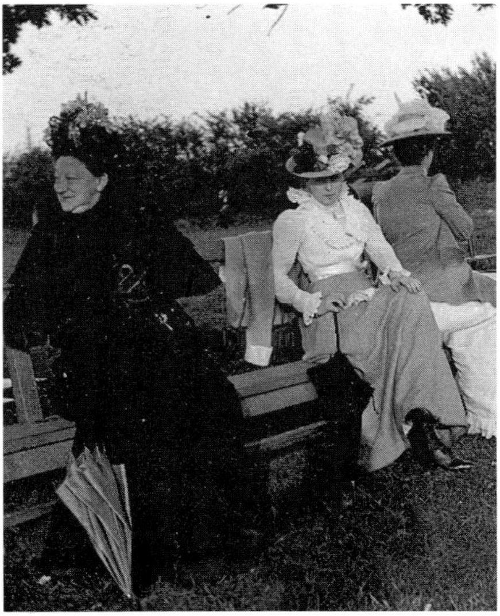

Mary Upton and Mrs Exham watching a cricket match in the early 1900s.

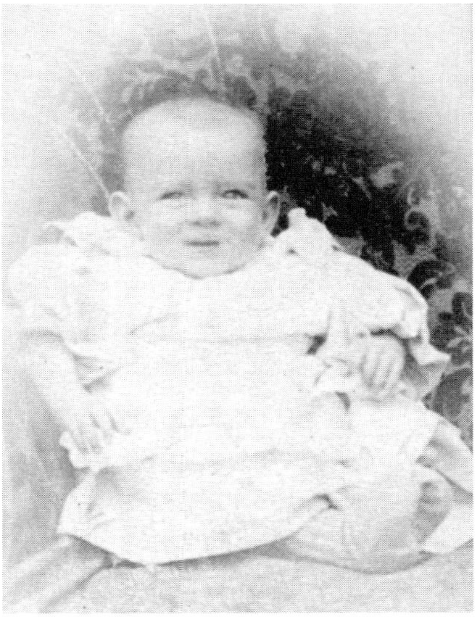

This photograph of a baby was found among the images of Mr Arnold, the local photographer, and dates from around 1880.

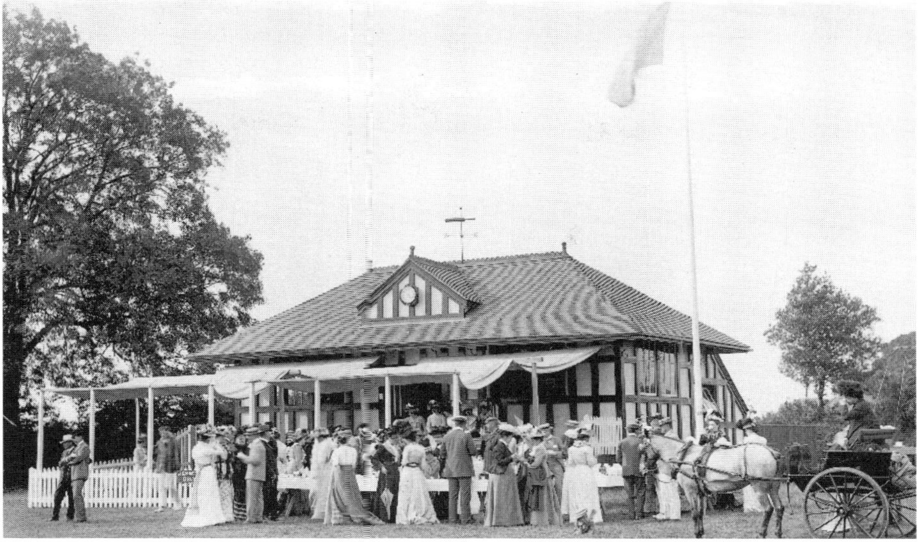

The green and yellow colours of the Market Drayton Cricket Club were also the racing colours of the Clifford family. The first known cricket match in Shropshire was played by the Shrewsbury Cricket Club in 1794. Local clubs, like the one in Market Drayton, emerged during the 1830s and '40s and members were mostly local gentry, the clergy and professional people. Tradespeople joined later on. The cricket pavilion, photographed here in 1901, was demolished in 1980.

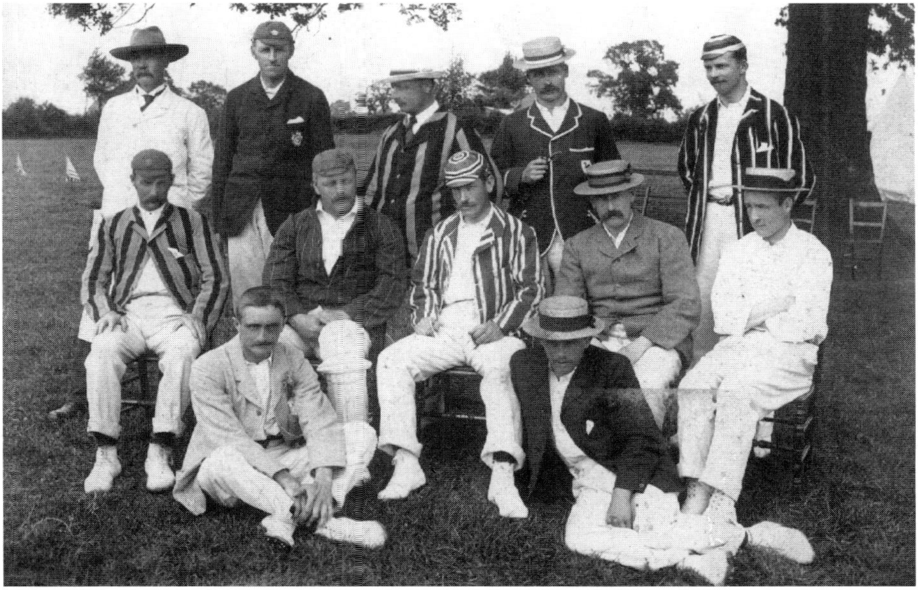

Some members of the Market Drayton cricket team, *c.* 1900. The team includes Mr Hodkins, H.R. Glennis, C.W. Clifford, Dr Exham, P.P. Arkinstall, and B.V. Eardley.

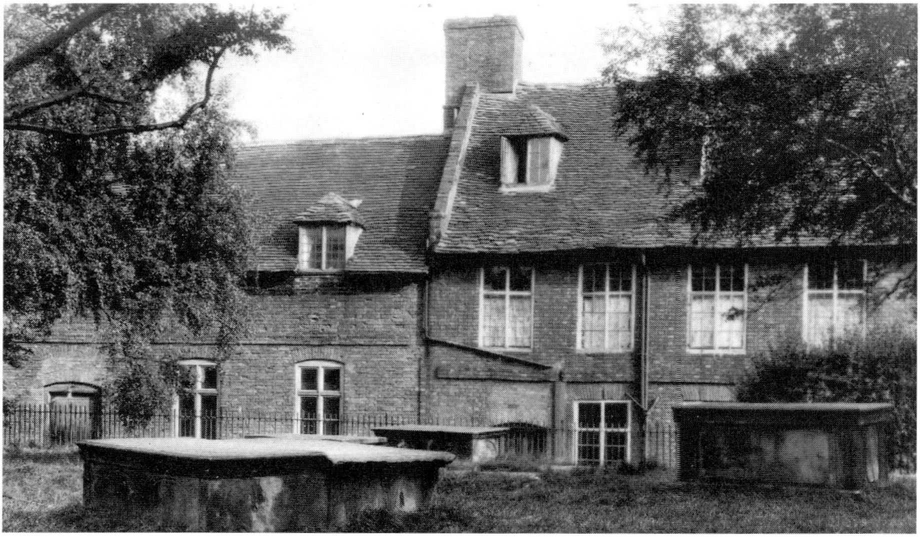

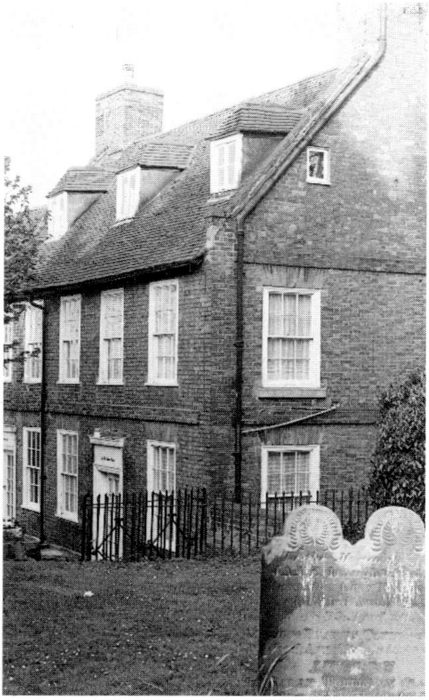

Sir Rowland Hill founded the Free Grammar School adjacent to St Mary's Church in 1555. English, Latin and Hebrew were the prescribed subjects and the church wardens acted as governors. Masters tended not to stay long at the school, for reasons not known. In 1719 the school was restored and a brick facing was added. Robert Clive attended the school at the beginning of 1737, breaking many of the rules. By 1811 the lord of the manor wrote that the place was falling into decay. More restoration work was carried out and the number of pupils increased to sixty-one. By 1867 the number had dwindled to twenty-four and the school building was once again in need of repair. After the Shropshire Education Committee was formed in 1902, the school was finally closed when the building was deemed unsuitable for repair or expansion. Above, the school around 1920; below, the building around 1979.

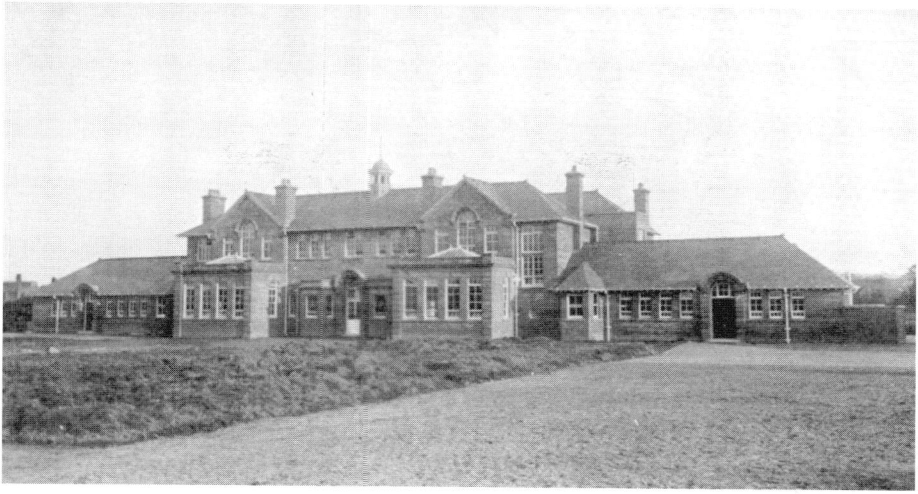

The County Grammar School, *c.* 1930. The new Grammar School at Mountfields began in 1910 as two separate schools for boys and girls. Permission was obtained to use part of the Clive coat of arms as the school's badge. Emphasis was placed on manual training and physical education and so there were rooms for cookery and woodwork. Twenty-nine girls, arriving by train, bicycles and pony-trap, attended the school in the first term. Only four scholarships were available, the rest of the pupils had to pay a fee. A kindergarten was added in the second year but was closed down in 1949. By 1933 over eighty boys and one hundred girls were registered; afterwards the school became co-educational. In 1965 the Grammar School and the Grove Secondary Modern were merged to form the new comprehensive.

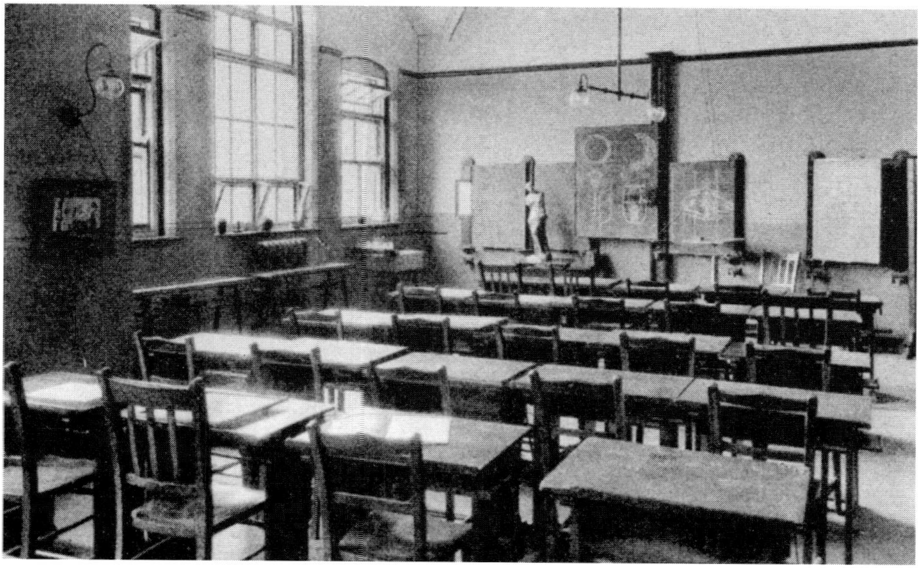

A typical classroom, *c.* 1930.

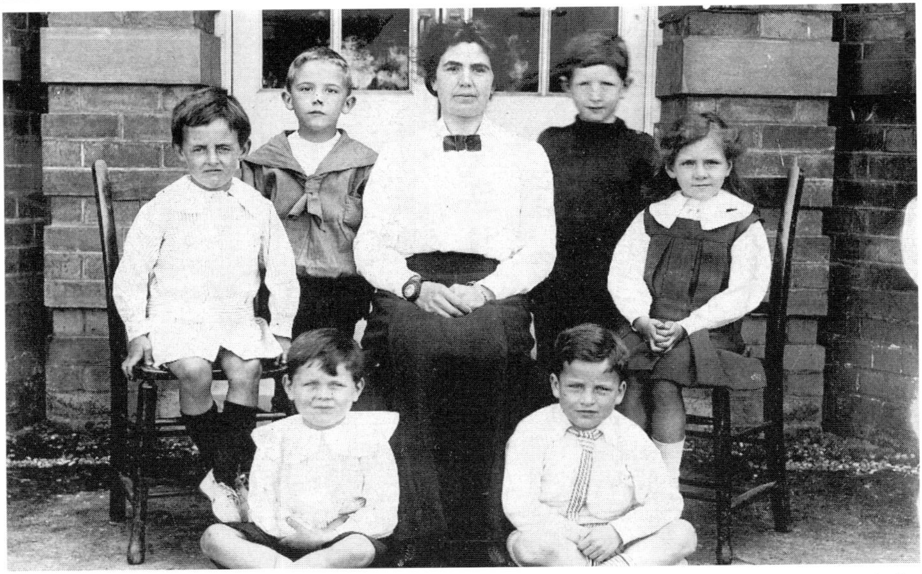

The name of the mistress of the kindergarten in 1914 is not known but one of the children featured here, sitting on the right-hand chair, is Evadna Etches. Her mother wrote on the back of the photograph: 'This is Vadnis class at school but not a very good photograph.'

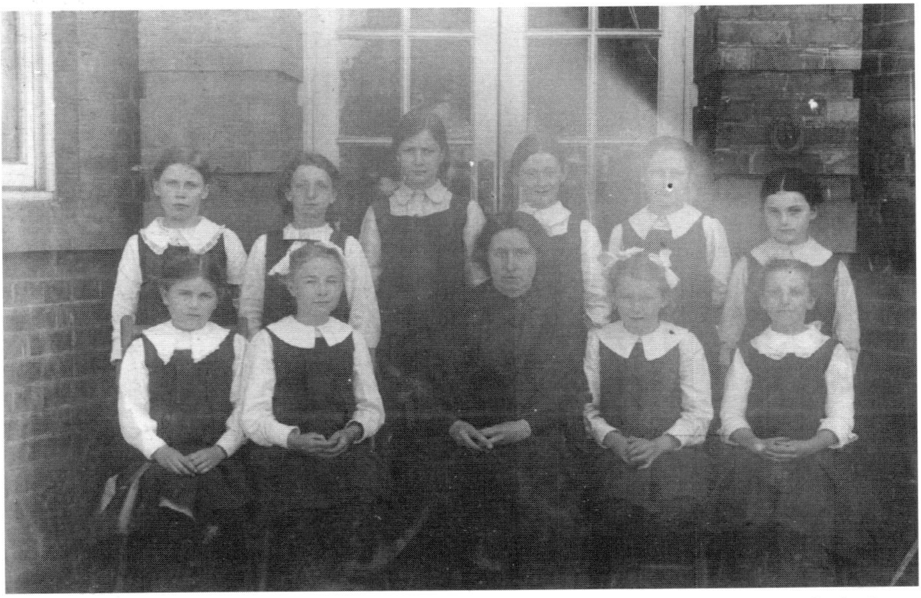

Girls Grammar School in 1912; only the art room was shared at that time with the boys school. The mathematics mistress is Miss Harry and the girls to the right and left of her are Mary Wood and Margaret Wood. Phyllis Byram is sitting next to Margaret Wood.

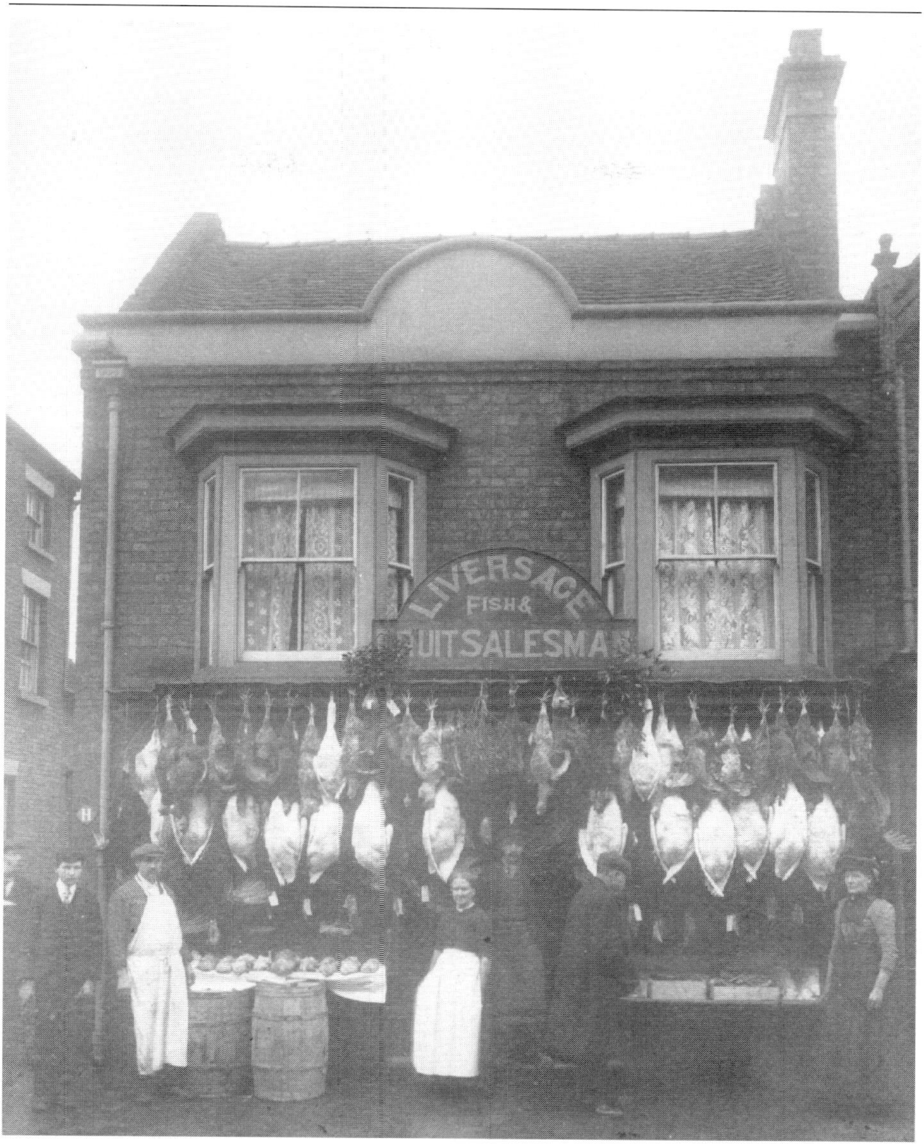

Liversage fish, poultry and fruit shop on Shropshire Street was known for its high-quality produce. This photograph from around 1898 shows from left to right: two shop boys, Mr Richard Liversage, Mrs Jones, Mr J.H. Boote, Mr Kettle and Sally Liversage. Richard Liversage died in September 1905 and left behind three children, Dorothy, Margaretta and Jessie. Mrs Liversage found it difficult to run the shop on her own and bring up three children. Eventually she married the foreman in the shop, J.H. Boote, although he was much younger than herself, in order to keep his help, but the marriage was not a happy one. An invoice from 1955 shows not only the prices but also that invoices were sometimes not settled for three months. The shop was demolished in 1979.

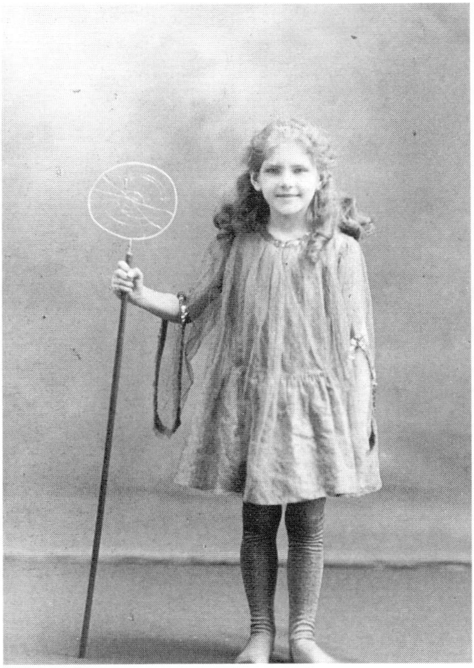

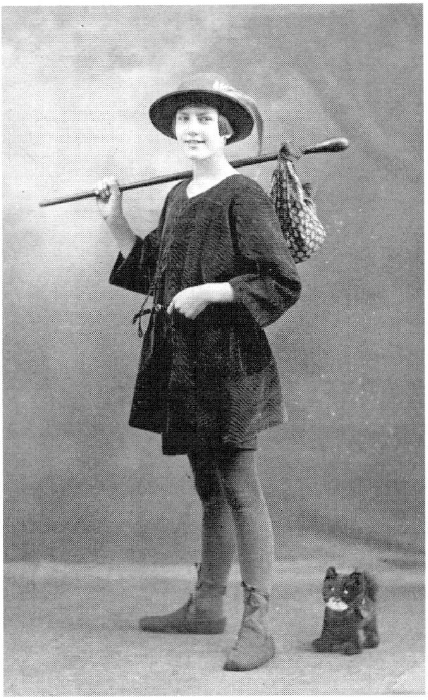

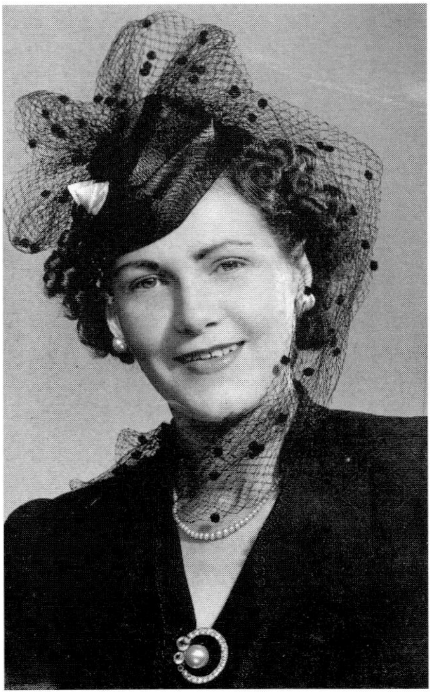

Three images of Evadna Etches, who lived at 32 Stafford Street until her death. The first photograph was taken by Mr Arnold, the local photographer, in his studio in 1918. The same location was used some years later for the image with the toy cat. At the time of the close-up, Evadna was about 28 years old and a glamorous aspiring actress in London. Evadna's father came to Market Drayton as an apprentice to the Gower iron foundry. A man of outstanding ability, he soon made a name for himself and the family prospered. Later on they moved into the Gower home. It appears that Mr Etches had an obsession about people's weight and he wrote down the measurements of every person he met.

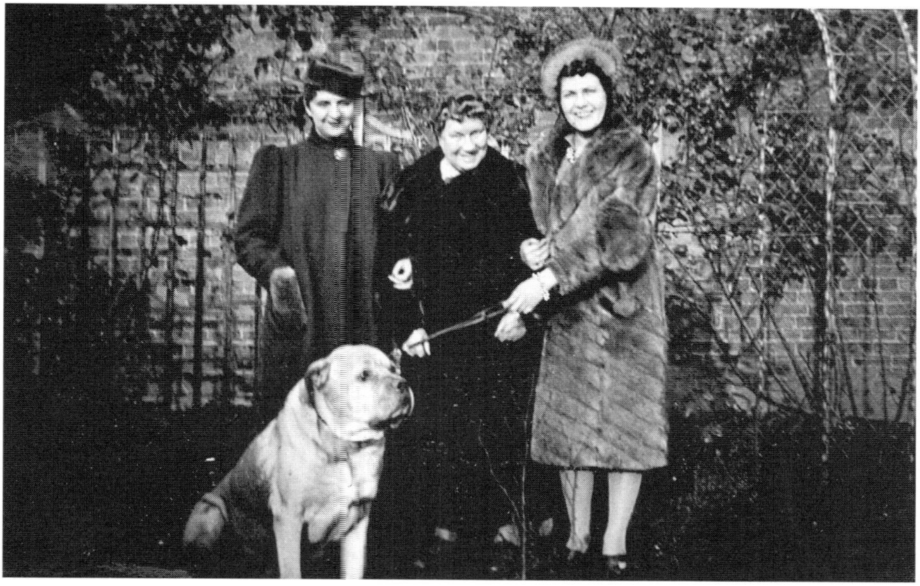

Evadna returned to Market Drayton from London first to look after her ailing mother (centre) and after her death she remained to support her father. With her dreams of a career as an actress in shreds, she never left Market Drayton again and became a recluse, writing plays for BBC radio.

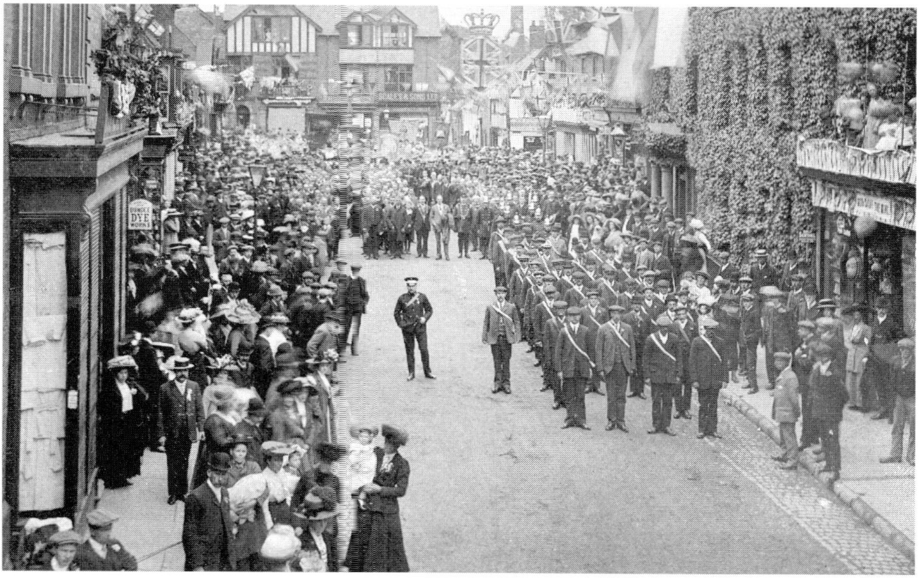

A photograph of Mr Arnold (centre) in 1911 at a coronation parade.

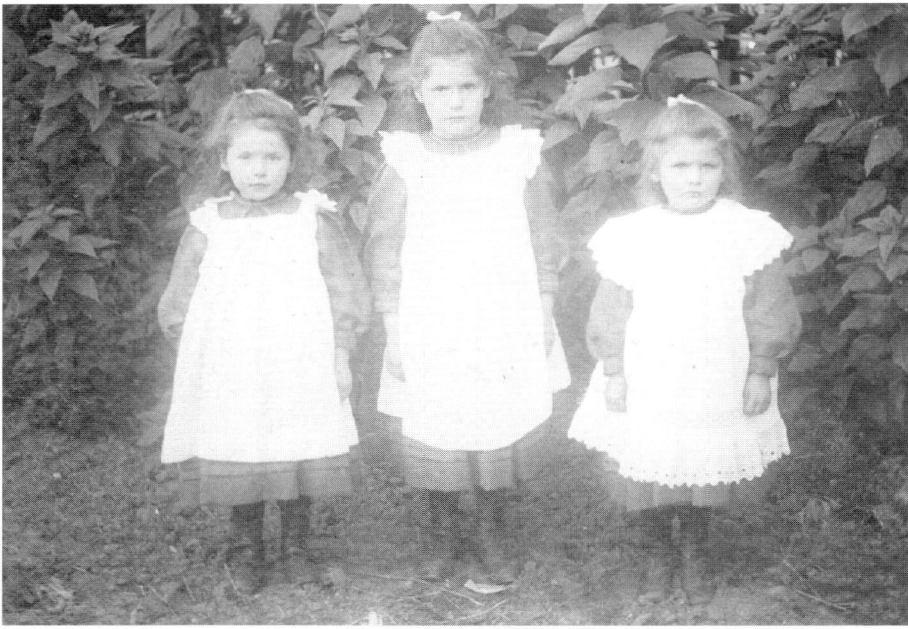

Dorothy, Margaretta and Jessie Liversage around 1898, ready to go to Sunday School (National School). It was always 'Sunday best' on these occasions.

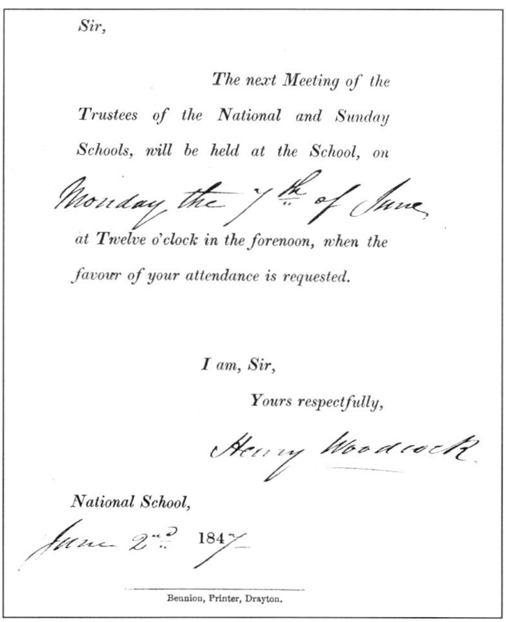

Sir,

The next Meeting of the Trustees of the National and Sunday Schools, will be held at the School, on

Monday the 7th of June

at Twelve o'clock in the forenoon, when the favour of your attendance is requested.

I am, Sir,

Yours respectfully,

Henry Woodcock

National School,

June 2nd 1847

Bennion, Printer, Drayton.

Invitation to a meeting of the trustees of the National School, dated 1847. It was here that the poll took place for the 1885 general election. Lord Newport stood for the Conservatives but was beaten by the Liberal candidate.

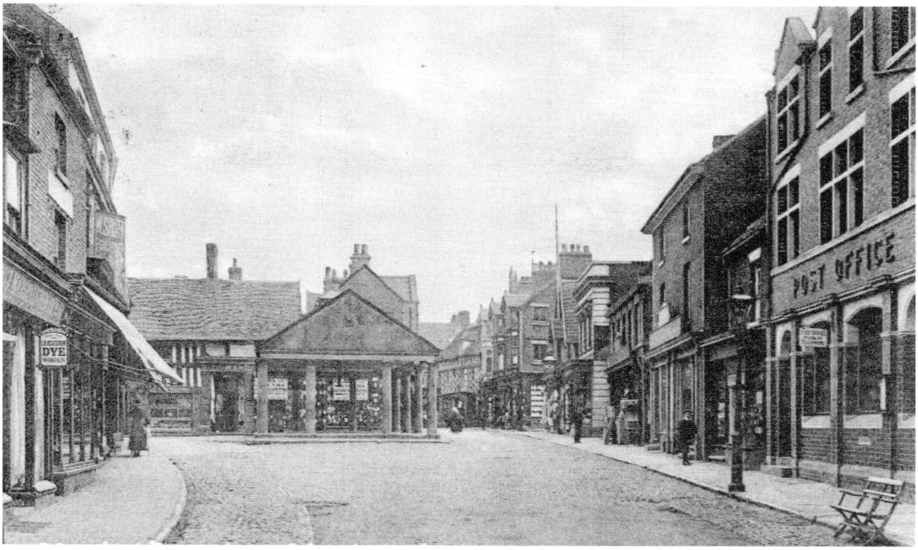

A map of 1787 shows what appear to have been two rectangular buildings on the site of the present Buttercross, which was not erected until 1824. Its purpose was to provide shelter for the sale of butter, eggs, cheese and poultry, as was still happening at the time of the Markets and Fairs Commission inquiry in 1888. When the present Buttercross, with its pediment and fourteen Tuscan columns was built, a 'round house' seems to have been added at one end (shown as a semi-circular building on the map of 1842), which was probably used as a prison. These photographs show the Buttercross with the post office in the 1920s and a close-up of the Buttercross in the late 1940s. The post office is still there but the roads have now lost their cobblestones.

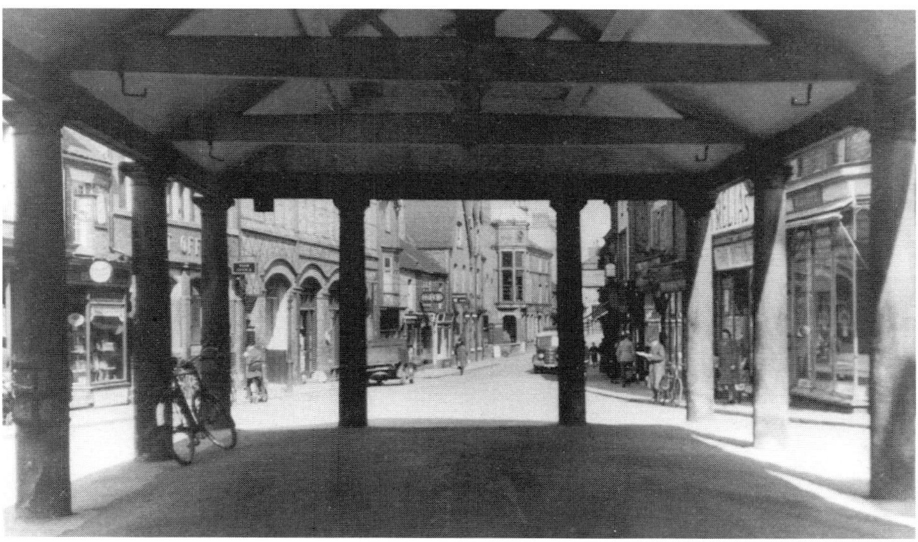

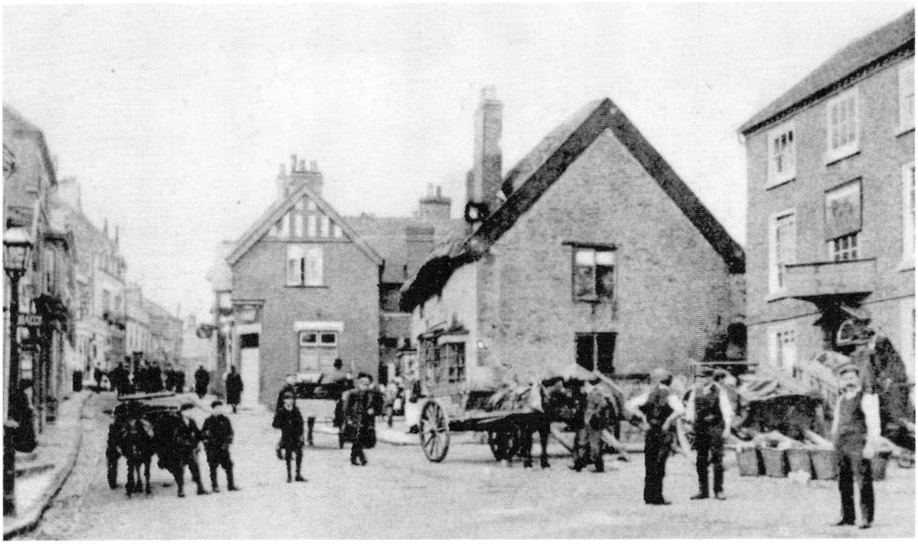

Some of the streets came to be known by their purpose on market days: Great Hales Street and Queen Street were known respectively as 'Stocke Lane' and 'Beast Market'; Stafford Street became 'Sheep Market' and Cheshire Street 'Horse Market'. At the time of this photograph in the late 1890s, damsons and other fruit were sold in Great Hales Street.

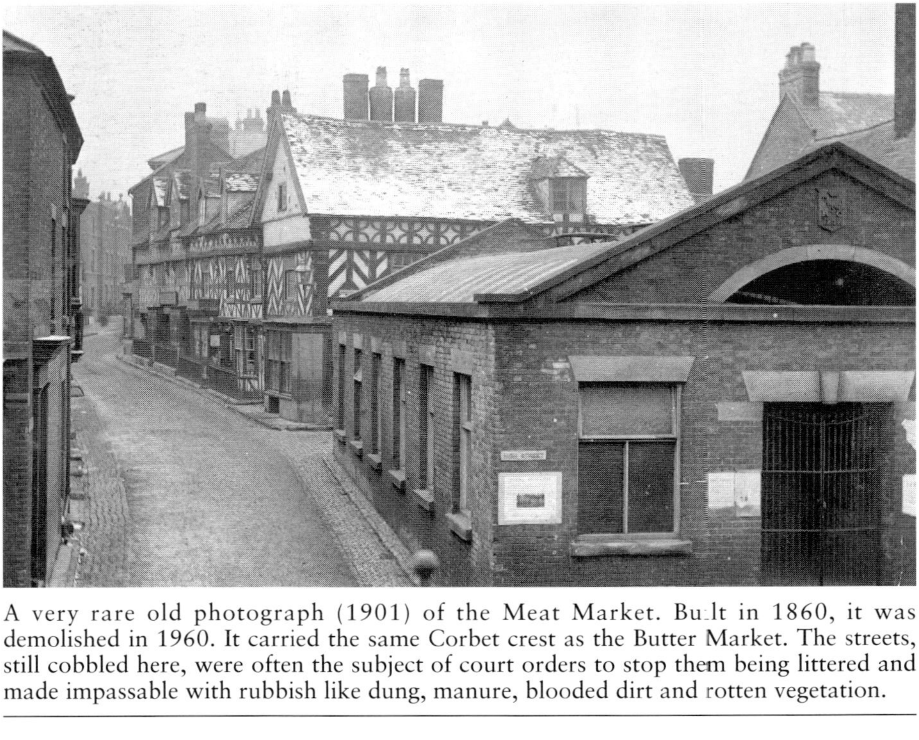

A very rare old photograph (1901) of the Meat Market. Built in 1860, it was demolished in 1960. It carried the same Corbet crest as the Butter Market. The streets, still cobbled here, were often the subject of court orders to stop them being littered and made impassable with rubbish like dung, manure, blooded dirt and rotten vegetation.

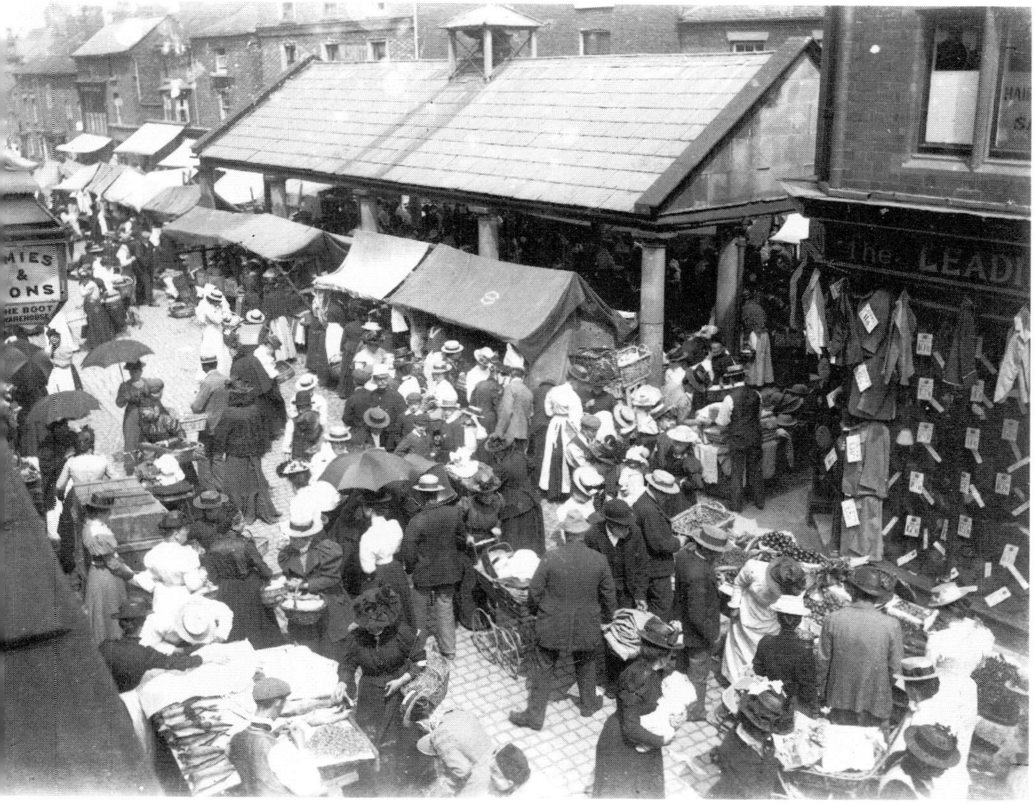

Market Drayton was granted its vital market charter by King Henry III at about the same time as Whitchurch. The founding fathers and Lords of the Manor, the Abbots of Combermere, involved themselves in almost all aspects of early life in the small community, particularly its trade. The market was the main reason for the growth of the town with tradesmen coming from miles around and some settling permanently in the district. Rental for the 'standings', made from movable poles, was charged by the Lord of the Manor. With the arrival of the canal and the railway in the mid-1880s the town grew still larger. Sadly the railway has been closed down and locals now call Market Drayton 'the forgotten market town'.

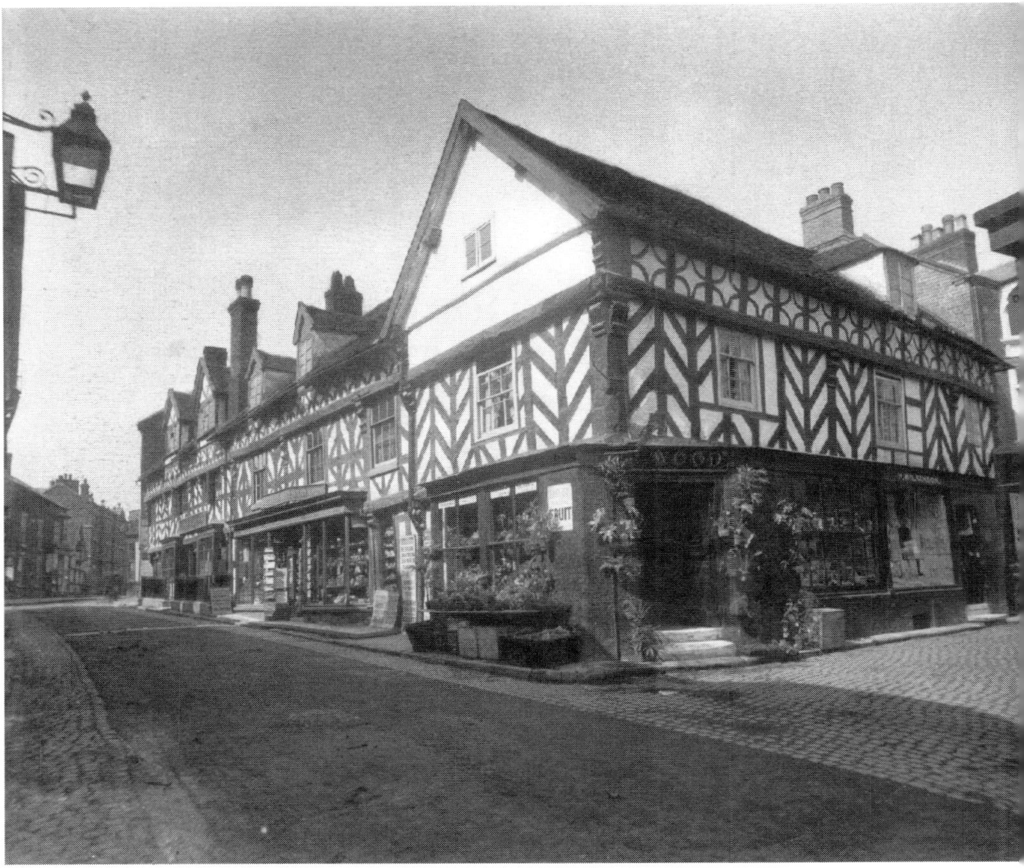

A sunny afternoon in 1909 with Wood's, the grocer and fruit shop at the corner of Cheshire Street. You can just about read the notice on the bill board: 'Women's Suffragette debate in the Commons,' advertising the *Daily News*. In the nineteenth century most shopkeepers lived above their shops, sometimes together with their assistant as well as the family.

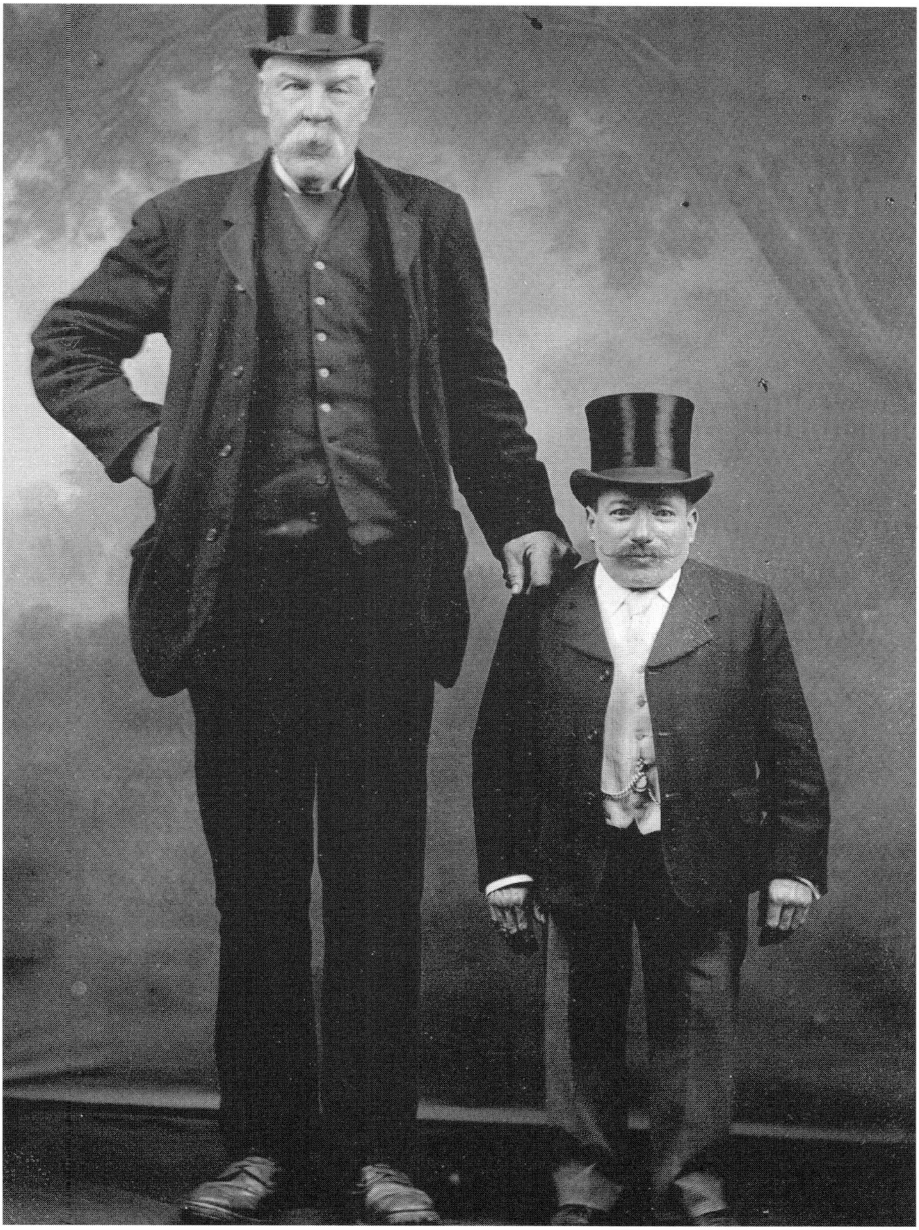

Tom Dutton was known as the Shropshire giant. This photograph, taken in Mr Arnold's studio, shows him together with Tom Sillitoe, who was much respected as a waistcoat designer. Among the bailiffs of Market Drayton in 1741 was a Mr Aaron Silito. This photograph was taken in 1918; both men died not long after, Tom Dutton in 1924 and Tom Sillitoe in 1926.

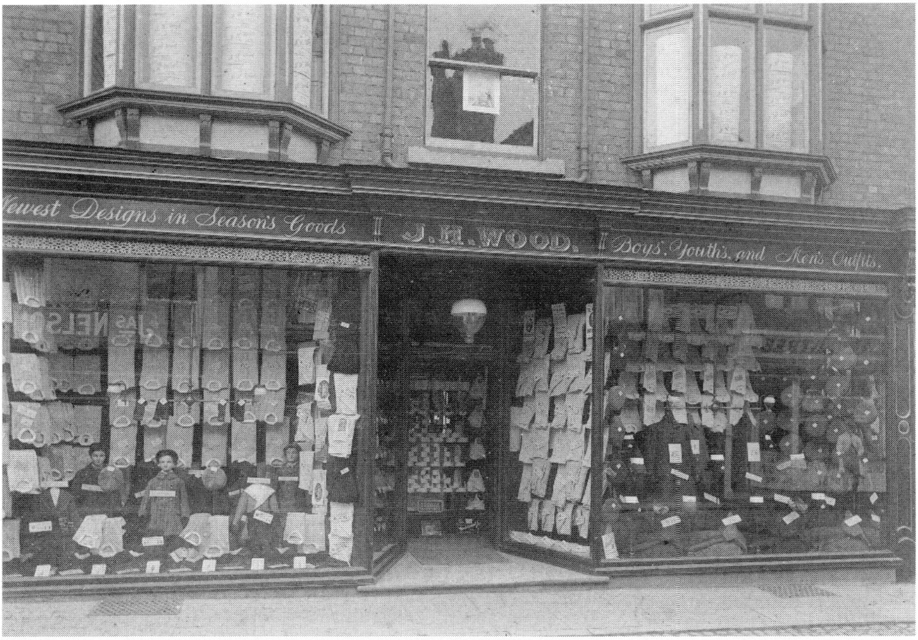

J.H. Wood, advertising the newest designs in 'Boys', Youths' and Mens' Outfits', in Cheshire Street, *c.* 1910. It was here that Tom Sillitoe worked.

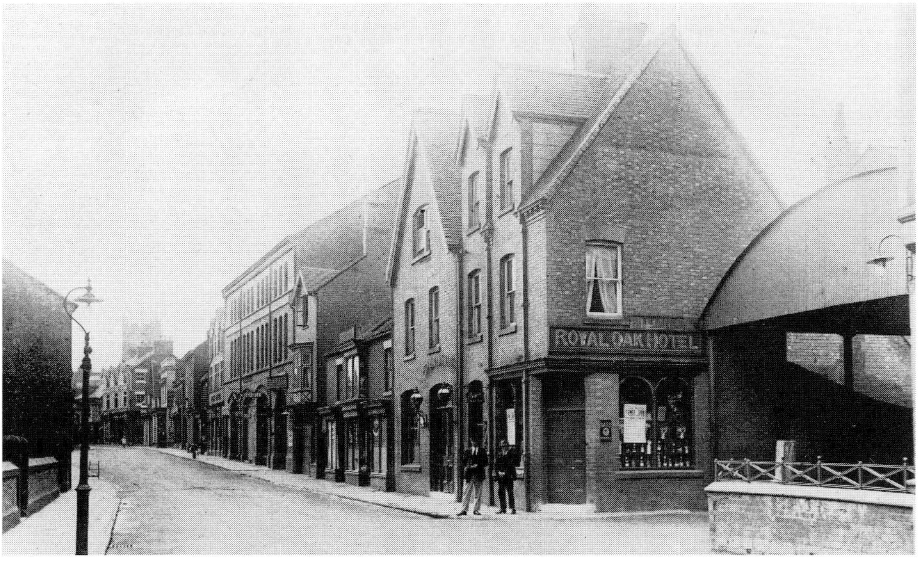

The Royal Oak Hotel, *c.* 1922. Established in 1652, it was advertised at this time as the 'Family and Commercial Hotel' by the proprietress Violet O. Hulme. The hotel no longer exists.

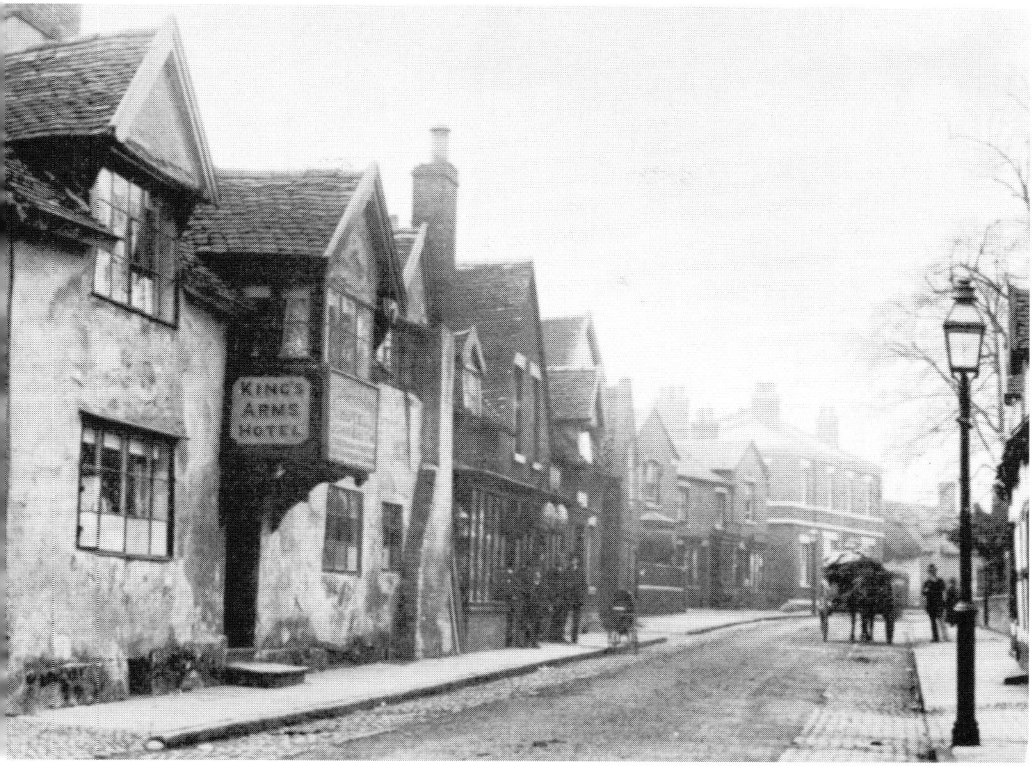

In 1890 the King's Arms Hotel in Shropshire Street still had the appearance of days long gone by. The fire in 1651 destroyed many of the old half-timbered houses in Market Drayton. Some of these were the one-bedroomed homes of the poorest; with walls made of mud or wattle and daub, and fires burning in the centre of earth floors. During the difficult times around 1800 about a fifth of the families of the parish received poor relief. With the arrival of the railway and the canal the town prospered and the population grew to over five thousand in the late 1800s. It had, however, an adverse effect on the many inns and coach-houses, as people would not generally need to stay overnight in the town.

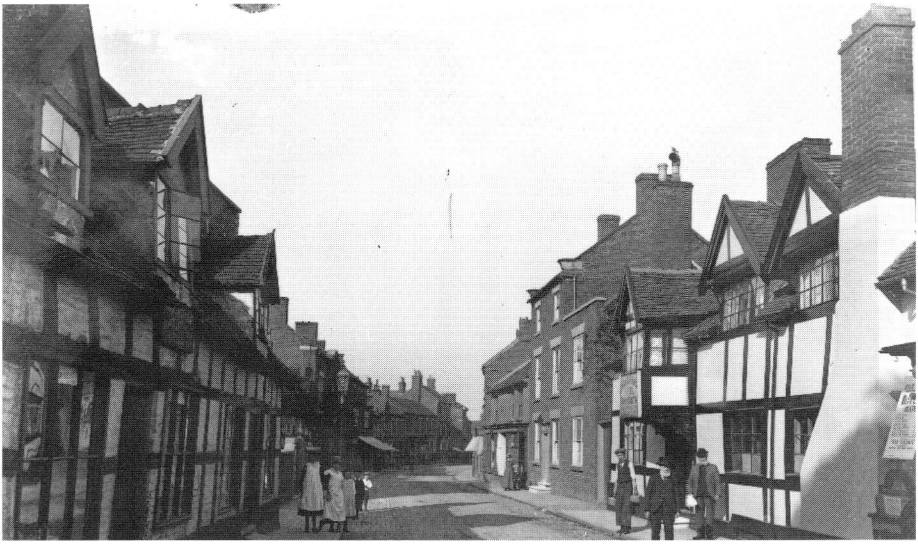

This 1905 photograph shows the dramatic changes that had taken place at the King's Arms Hotel over just fifteen years: the chimney-stack has been rendered and a mock-tudor front gives the building a contemporary appearance. The proprietor John Smith poses proudly in front of his smart hotel. The cottages on the other side burned down in a fire in 1937. The hotel has changed very little today.

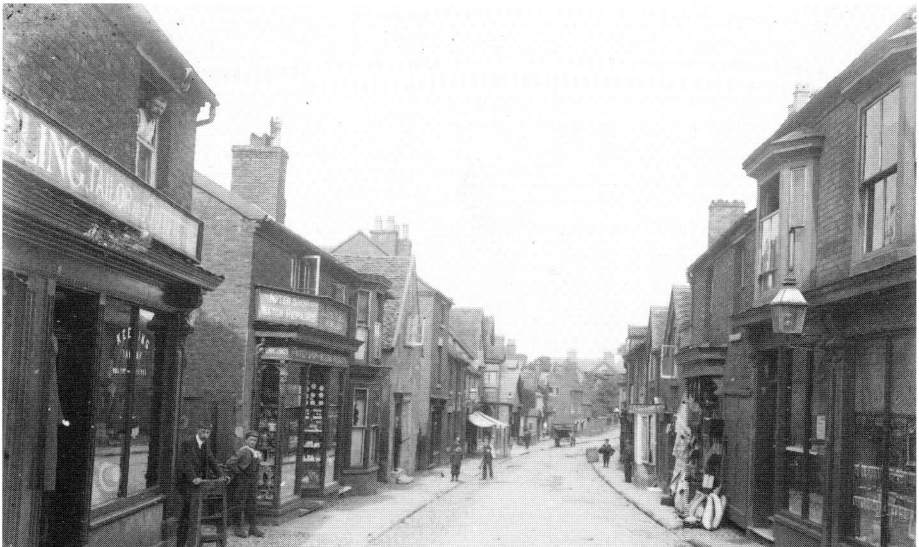

A typical street scene in Market Drayton at the beginning of 1900, with the barber shop on the right-hand side, a tailor opposite, a small tea-room and a jeweller. Soon after this a scheme began all over Shropshire to improve the roads, and the cobblestones disappeared from the townscape.

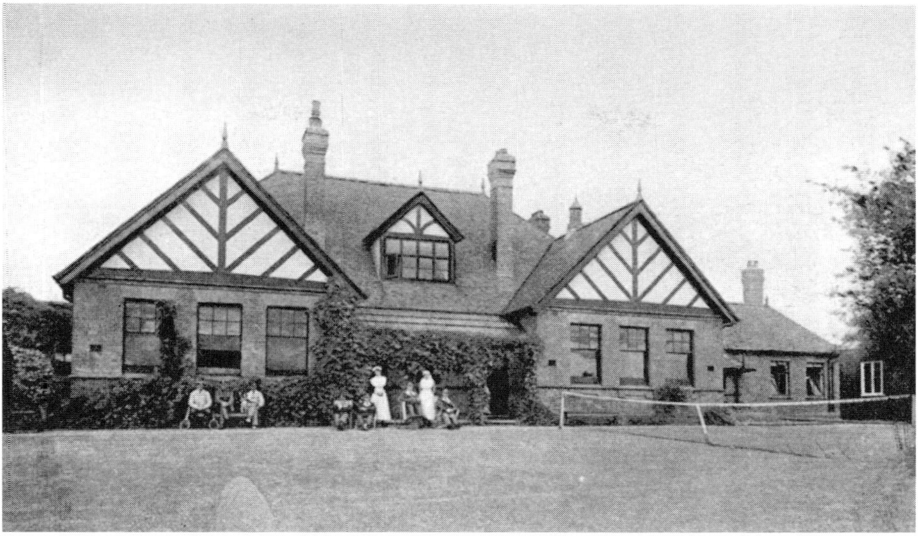

The Cottage Hospital was built with money raised by public subscription in the late 1890s. It has now closed but efforts are being made to retain the building for the town. This photograph was taken around 1917.

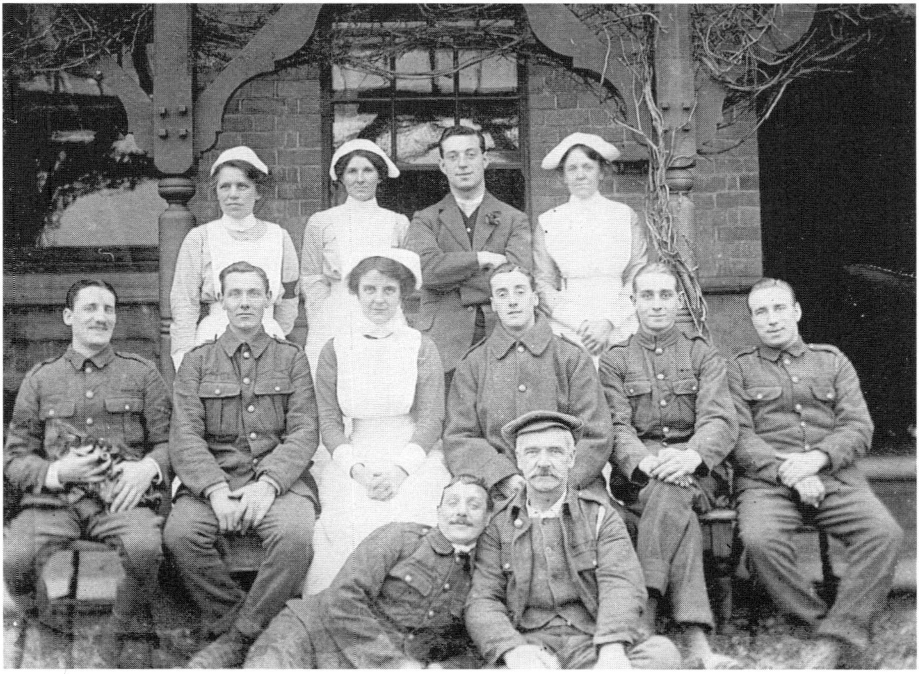

Miss E. Good had succeeded Miss Armitage as matron at the hospital at the time of this image in 1918.

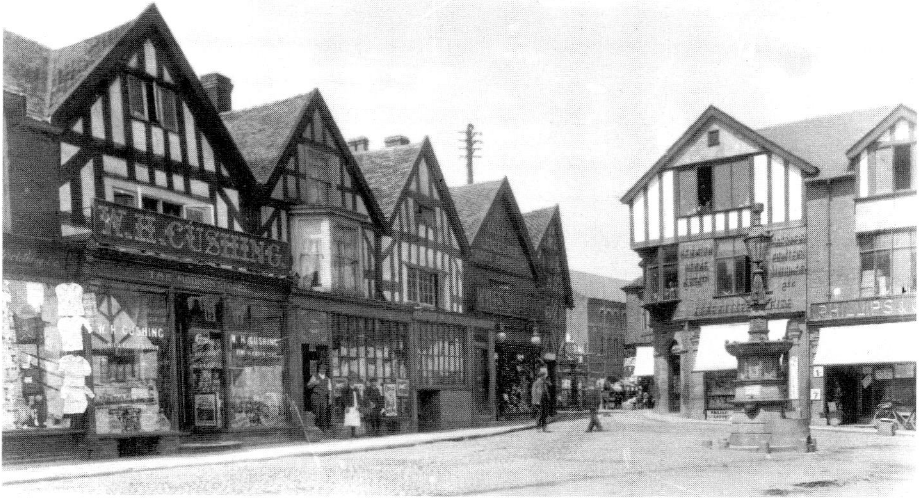

Nineteenth-century directories show that there was a large traffic in grain in Market Drayton. Tolls had to be paid for the privilege of selling corn and grain at the market. In 1740, a year of great famine, the quarter session records show that, 'four women and one man were charged with seizing a horse and waggon, laden with corn'. Hidden underneath the surface of the road in this photograph of 1895 are the weighing machines of the Corn Shop in the High Street. The building behind the fountain had recently received a mock-tudor front.

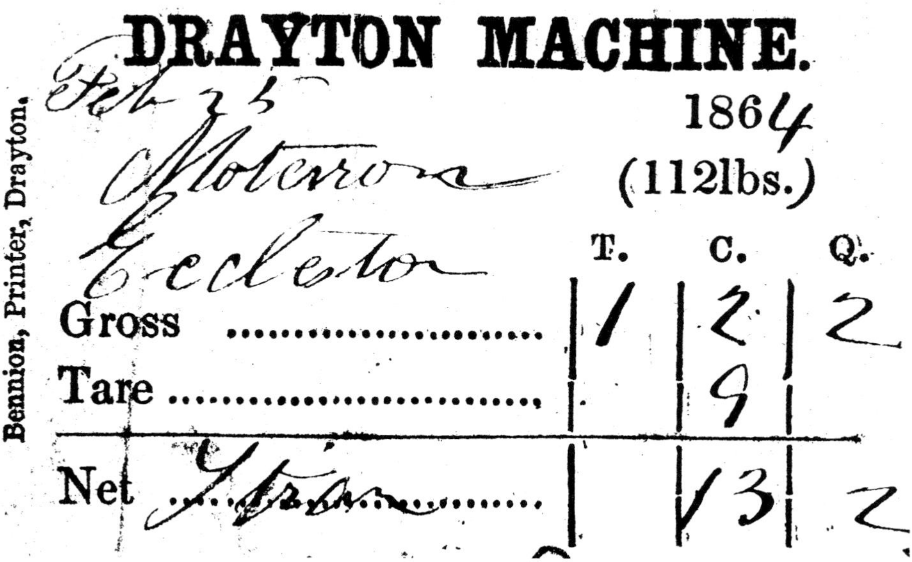

DRAYTON MACHINE.

Feb 25 1864

(112lbs.)

	T.	C.	Q.
Gross	1	2	2
Tare		9	
Net	1	13	2

Bennion, Printer, Drayton.

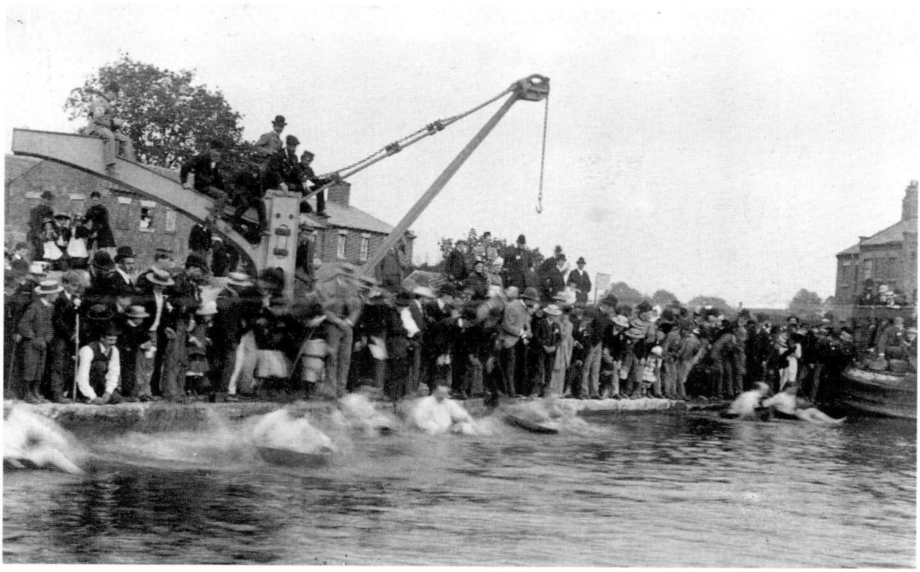

There is conflicting information as to the date of these two photographs taken on the same day. The occasion was either the Golden or the Diamond Jubilee of Queen Victoria, 1887 or 1897. But taking part in the fun of the tub race is definitely Mr Upton. The location was the canal in Market Drayton.

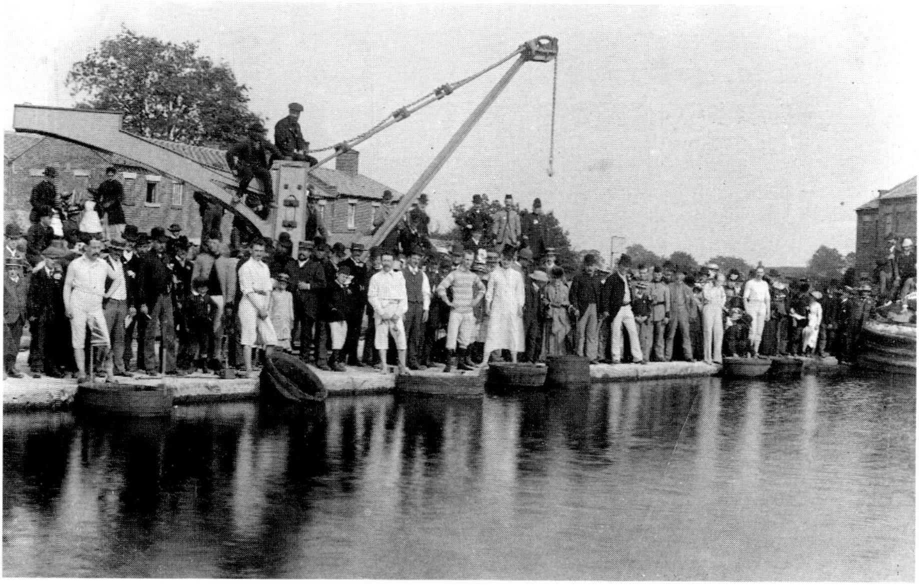

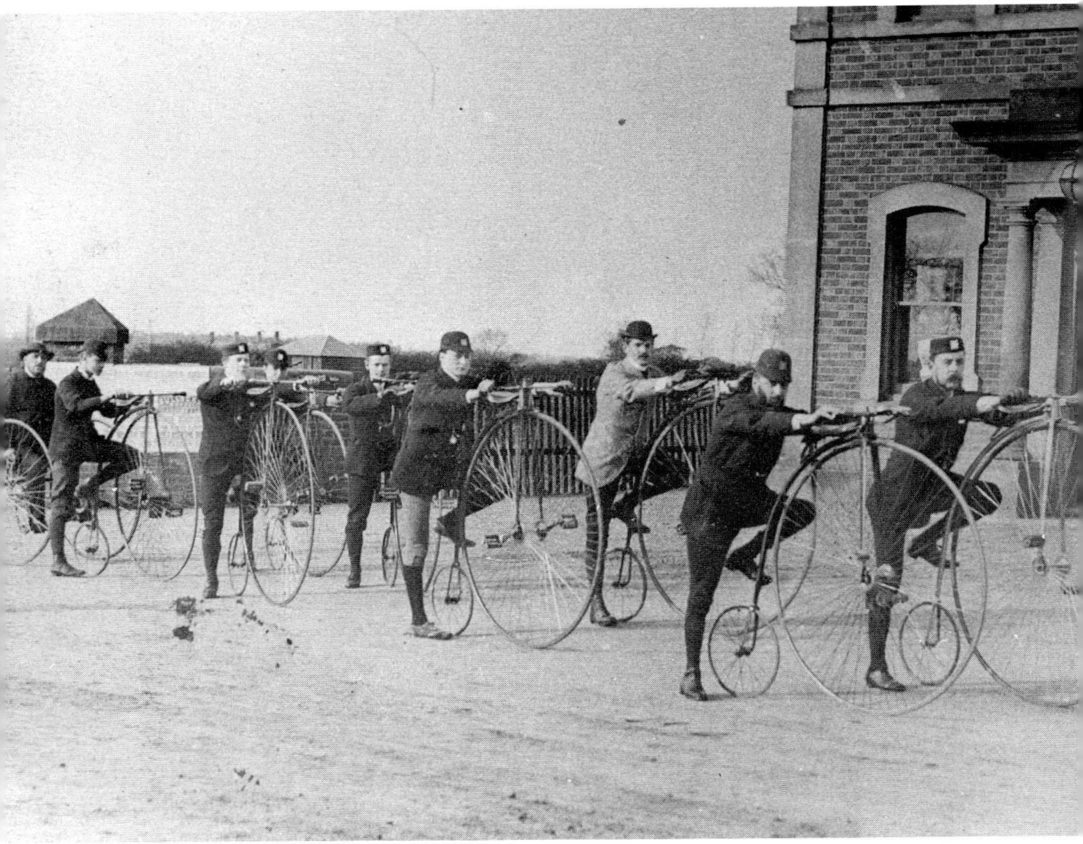

The Market Drayton Bicycle Club in front of the Raven Hotel, *c.* 1880. The invention of the bicycle gave new freedom to many people in the countryside; unless you had money and land to support a carriage horse and could provide stabling, the only transport was on foot. For a long time it was, however, impossible for women to ride a bike, as the fashion of that time was impractical. Even today many clubs around the country remain all-male bastions.

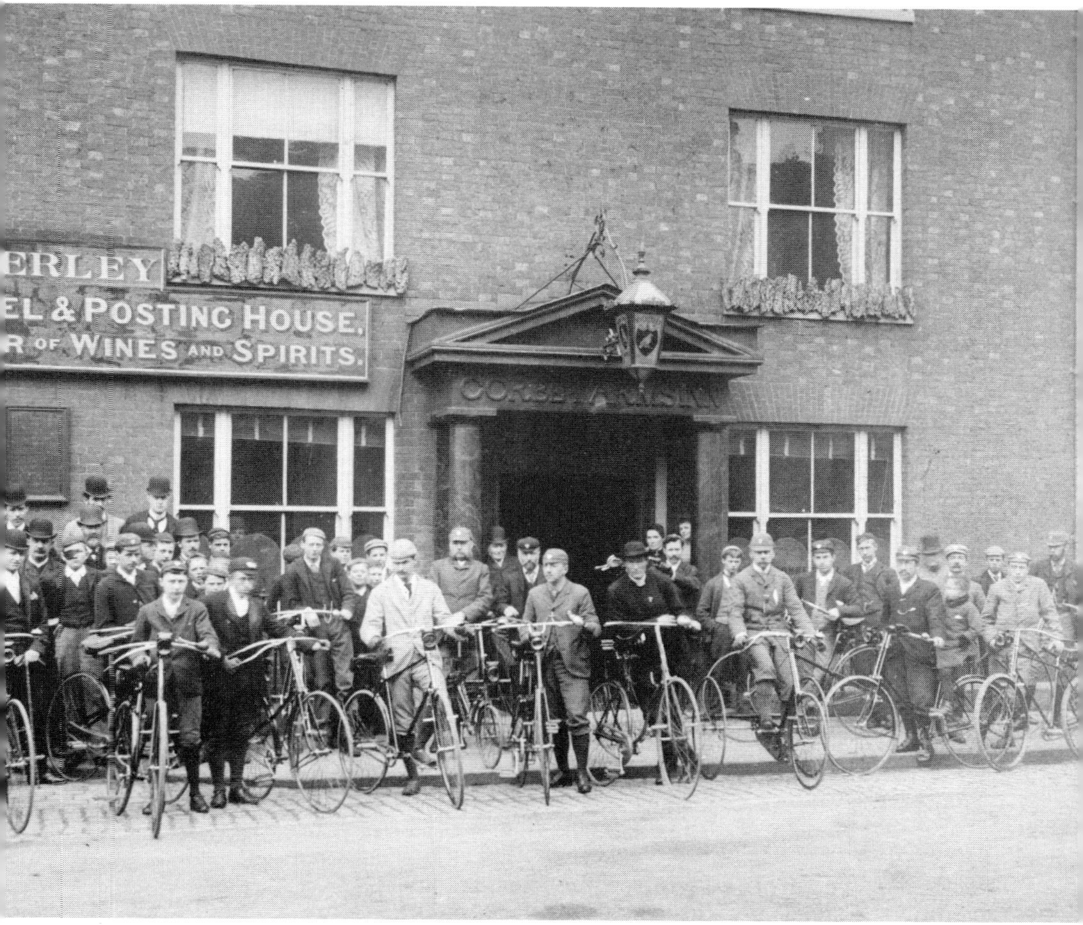

The Market Drayton Bicycle Club outside the Corbet Arms, *c*. 1900.

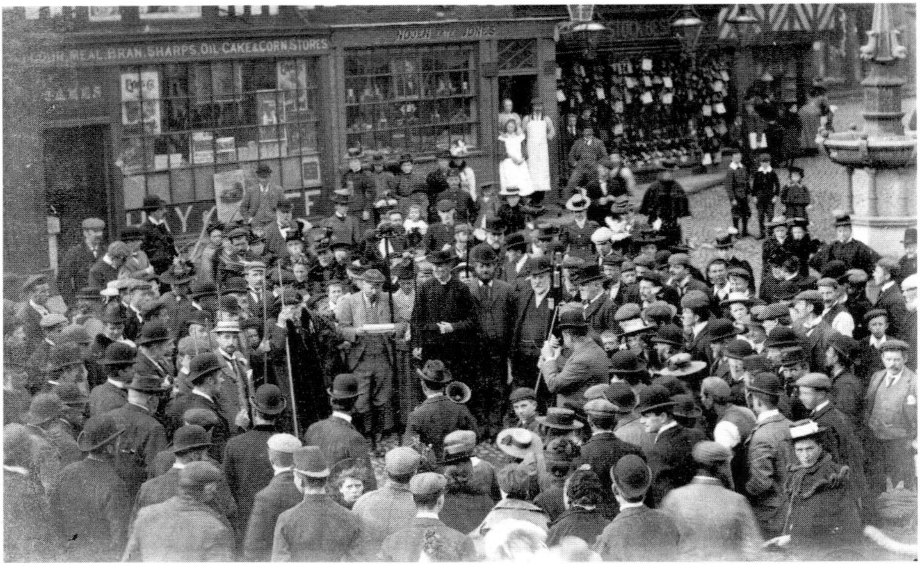

When the Lordship of Drayton Magna passed from the Abbots of Combermere into the hands of Sir Rowland Hill in 1550, he secured from King Edward VI a confirmation of the charter for the market and fair. To this was added the Court of Pie Powder (Pieds poudres) – courts to settle on the spot smaller disputes involving visitors 'with dusty feet'. Some rules of the Court Leet have a familiar ring. In 1556, for instance, the bailiff announced that: 'No inhabitant shall kepe any mastiffe dogge above the age of three quarters of a yeare olde unlesse the same mastiffe by tyed or musseled.' By the time of this photograph in 1903 the Court Leet was mainly carried out as an entertainment for the locals.

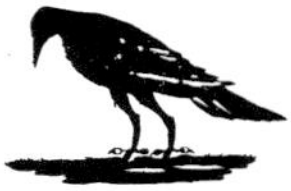

Court Leet of Market Drayton.

Oyez ! Oyez ! Oyez !

The Fair falls on   the instant. All Officers are in duty bound to attend at the Corbet Arms, at 11 o'oclock a.m., to proclaim the same.

Death is never far away in a small community. It is looked upon in the country as being as inevitable as autumn turning to winter. Neighbours in life become neighbours in death. But seldom does tragedy occur on such a scale as in the case of the Lewis family. The gravestone at Market Drayton cemetery relates this heartfelt sorrow: 'William Poole Lewis/Died February 11th 1894. Aged 35 years/Six of our children/Edith Mary born Oct. 18th 1883 died Nov. 9th 1888/Bernard born Nov. 13th 1891 died Jan. 26th 1894/Mabel Marion born Jan. 26th 1885 died Jan. 28th 1894/Ivan William born Jul. 10th 1888 died Feb. 4th 1894/George Wallace born Aug. 19th 1886 died Feb. 12th 1894/Frank Poole born Sept. 19th 1889 died Feb. 13th 1894/Peace Perfect Peace/Death shadowing us and ours./Jesus had vanquished death/And all its powers.' All died from diphtheria.

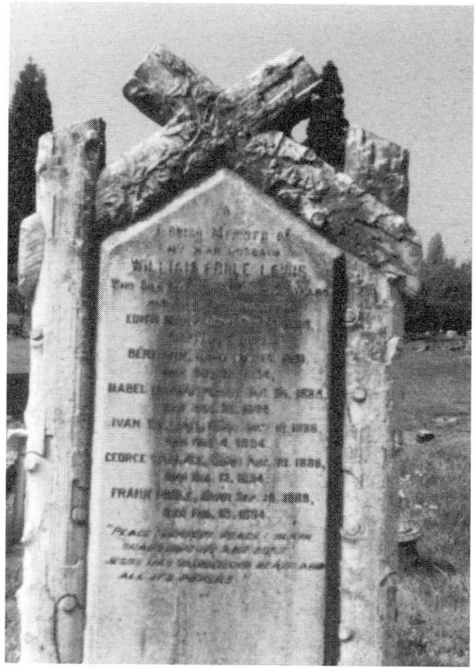

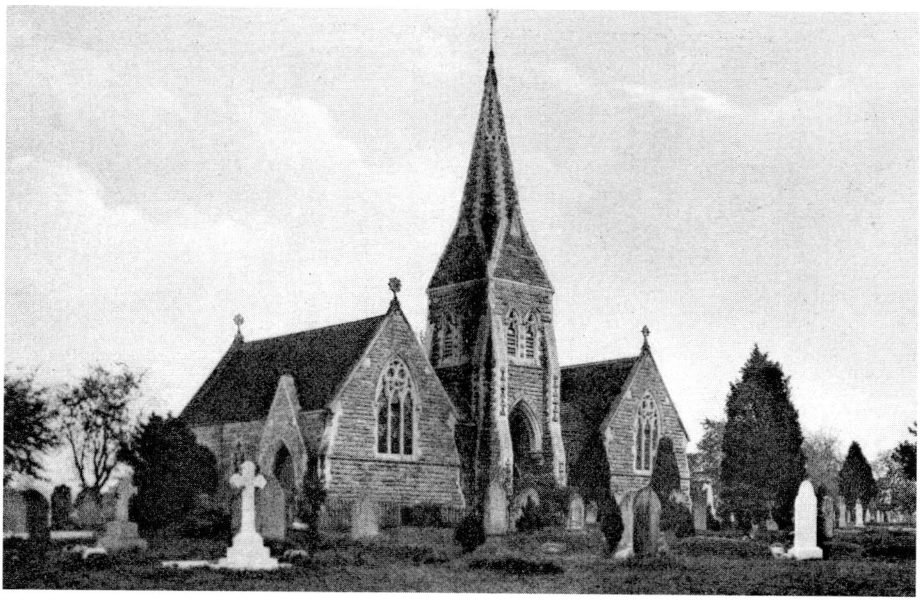

Market Drayton cemetery.

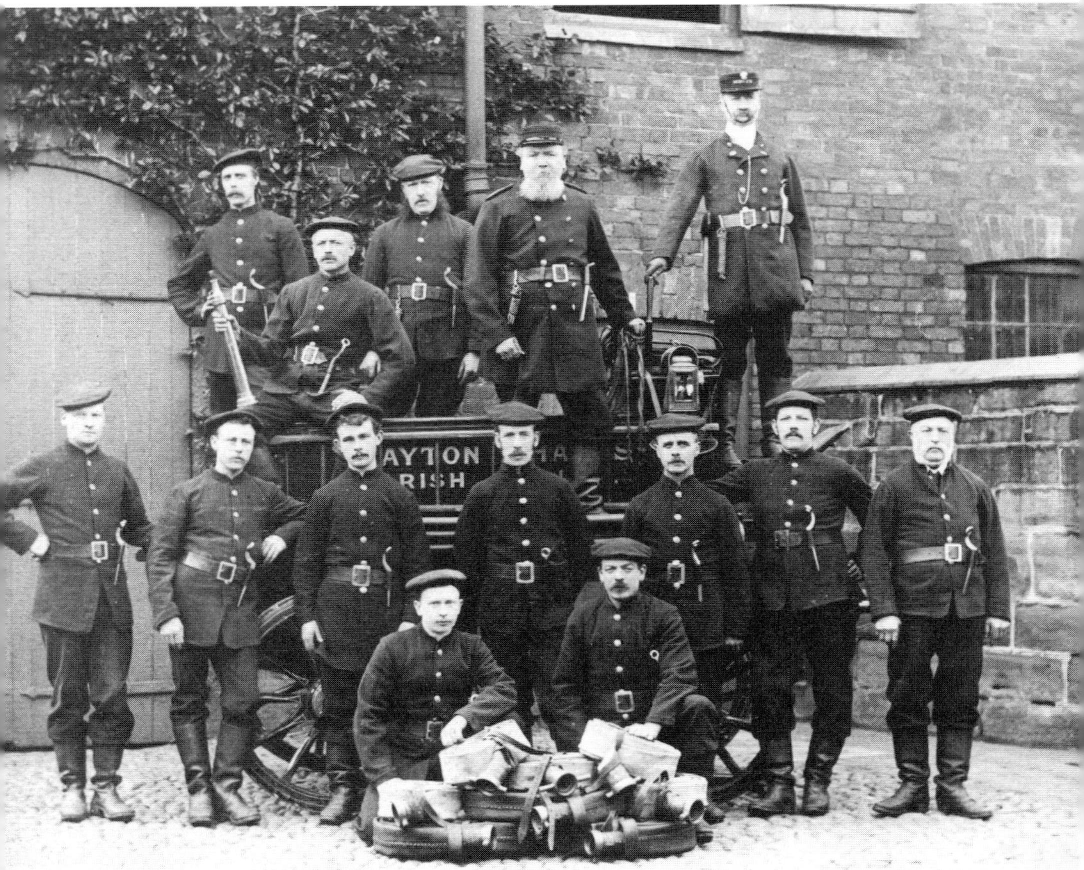

In 1828 a timber merchant, Samuel Burley, was the agent for the Norwich Union Insurance Company, representing the Salop Fire Office at the same time. The horse-drawn fire-engines were located at a house in the Beast Market. This photograph from 1900 shows the volunteer fire brigade, minus the horse.

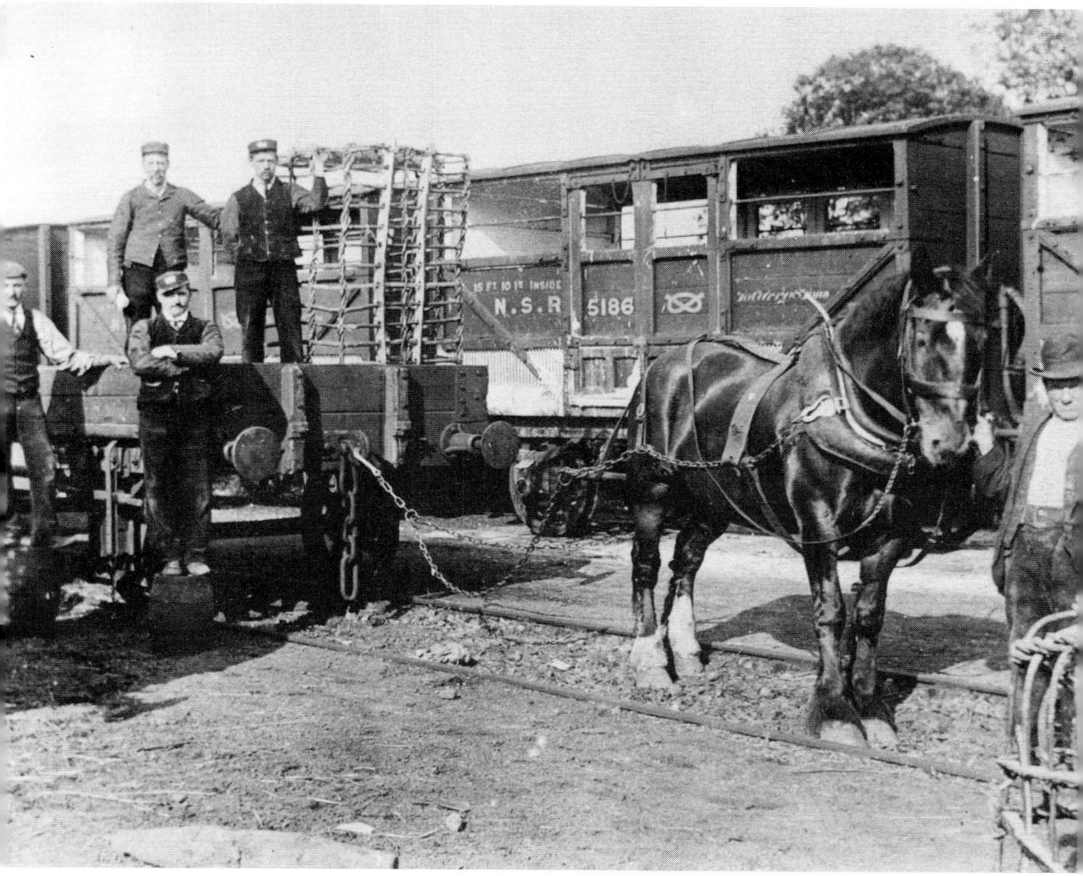

Horses were used for yard shunting duties until the beginning of this century. This photograph with carriages and staff of the North Shropshire Railway was taken around 1906. The railway arrived in Market Drayton in 1863, first the line from Nantwich to Market Drayton, followed by the line to Wellington in 1867, and the North Staffs Railway in 1870.

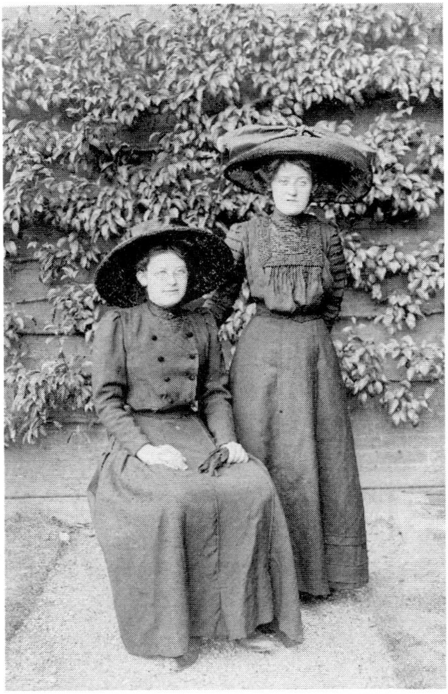

The sisters Harriet and Alice George of Great Hales Street in Market Drayton were in charge of the distribution and display of bill-boards all over the area. After their deaths, Harriet in 1975 and Alice in 1978, it was discovered that the sisters actually lived in the shed adjoining their cottage. It was difficult to gain access to the cottage itself as it was full from top to bottom with old bill-boards and newspapers.

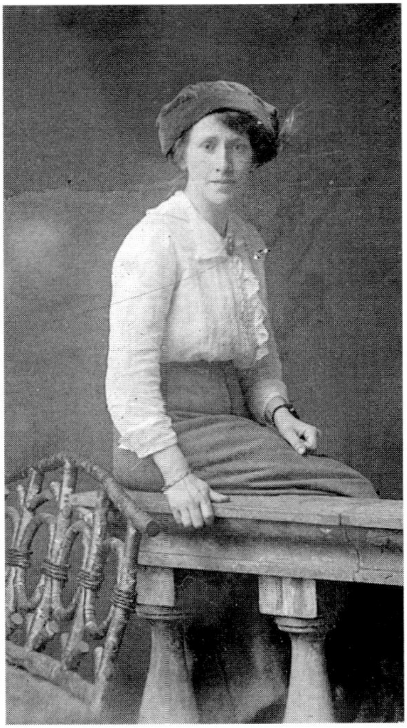

Harriet George photographed during a holiday at Blackpool. The photograph was taken by Mr Arnold around 1918.

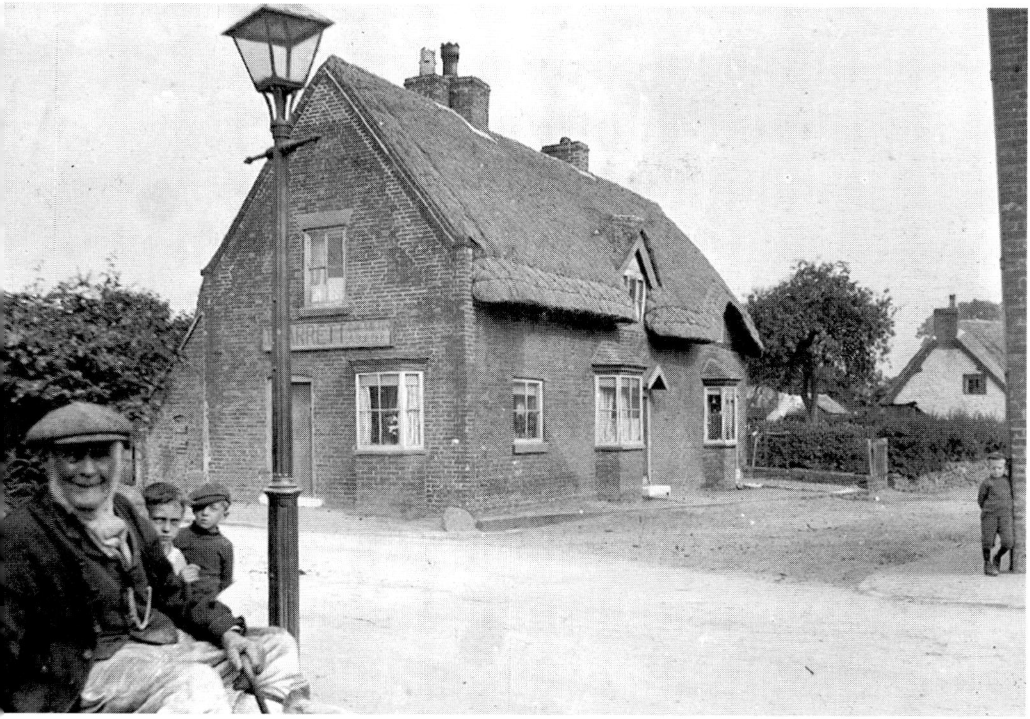

Mr Barrow at Doublegates, *c.* 1900. Thatched cottages, now the ideal country retreat of the city dweller, were often the homes of the poorer townspeople, with more than one generation sharing the small space. Straw was used for thatching, pinned down with split hazel. The arrival of the combine harvester demanded a shorter-stalked, hybrid wheat, unsuitable for thatching. As most of these cottages belonged to the estates, the roofs were not renewed after the farmworkers were no longer needed. It was also looked upon as old-fashioned to have a thatched roof, which was an added fire hazard. But with the demand by the commuter for traditional country cottages, the craft of thatching has made a come-back.

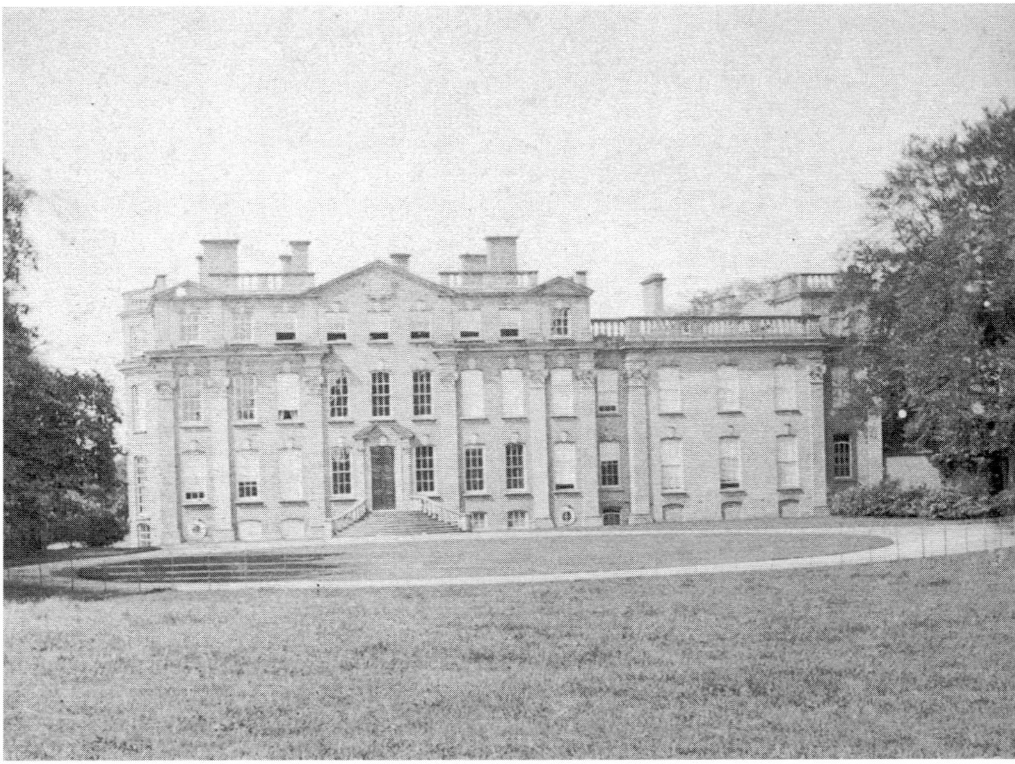

Buntingdale Hall, photographed around 1870, was built by Bulkeley Mackworth in 1701, replacing a timber-framed property. The hall was bought by William Tayleur in the eighteenth century for £7,000. In 1923 the house was sold by the sister of John Tayleur and the ten people who inherited a share of the property in order to satisfy the Inland Revenue. Mr Jones, who lived there for ten years, sold it to the RAF. Now once again a Tayleur owns part of the hall and it is being lovingly restored.

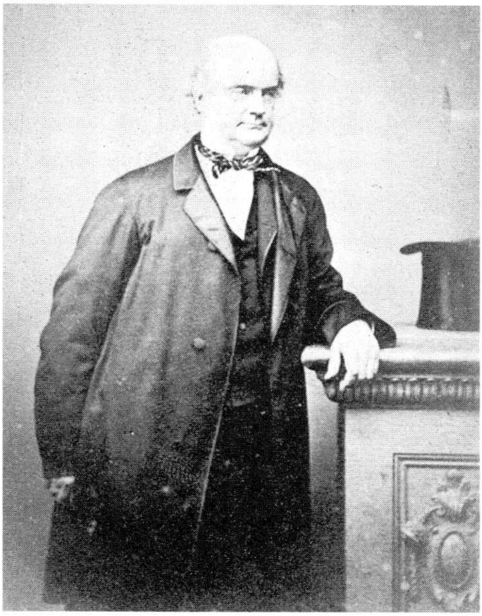

William Tayleur, photographed here not long before his death in 1873, added a new wing to Buntingdale Hall. He had inherited the hall from his father John, who was an autocratic eccentric. He would neither prosecute poachers nor give away his butler who stole the family diamonds. He would shoot rabbits from one of the top-floor windows, with the gun supported on the back of a footman.

Mr and Mrs Tayleur

request the pleasure of

The Revd. Mr Upton Mrs Upton & family's Company

at a Garden Party on

Thursday 8th Septr 3 to 7

Buntingdale

R.S.V.P.

The invitation to a garden party given by Mr and Mrs Tayleur is addressed to Mr and Mrs Upton of Market Drayton. Mr John Tayleur, owner of the hall from 1873 onwards, was the nephew of William. He and his wife Katherine were much respected in Market Drayton.

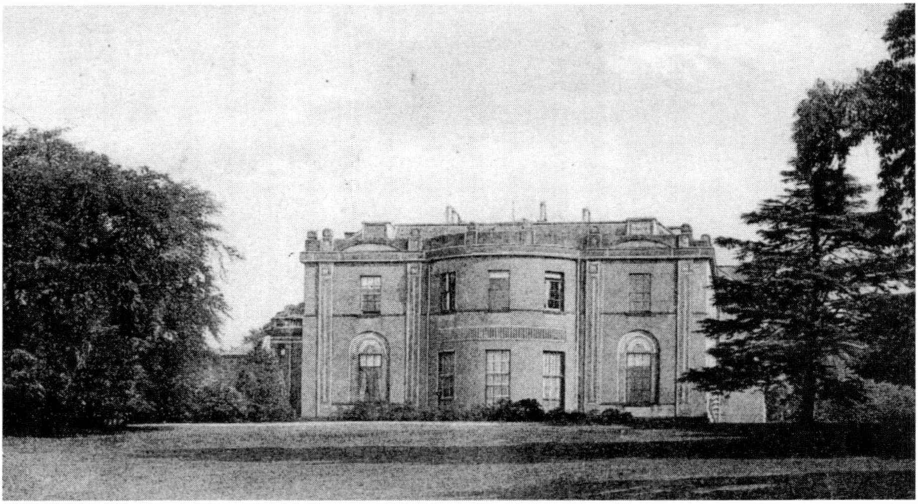

Pell Wall Hall was built by Sir John Soane in 1825 for the Sillitoes of Market Drayton and is said to be one of his finest houses. The famous greenhouses of the estate provided enough to give free meals to the poor of the area, as well as for the lavish parties at the house. The hall was sold to Munroe Walker, the distiller from Manchester. Even during the hard times in the late 1920s he gave parties of outrageous proportions at the hall. Later the hall fell into ruin and the County Council bought it for £1 from the then owner under the Compulsory Purchase Act. A group of trustees and English Heritage are now trying to restore the hall to its former glory. Above, the hall in 1918; below, in 1963.

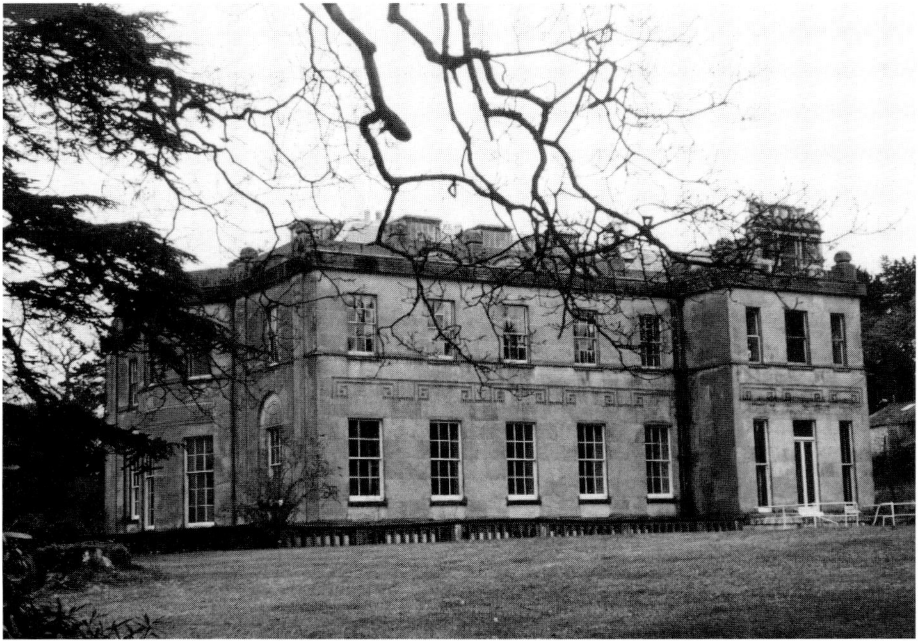

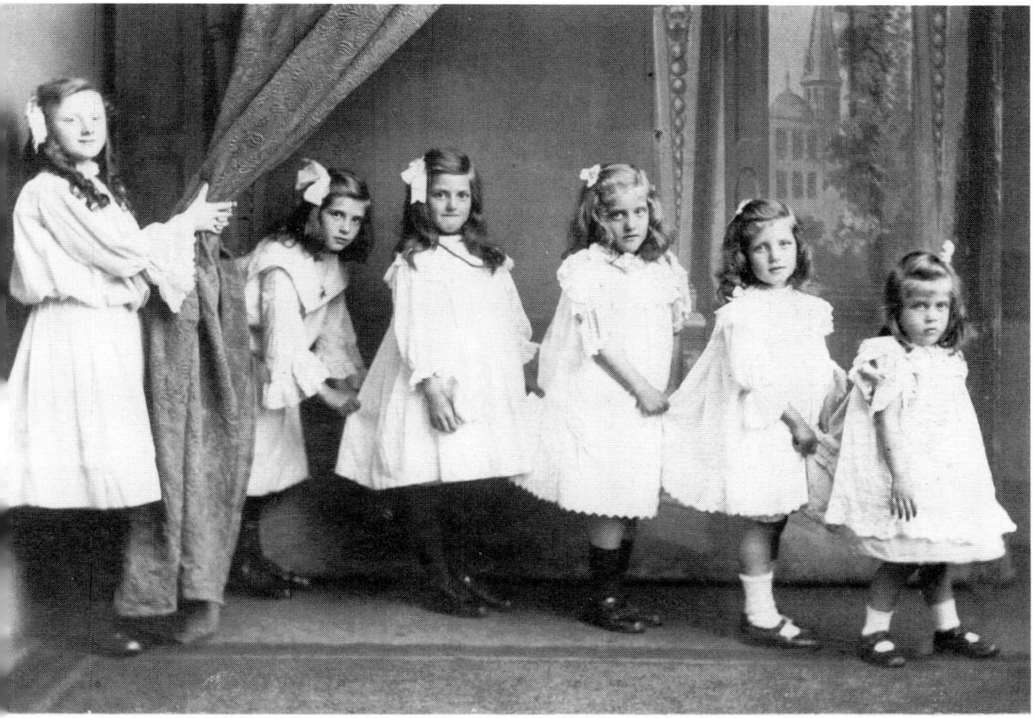

The photographer Richard G. Arnold worked in Market Drayton from 1877 until his death in 1919. Market Drayton owes him some of the most memorable images of that time. His portraits have a contemporary look because he tried not only to get a 'likeness' but also tell us something of the character of the sitter. Despite the fact that in those days the equipment was cumbersome, he carried it to the most remote spots, photographing buildings, landscapes and everyday events in the street. He understood the essence of photography, that by pressing of a button you can record history, capturing a moment that can never be repeated. His daughter continued the business after his death. The date of this photograph at the National School is not known.

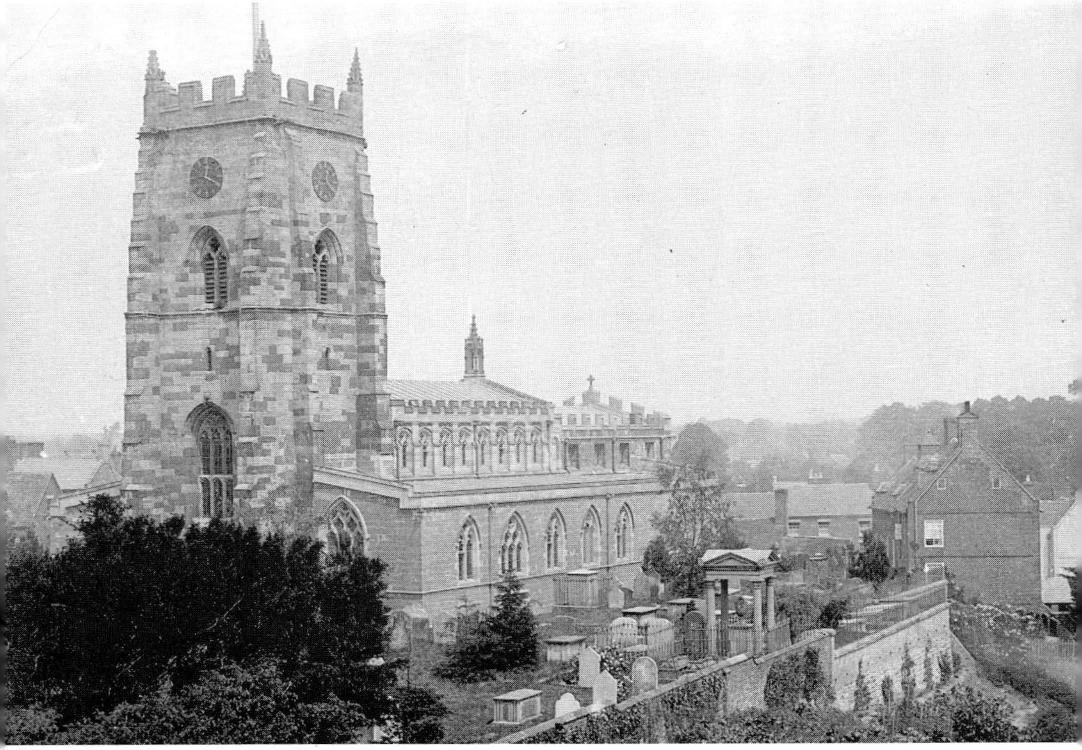

St Mary's Church was probably Saxon in origin with additions made in the twelfth and fourteenth centuries. The dedication to St Mary may be explained by the connection of the town with the abbey of Combermere. In 1782 it was decided to apply for a 'brief' (a collection towards a deserving project). The sum of £2,164 was raised and the rebuilding of the church was completed in 1787, giving the interior an eighteenth-century appearance. However, many beautiful features disappeared in the process. It is well documented that Robert Clive climbed to the top of the tower, or as some state, simply walked up from the inside (the second option sounds more reasonable). He is known also to have sat on one of the gargoyles on the tower, trying to remove a stone from its mouth.

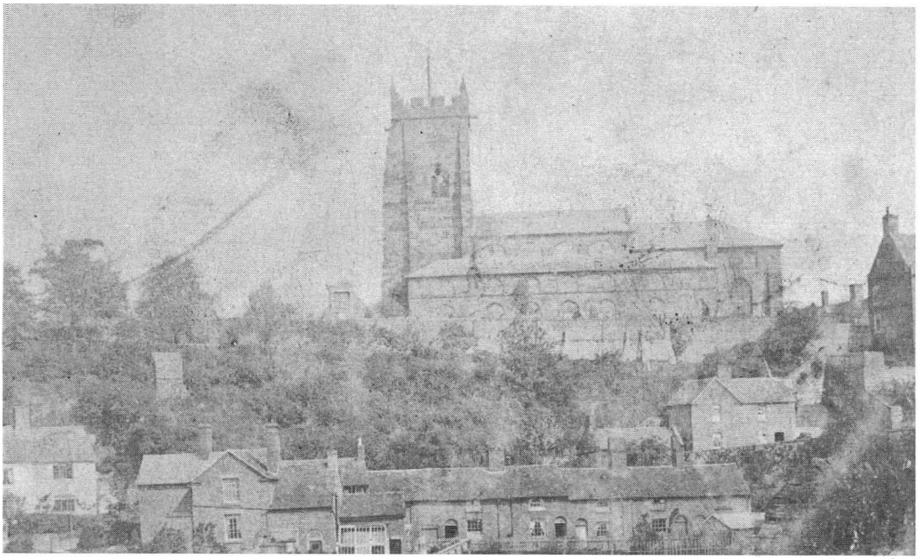

A very old photograph by Mr Arnold of the church before 1884. Alterations were carried out after that time to change the windows and the roof. Notice the old paper mill in the foreground with the mill cottage.

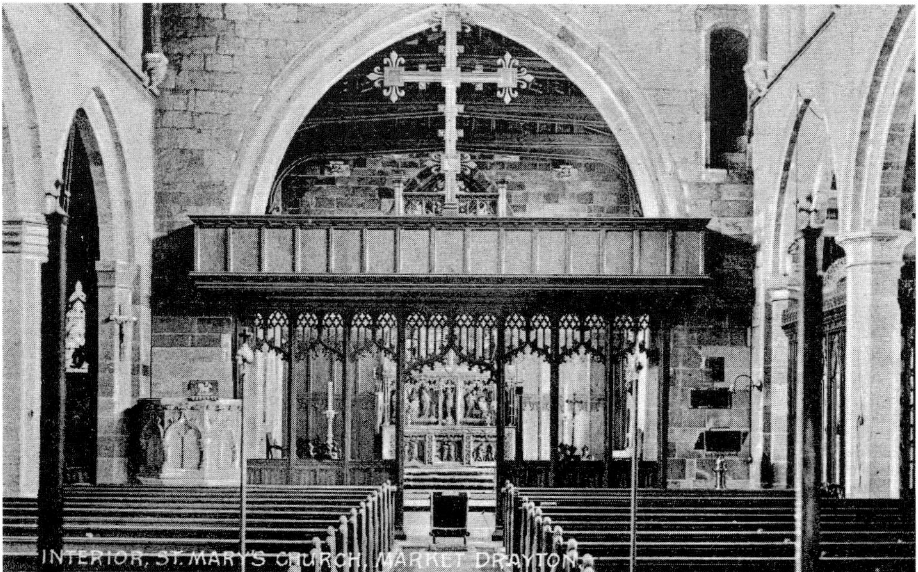

After further alterations the rood screen and the gallery finally disappeared. What remains is the east window featuring the appearance of the risen Christ, in memory of Richard and Eleanor Corbet.

Acknowledgements

My grateful thanks are due to the late Harold Jones, Hilda Cliff, the late Bill Cliff, Donald Wynn, Vicky Sarginson, Oswestry Library, Shropshire Local Studies Library. Special thanks are due to all the people who trusted me with their priceless photographs and gave me so much of their time, and most of all encouraged me by believing in the project:

Joan Barton, Whitchurch Archaeological Society • John Dickerson, Shawbury
Margaret Dutton, Moreton Say • Diana Parsons, Redbrook Maelor
Marie Sarginson, Whitchurch • Shropshire Local Studies Library
Mrs F. Upton, Civic Society, Market Drayton•
Roger West, Fauls, Lower Heath